AT SEA
WITH
PIRATES

EYEWITNESS ACCOUNTS

AT SEA WITH WITH PIRATES

WILLIAM DAMPIER

AMBERLEY

First published 2014

Amberley Publishing
The Hill, Stroud
Gloucestershire, GL5 4EP

www.amberley-books.com

British Library Cataloguing in Publication Data.
A catalogue record for this book is available from the British Library.

ISBN 978 1 4456 4280 2 (print)
ISBN 978 1 4456 4293 2 (ebook)

Typeset in 10pt on 12pt Sabon.
Typesetting and Origination by Amberley Publishing.
Printed in the UK.

Contents

Preface

Before the reader proceed any further in the perusal of this work I must bespeak a little of his patience here to take along with him this short account of it. It is composed of a mixed relation of places and actions in the same order of time in which they occurred: for which end I kept a journal of every day's observations.

In the description of places, their product, etc., I have endeavoured to give what satisfaction I could to my countrymen; though possibly to the describing several things that may have been much better accounted for by others: choosing to be more particular than might be needful, with respect to the intelligent reader, rather than to omit what I thought might tend to the information of persons no less sensible and inquisitive, though not so learned or experienced. For which reason my chief care has been to be as particular as was consistent with my intended brevity in setting down such observables as I met with. Nor have I given myself any great trouble since my return to compare my discoveries with those of others: the rather because, should it so happen that I have described some places or things which others have done before me, yet in different accounts, even of the same things, it can hardly be but there will be some new light afforded by each of them. But after all, considering that the main of this voyage has its scene laid in long tracts of the remoter parts both of the East and West Indies, some of which very seldom visited by Englishmen, and others as rarely by any Europeans, I may without vanity encourage the reader to expect many things wholly new to him, and many others more fully described than he may have seen elsewhere; for which not only in this voyage, though itself of many years continuance, but also several former long and distant voyages have qualified me.

As for the actions of the company among whom I made the greatest part of this voyage, a thread of which I have carried on through it, it is not to divert the reader with them that I mention them, much less that I take any pleasure in relating them: but for method's sake, and for the reader's satisfaction; who could not so well acquiesce in my description of places, etc., without knowing the particular traverses I made among them; nor in these, without an account of the concomitant circumstances: besides, that I would not prejudice the truth and sincerity of my relation, though by omissions only. And as for the traverses themselves, they make for the reader's advantage, how little soever for mine; since thereby I have been the better enabled to gratify his curiosity; as one who rambles about a country can give usually a better account of it than a carrier who jogs on to his inn without ever going out of his road.

As to my style, it cannot be expected that a seaman should affect politeness; for were I able to do it, yet I think I should be little solicitous about it in a work of this nature. I have frequently indeed divested myself of sea-phrases to gratify the land reader; for which the seamen will hardly forgive me: and yet, possibly, I shall not seem complaisant enough to the other; because I still retain the use of so many sea-terms. I confess I have not been at all scrupulous in this matter, either as to the one or the other of these; for I am persuaded that, if what I say be intelligible, it matters not greatly in what words it is expressed.

For the same reason I have not been curious as to the spelling of the names of places, plants, fruits, animals, etc., which in any of these remoter parts are given at the pleasure of travellers, and vary according to their different humours: neither have I confined myself to such names as are given by learned authors, or so much as enquired after many of them. I write for my countrymen; and have therefore, for the most part, used such names as are familiar to our English seamen, and those of our colonies abroad, yet without neglecting others that occurred. As it might suffice me to have given such names and descriptions as I could I shall leave to those of more leisure and opportunity the trouble of comparing these with those which other authors have assigned.

The reader will find as he goes along some references to an appendix which I once designed to this book; as, to a chapter about the winds in different parts of the world; to a description of the Bay of Campeachy in the West Indies, where I lived long in a former voyage; and to a particular chorographical description of all the South Sea coast of America, partly from a Spanish manuscript, and partly from my own and other travellers' observations, besides those contained in this book. But such an appendix would have swelled it too unreasonably: and therefore I chose rather to publish it hereafter by itself, as opportunity shall serve. And the same must be said also as to a particular voyage from Achin in the isle of Sumatra, to Tonquin, Malacca, etc., which should have been inserted as part of this general one; but it would have been too long, and therefore, omitting it for the present, I have carried on this, next way from Sumatra to England; and so made the tour of the world correspondent to the title.

For the better apprehending the course of the voyage and the situation of the places mentioned in it I have caused several maps to be engraven, and some particular charts of my own composure. Among them there is in the map of the American Isthmus, a new scheme of the adjoining Bay of Panama and its islands, which to some may seem superfluous after that which Mr. Ringrose has published in the History of the Buccaneers; and which he offers as a very exact chart. I must needs disagree with him in that, and doubt not but this which I here publish will be found more agreeable to that bay, by one who shall have opportunity to examine it; for it is a contraction of a larger map which I took from several stations in the bay itself. The reader may judge how well I was able to do it by my several traverses about it, mentioned in this book; those, particularly, which are described in the 7th chapter, which I have caused to be marked out with a pricked line; as the course of my voyage is generally in all the maps, for the reader's more easy tracing it.

I have nothing more to add, but that there are here and there some mistakes made as to expression and the like, which will need a favourable correction as they occur upon reading. For instance, the log of wood lying out at some distance from sides of the boats described at Guam, and parallel to their keel, which for distinction's sake I have called the little boat, might more clearly and properly have been called the side log, or by some such name; for though fashioned at the bottom and ends boatwise, yet is not hollow at top, but solid throughout. In other places also I may not have expressed myself so fully as I ought: but any considerable omission that I shall recollect or be informed of I shall endeavour to make up in those accounts I have yet to publish; and for any faults I leave the reader to the joint use of his judgment and candour.

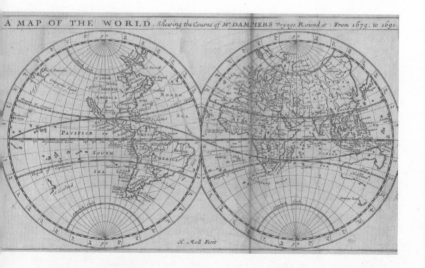

This contemporary map of the world shows the extent of Dampier's voyages.

CHAPTER 1

England to Juan Fernandez

The author's departure from England, and arrival in Jamaica.

I first set out of England on this voyage at the beginning of the year 1679, in the Loyal Merchant of London, bound for Jamaica, Captain Knapman Commander. I went a passenger, designing when I came thither to go from thence to the Bay of Campeachy in the Gulf of Mexico, to cut log-wood: where in a former voyage I had spent about three years in that employ; and so was well acquainted with the place and the work.

We sailed with a prosperous gale without any impediment or remarkable passage in our voyage: unless that when we came in sight of the island Hispaniola, and were coasting along on the south side of it by the little isles of Vacca, or Ash, I observed Captain Knapman was more vigilant than ordinary, keeping at a good distance off shore, for fear of coming too near those small low islands; as he did once, in a voyage from England, about the year 1673, losing his ship there, by the carelessness of his mates. But we succeeded better; and arrived safe at Port Royal in Jamaica some time in April 1679, and went immediately ashore.

I had brought some goods with me from England which I intended to sell here, and stock myself with rum and sugar, saws, axes, hats, stockings, shoes, and such other commodities, as I knew would sell among the Campeachy log-wood-cutters. Accordingly I sold my English cargo at Port Royal; but upon some maturer considerations of my intended voyage to Campeachy I changed my thoughts of that design, and continued at Jamaica all that year in expectation of some other business.

I shall not trouble the reader with my observations at that isle, so well known to Englishmen; nor with the particulars of my own affairs during my stay there. But in short, having there made a purchase of a small estate in Dorsetshire, near my native country of Somerset, of one whose title to it I was well assured of, I was just embarking myself for England, about Christmas 1679, when one Mr. Hobby invited me to go first a short trading voyage to the country of the Moskitos, of whom I shall speak in my first chapter. I was willing to get up some money before my return, having laid out what I had at Jamaica; so I sent the writing of my new purchase along with the same friends whom I should have accompanied to England, and went on board Mr. Hobby.

Soon after our setting out we came to an anchor again in Negril Bay, at the west end of Jamaica; but finding there Captain Coxon, Sawkins, Sharp, and other privateers, Mr. Hobby's men all left him to go with them upon an expedition they had contrived, leaving not one with him beside myself; and being thus left alone, after three or four days' stay with Mr. Hobby I was the more easily persuaded to go with them too.

His first going over the Isthmus of America into the south seas.

It was shortly after Christmas 1679 when we set out. The first expedition was to Portobello; which being accomplished it was resolved to march by land over the Isthmus of Darien upon some new adventures in the South Seas. Accordingly on the 5th of April 1680 we went ashore on the Isthmus, near Golden Island, one of the Samballoes, to the number of between three and four hundred men, carrying with us such provisions as were necessary, and toys wherewith to gratify the wild Indians through whose country we were to pass. In about nine days' march we arrived at Santa Maria and took it, and after a stay there of about three days we went on to the South Sea coast, and there embarked ourselves in such canoes and periagos as our Indian friends furnished us withal. We were in sight of Panama by the 23rd of April, and having in vain attempted Puebla Nova, before which Sawkins, then commander in chief, and others, were killed, we made some stay at the neighbouring isles of Quibo.

His coasting Peru and Chile, and back again, to his parting with Captain Sharp near the Isle of Plata, in order to return overland.

Here we resolved to change our course and stand away to the southward for the coast of Peru. Accordingly we left the keys or isles of Quibo the 6th of June, and spent the rest of the year in that southern course; for, touching at the isles of Gorgona and Plata, we came to Ylo, a small town on the coast of Peru, and took it. This was in October, and in November we went thence to Coquimbo on the same coast, and about Christmas were got as far as the isle of Juan Fernandez, which was the farthest of our course to the southward.

After Christmas we went back again to the northward, having a design upon Arica, a strong town advantageously situated in the hollow of the elbow, or bending, of the Peruvian coast. But being there repulsed with great loss, we continued our course northward, till by the middle of April we were come in sight of the isle of Plata, a little to the southward of the Equinoctial Line.

I have related this part of my voyage thus summarily and concisely, as well because the world has accounts of it already, in the relations that Mr. Ringrose and others have given of Captain Sharp's expedition, who was made chief commander upon Sawkins' being killed; as also because in the prosecution of this voyage I shall come to speak of these parts again, upon occasion of my going the second time into the South Seas: and shall there describe at large the places both of the North and South America as they occurred to me. And for this reason, that I might avoid needless repetitions, and hasten to such particulars as the public has hitherto had no account of, I have chosen to comprise the relation of my voyage hitherto in this short compass, and place it as an Introduction before the rest, that the reader may the better perceive where I mean to begin to be particular; for there I have placed the title of my first chapter.

All therefore that I have to add to the Introduction is this; that, while we lay at the isle of Juan Fernandez, Captain Sharp was, by general consent, displaced from being commander;

the company being not satisfied either with his courage or behaviour. In his stead Captain Watling was advanced: but, he being killed shortly after before Arica, we were without a commander during all the rest of our return towards Plata. Now Watling being killed, a great number of the meaner sort began to be as earnest for choosing Captain Sharp again into the vacancy as before they had been as forward as any to turn him out: and on the other side the abler and more experienced men, being altogether dissatisfied with Sharp's former conduct, would by no means consent to have him chosen. In short, by that time we were come in sight of the island Plata, the difference between the contending parties was grown so high that they resolved to part companies; having first made an agreement that, which party soever should upon polling appear to have the majority, they should keep the ship: and the other should content themselves with the launch, or longboat, and canoes, and return back over the Isthmus, or go to seek their fortune other-ways, as they would.

Accordingly we put it to the vote; and, upon dividing, Captain Sharp's party carried it. I, who had never been pleased with his management, though I had hitherto kept my mind to myself, now declared myself on the side of those that were out-voted; and, according to our agreement, we took our shares of such necessaries as were fit to carry overland with us (for that was our resolution) and so prepared for our departure.

CHAPTER 2

From the South Sea to the North

The author's land journey from the South to the North Sea, over the terra firma, or Isthmus of Darien.

Being landed May the 1st, we began our march about 3 o'clock in the afternoon, directing our course by our pocket compasses north-east and, having gone about 2 miles, we came to the foot of a hill where we built small huts and lay all night; having excessive rains till 12 o'clock.

The 2nd day in the morning having fair weather we ascended the hill, and found a small Indian path which we followed till we found it run too much easterly, and then, doubting it would carry us out of the way, we climbed some of the highest trees on the hill, which was not meanly furnished with as large and tall trees as ever I saw: at length we discovered some houses in a valley on the north side of the hill, but it being steep could not descend on that side, but followed the small path which led us down the hill on the east side, where we presently found several other Indian houses. The first that we came to at the foot of the hill had none but women at home who could not speak Spanish, but gave each of us a good calabash or shell-full of corn-drink. The other houses had some men at home, but none that spoke Spanish; yet we made a shift to buy such food as their houses or plantations afforded, which we dressed and ate all together; having all sorts of our provision in common, because none should live better than others, or pay dearer for anything than it was worth. This day we had marched 6 mile.

In the evening the husbands of those women came home and told us in broken Spanish that they had been on board of the guard-ship, which we fled from two days before, that we were now not above 3 mile from the mouth of the river Congo, and that they could go from thence aboard the guard-ship in half a tide's time.

This evening we supped plentifully on fowls and peccary; a sort of wild hogs which we bought of the Indians; yams, potatoes, and plantains served us for bread, whereof we had enough. After supper we agreed with one of these Indians to guide us a day's march into the country, towards the north side; he was to have for his pains a hatchet, and his bargain was to bring us to a certain Indian's habitation, who could speak Spanish, from whom we were in hopes to be better satisfied of our journey.

The 3rd day having fair weather we began to stir betimes, and set out between 6 and 7 o'clock, marching through several old ruined plantations. This morning one of our men being tired gave us the slip. By 12 o'clock we had gone 8 mile, and arrived at the Indian's house, who lived on the bank of the river Congo and spoke very good Spanish; to whom we declared the reason of this visit.

At first he seemed to be very dubious of entertaining any discourse with us, and gave impertinent answers to the questions that we demanded of him; he told us he knew no way to the north side of the country, but could carry us to Cheapo, or Santa Maria, which we knew to be Spanish garrisons; the one lying to the eastward of us, the other to the westward: either of them at least 20 miles out of our way. We could get no other answer from him, and all his discourse was in such an angry tone as plainly declared he was not our friend. However we were forced to make a virtue of necessity and humour him, for it was neither time nor place to be angry with the Indians; all our lives lying in their hand.

We were now at a great loss, not knowing what course to take, for we tempted him with beads, money, hatchets, machetes, or long knives; but nothing would work on him, till one of our men took a sky-coloured petticoat out of his bag and put it on his wife; who was so much pleased with the present that she immediately began to chatter to her husband, and soon brought him into a better humour. He could then tell us that he knew the way to the north side, and would have gone with us, but that he had cut his foot two days before, which made him incapable of serving us himself: but he would take care that we should not want a guide; and therefore he hired the same Indian who brought us hither to conduct us two days' march further for another hatchet. The old man would have stayed us here all the day because it rained very hard; but our business required more haste, our enemies lying so near us, for he told us that he could go from his house aboard the guard-ship in a tide's time; and this was the 4th day since they saw us. So we marched 3 miles farther, and then built huts, where we stayed all night; it rained all the afternoon, and the greatest part of the night.

The 4th day we began our march betimes, for the forenoons were commonly fair, but much rain after noon: though whether it rained or shined it was much at one with us, for I verily believe we crossed the rivers 30 times this day: the Indians having no paths to travel from one part of the country to another; and therefore guided themselves by the rivers. We marched this day 12 miles, and then built our hut, and lay down to sleep; but we always kept two men on the watch; otherwise our own slaves might have knocked us on the head while we slept. It rained violently all the afternoon and most part of the night. We had much ado to kindle a fire this evening: our huts were but very mean or ordinary, and our fire small, so that we could not dry our clothes, scarce warm ourselves, and no sort of food for the belly; all which made it very hard with us. I confess these hardships quite expelled the thoughts of an enemy, for now, having been 4 days in the country, we began to have but few other cares than how to get guides and food, the Spaniards were seldom in our thoughts.

The 5th day we set out in the morning betimes, and, having travelled 7 miles in those wild pathless woods, by 10 o'clock in the morning we arrived at a young Spanish Indian's house, who had formerly lived with the Bishop of Panama. The young Indian was very brisk, spoke very good Spanish, and received us very kindly. This plantation afforded us store of provisions, yams, and potatoes, but nothing of any flesh besides 2 fat monkeys we shot, part whereof we distributed to some of our company, who were weak and sickly; for others we got eggs and such refreshments as the Indians had, for we still provided for the sick and weak. We had a Spanish Indian in our company, who first took up arms with Captain Sawkins, and had been with us ever since his death. He was persuaded to live here by the master of the house, who promised him his sister in marriage, and to be assistant to him in clearing a plantation: but we would not consent to part from him here for fear of some treachery, but promised to release him in two or three days, when we were certainly out of danger of our enemies. We stayed here all the afternoon, and dried our clothes and ammunition, cleared our guns, and provided ourselves for a march the next morning.

Our surgeon, Mr. Wafer, came to a sad disaster here: being drying his powder, a careless fellow passed by with his pipe lighted and set fire to his powder, which blew up and scorched his knee, and reduced him to that condition that he was not able to march; wherefore we allowed him a slave to carry his things, being all of us the more concerned at the accident, because liable ourselves every moment to misfortune, and none to look after us but him. This Indian plantation was seated on the bank of the river Congo, in a very fat soil, and thus far we might have come in our canoe if I could have persuaded them to it.

The 6th day we set out again, having hired another guide. Here we first crossed the river Congo in a canoe, having been from our first landing on the west side of the river, and, being over, we marched to the eastward two miles, and came to another river, which we forded several times though it was very deep. Two of our men were not able to keep company with us, but came after us as they were able. The last time we forded the river it was so deep that our tallest men stood in the deepest place and handed the sick, weak and short men; by which means we all got over safe, except those two who were behind. Foreseeing a necessity of wading through rivers frequently in our land-march, I took care before I left the ship to provide myself a large joint of bamboo, which I stopped at both ends, closing it with wax, so as to keep out any water. In this I preserved my journal and other writings from being wet, though I was often forced to swim. When we were over this river, we sat down to wait the coming of our consorts who were left behind, and in half an hour they came. But the river by that time was so high that they could not get over it, neither could we help them over, but bid them be of good comfort, and stay till the river did fall: but we marched two miles farther by the side of the river, and there built our huts, having gone this day six miles. We had scarce finished our huts before the river rose much higher, and, overflowing the banks, obliged us to remove into higher ground: but the next night came on before we could build more huts, so we lay straggling in the woods, some under one tree, some under another, as we could find conveniency, which might have been indifferent comfortable if the weather had been fair; but the greatest part of the night we had extraordinary hard rain, with much lightning, and terrible claps of thunder. These hardships and inconveniencies made us all careless, and there was no watch kept (though I believe nobody did sleep) so our slaves, taking the opportunity, went away in the night; all but one who was hid in some hole and knew nothing of their design, or else fell asleep. Those that went away carried with them our surgeon's gun and all his money.

The next morning being the 8th day, we went to the river's side, and found it much fallen; and here our guide would have us ford it again, which, being deep and the current running swift, we could not. Then we contrived to swim over; those that could not swim we were resolved to help over as well as we could: but this was not so feasible: for we should not be able to get all our things over. At length we concluded to send one man over with a line, who should haul over all our things first, and then get the men over. This being agreed on, one George Gayny took the end of a line and made it fast about his neck, and left the other end ashore, and one man stood by the line to clear it away to him. But when Gayny was in the midst of the water the, line in drawing after him, chanced to kink or grow entangled; and he that stood by to clear it away stopped the line, which turned Gayny on his back, and he that had the line in his hand threw it all into the river after him, thinking he might recover himself; but the stream running very swift, and the man having three hundred dollars at his back, was carried down, and never seen more by us. Those two men whom we left behind the day before, told us afterwards that they found him lying dead in a creek where the eddy had driven him ashore, and the money on his back; but they meddled not with any of it, being only in care how to work their way through a wild unknown country. This put a period to that contrivance. This was the fourth man that we lost in this land-journey; for these two men that we left the day before did not come to us till we were in the North Seas, so we yielded them also for lost. Being frustrated at getting over the river this way, we looked about for a tree to fell across the river. At length we found one, which we cut down, and it reached clear over: on this we passed to the other side, where we found a small plantain-walk, which we soon ransacked.

While we were busy getting plantains our guide was gone, but in less than two hours came to us again, and brought with him an old Indian to whom he delivered up his charge; and we gave him a hatchet and dismissed him, and entered ourselves under the conduct of our new guide: who immediately led us away, and crossed another river, and entered into a large valley of the fattest land I did ever take notice of; the trees were not very thick, but the largest that I saw in all my travels; we saw great tracks which were made by the peccaries, but saw none of them. We marched in this pleasant country till 3 o'clock in the afternoon, in all about 4 miles, and then arrived at the old man's country house, which was only a habitation for hunting: there was a small plantain-walk, some yams, and potatoes. Here we took up our quarters for this day and refreshed ourselves with such food as the place afforded, and dried our clothes and ammunition. At this place our young Spanish Indian provided to leave us, for now we thought ourselves past danger. This was he that was persuaded to stay at the last house we came from, to marry the young man's sister; and we dismissed him according to our promise.

The 9th day the old man conducted us towards his own habitation. We marched about 5 miles in this valley; and then ascended a hill and travelled about 5 miles farther over two or three small hills before we came to any settlement. Half a mile before we came to the plantations we light of a path, which carried us to the Indians habitations. We saw many wooden crosses erected in the way, which created some jealousy in us that here were some Spaniards: therefore we new-primed all our guns, and provided ourselves for an enemy; but coming into the town found none but Indians, who were all got together in a large house to receive us: for the old man had a little boy with him that he sent before.

They made us welcome to such as they had, which was very mean; for these were new plantations, the corn being not eared. Potatoes, yams, and plantains they had none but what they brought from their old plantations. There was none of them spoke good Spanish: two young men could speak a little, it caused us to take more notice of them. To these we made a present, and desired them to get us a guide to conduct us to the north side, or part of the way, which they promised to do themselves; if we would reward them for it, but told us we must lie still the next day. But we thought ourselves nearer the North Sea than we were, and proposed to go without a guide rather than stay here a whole day: however some of our men who were tired resolved to stay behind; and Mr. Wafer our surgeon, who marched in great pain ever since his knee was burned with powder, was resolved to stay with them.

The 10th day we got up betimes, resolving to march, but the Indians opposed it as much as they could; but, seeing they could not persuade us to stay, they came with us; and, having taken leave of our friends, we set out.

Here therefore we left the surgeon and two more, as we said, and marched away to the eastward following our guides. But we often looked on our pocket compasses and showed them to the guides, pointing at the way that we would go, which made them shake their heads and say they were pretty things, but not convenient for us. After we had descended the hills on which the town stood we came down into a valley, and guided ourselves by a river, which we crossed 22 times; and, having marched 9 miles, we built huts and lay there all night: this evening I killed a quaum, a large bird as big as a turkey, wherewith we treated our guides, for we brought no provision with us. This night our last slave ran away.

The eleventh day we marched 10 mile farther, and built huts at night; but went supperless to bed.

The twelfth in the morning we crossed a deep river, passing over it on a tree, and marched 7 mile in a low swampy ground; and came to the side of a great deep river, but could not get over. We built huts upon its banks and lay there all night, upon our barbecues, or frames of sticks raised about 3 foot from the ground.

The thirteenth day when we turned out the river had overflowed its banks, and was 2 foot deep in our huts, and our guides went from us, not telling us their intent, which made us think they were returned home again. Now we began to repent our haste in coming from the settlements, for we had no food since we came from thence. Indeed we got macaw-berries in this place, wherewith we satisfied ourselves this day though coarsely.

The fourteenth day in the morning betimes our guides came to us again; and, the waters being fallen within their bounds, they carried us to a tree that stood on the bank of the river, and told us if we could fell that tree across it we might pass: if not, we could pass no farther. Therefore we set two of the best axe-men that we had, who felled it exactly across the river, and the boughs just reached over; on this we passed very safe. We afterwards crossed another river three times, with much difficulty, and at 3 o'clock in the afternoon we came to an Indian settlement, where we met a drove of monkeys, and killed 4 of them, and stayed here all night, having marched this day 6 miles. Here we got plantains enough, and a kind reception of the Indian that lived here all alone, except one boy to wait on him.

The fifteenth day when we set out, the kind Indian and his boy went with us in a canoe, and set us over such places as we could not ford: and, being past those great rivers, he returned back again, having helped us at least 2 mile. We marched afterwards 5 mile, and came to large plantain-walks, where we took up our quarters that night; we there fed plentifully on plantains, both ripe and green, and had fair weather all the day and night. I think these were the largest plantain-walks, and the biggest plantains that ever I saw, but no house near them: we gathered what we pleased by our guide's orders.

The sixteenth day we marched 3 mile and came to a large settlement where we abode all day: not a man of us but wished the journey at an end; our feet being blistered, and our thighs stripped with wading through so many rivers; the way being almost continually through rivers or pathless woods. In the afternoon five of us went to seek for game and killed 3

monkeys, which we dressed for supper. Here we first began
to have fair weather, which continued with us till we came to
the North Seas.

The eighteenth day we set out at 10 o'clock, and the Indians
with 5 canoes carried us a league up a river; and when we
landed the kind Indians went with us and carried our burdens.
We marched 3 mile farther, and then built our huts, having
travelled from the last settlements 6 mile.

The nineteenth day our guides lost their way, and we did not
march above 2 mile.

The twentieth day by 12 o'clock we came to Cheapo River.
The rivers we crossed hitherto run all into the South Seas; and
this of Cheapo was the last we met with that run that way. Here
an old man who came from the last settlements distributed his
burthen of plantains amongst us and, taking his leave, returned
home. Afterward we forded the river and marched to the foot
of a very high mountain, where we lay all night. This day we
marched about 9 miles.

The 21st day some of the Indians returned back, and we
marched up a very high mountain; being on the top, we went
some miles on a ridge, and steep on both sides; then descended
a little, and came to a fine spring, where we lay all night,
having gone this day about 9 miles, the weather still very fair
and clear.

The 22nd day we marched over another very high mountain,
keeping on the ridge 5 miles. When we came to the north end
we, to our great comfort, saw the sea; then we descended, and
parted ourselves into 3 companies, and lay by the side of a river,
which was the first we met that runs into the North Sea.

The 23rd day we came through several large plantain-walks,
and at 10 o'clock came to an Indian habitation not far from
the North Seas. Here we got canoes to carry as down the
river Concepcion to the seaside; having gone this day 7 miles.
We found a great many Indians at the mouth of the river.
They had settled themselves here for the benefit of trade with
the privateers; and their commodities were yams, potatoes,
plantains, sugarcane, fowls, and eggs.

The Indians told us that there had been a great many
English and French ships here, which were all gone but one
barcolongo, a French privateer that lay at La Sounds Key or

Island. This island is about 3 leagues from the mouth of the river Concepcion, and is one of the Samballoes, a range of islands reaching for about 20 leagues from Point Samballas to Golden Island eastward. These islands or keys, as we call them, were first made the rendezvous of privateers in the year 1679, being very convenient for careening, and had names given to some of them by the captains of the privateers: as this La Sounds Key particularly.

Thus we finished our journey from the South Sea to the North in 23 days; in which time by my account we travelled 110 miles, crossing some very high mountains; but our common march was in the valleys among deep and dangerous rivers. At our first landing in this country, we were told that the Indians were our enemies; we knew the rivers to be deep, the wet season to be coming in; yet, excepting those we left behind, we lost but one man, who was drowned, as I said. Our first landing place on the south coast was very disadvantageous, for we travelled at least fifty miles more than we need to have done, could we have gone up Cheapo River, or Santa Maria River; for at either of these places a man may pass from sea to sea in three days time with ease. The Indians can do it in a day and a half, by which you may see how easy it is for a party of men to travel over. I must confess the Indians did assist us very much, and I question whether ever we had got over without their assistance, because they brought us from time to time to their plantations where we always got provision, which else we should have wanted. But if a party of 500 or 600 men or more were minded to travel from the North to the South Seas they may do it without asking leave of the Indians; though it be much better to be friends with them.

The 24th of May (having lain one night at the river's mouth) we all went on board the privateer, who lay at La Sound's Key. It was a French vessel, Captain Tristian commander. The first thing we did was to get such things as we could to gratify our Indian guides, for we were resolved to reward them to their hearts' content. This we did by giving them beads, knives, scissors, and looking-glasses, which we bought of the privateer's crew: and half a dollar a man from each of us; which we would have bestowed in goods also, but could not get any, the privateer having no more toys. They were so well satisfied with these that they returned with joy to their friends; and were very kind to our consorts whom we left behind; as Mr. Wafer our surgeon and the rest of them told us when they came to us some months afterwards, as shall be said hereafter.

I might have given a further account of several things relating to this country; the inland parts of which are so little known to the Europeans. But I shall leave this province to Mr. Wafer, who made a longer abode in it than I, and is better able to do it than any man that I know, and is now preparing a particular description of this country for the press.

Contemporary map of the Isthmus of Darien.

CHAPTER 3

Samballoes Isles to Virginia

The author's cruising with the privateers in the north seas on the West India coast.

The privateer on board which we went being now cleaned, and our Indian guides thus satisfied and set ashore, we set sail in two days for Springer's Key, another of the Samballoes Isles, and about 7 or 8 leagues from La Sound's Key. Here lay 8 sail of privateers more, namely:

English commanders and Englishmen:
Captain Coxon, 10 guns, 100 men.
Captain Payne, 10 guns, 100 men.
Captain Wright, a barcolongo. 4 guns, 40 men.
Captain Williams, a small barcolongo.
Captain Yankes, a barcolongo, 4 guns, about 60 men, English, Dutch and French; himself a Dutchman.
French Commanders and men:
Captain Archemboe, 8 guns, 40 men.
Captain Tucker, 6 guns, 70 men.
Captain Rose, a barcolongo.

An hour before we came to the fleet Captain Wright, who had been sent to Chagra River, arrived at Springer's Key with a large canoe or periago laden with flour, which he took there. Some of the prisoners belonging to the periago came from Panama not above six days before he took her, and told the news of our coming overland, and likewise related the condition and strength of Panama, which was the main thing they enquired after; for Captain Wright was sent thither purposely to get a prisoner that was able to inform them of the strength of that city, because these privateers designed to join all their force, and, by the assistance of the Indians (who had promised to be their guides) to march overland to Panama; and there is no other way of getting prisoners for that purpose but by absconding between Chagra and Portobello, because there are much goods brought that way from Panama; especially when the armada lies at Portobello. All the commanders were aboard of Captain Wright when we came into the fleet; and were mighty inquisitive of the prisoners to know the truth of what they related concerning us. But as soon as they knew we were come they immediately came aboard of Captain Tristian, being all overjoyed to see us; for Captain Coxon and many others had left us in the South Seas about 12 months since, and had never heard what became of us since that time. They enquired of us what we did there? how we lived? how far we had been? and what discoveries we made in those seas? After we had answered these general questions they began to be more particular in examining us concerning our passage through the country from the South Seas. We related the whole matter; giving them an account of the fatigues of our march, and the inconveniencies we suffered by the rains; and disheartened them quite from that design.

Then they proposed several other places where such a party of men as were now got together might make a voyage; but the objections of some or other still hindered any proceeding: for the privateers have an account of most towns within 20 leagues of the sea, on all the coast from Trinidad down to La Vera Cruz; and are able to give a near guess of the strength and riches of them: for they make it their business to examine all prisoners that fall into their hands concerning the country, town, or city that they belong to; whether born there, or how long they have known it? how many families, whether most Spaniards? or whether the major I part are not copper-coloured, as Mulattoes, Mestizos, or Indians? whether rich, and what their riches do consist in? and what their chiefest manufactures? if fortified, how many great guns, and what number of small arms? whether it is possible to come undescribed on them? How many lookouts or sentinels; for such the Spaniards always keep? and how the lookouts are placed? Whether possible to avoid the lookouts, or take them? If any river or creek comes near it, or where the best landing;

with innumerable other such questions, which their curiosities led them to demand. And if they have had any former discourse of such places from other prisoners they compare one with the other; then examine again, and enquire if he or any of them are capable to be guides to conduct a party of men thither: if not, where and how any prisoner may be taken that may do it; and from thence they afterwards lay their schemes to prosecute whatever design they take in hand.

It was 7 or 8 days after before any resolution was taken, yet consultations were held every day. The French seemed very forward to go to any town that the English could or would propose, because the governor of Petit Guavres (from whom the privateers take commissions) had recommended a gentleman lately come from France to be general of the expedition, and sent word by Captain Tucker, with whom this gentleman came, that they should, if possible, make an attempt on some town before he returned again. The English, when they were in company with the French, seemed to approve of what the French said, but never looked on that general to be fit for the service in hand.

They go to the isle of San Andreas.
Of the cedars there.

At length it was concluded to go to a town, the name of which I have forgot; it lies a great way in the country, but not such a tedious march as it would be from hence to Panama. Our way to it lay up Carpenter's River, which is about 60 leagues to the westward of Portobello. Our greatest obstruction in this design was our want of boats: therefore it was concluded to go with all our fleet to San Andreas, a small uninhabited island lying near the isle of Providence, to the westward of it, in 13 degrees 15 minutes north latitude, and from Portobello north-north-west about 70 leagues; where we should be but a little way from Carpenter's River. And besides, at this island we might build canoes, it being plentifully stored with large cedars for such a purpose; and for this reason the Jamaica men come hither frequently to build sloops; cedar being very fit for building, and it being to be had here at free cost; beside other wood.

All things being thus concluded on, we sailed from thence, directing our course towards San Andreas. We kept company the first day, but at night it blew a hard gale at north-east and some of our ships bore away: the next day others were forced to leave us, and the second night we lost all our company. I was now belonging to Captain Archembo, for all the rest of the fleet were over-manned: Captain Archembo wanting men, we that came out of the South Seas must either sail with him or remain among the Indians. Indeed we found no cause to dislike the captain; but his French seamen were the saddest creatures that ever I was among; for though we had bad weather that required many hands aloft, yet the biggest part of them never stirred out of their hammocks but to eat or ease themselves. We made a shift to find the island the fourth day, where we met Captain Wright, who came thither the day before, and had taken a Spanish tartane, wherein were 30 men, all well armed: she had 4 patereroes and some long guns placed in the swivel on the gunwale. They fought an hour before they yielded. The news they related was that they came from Cartagena in company of 11 armadillos (which are small vessels of war) to seek for the fleet of privateers lying in the Samballoes: that they parted from the armadillos 2 days before: that they were ordered to search the Samballoes for us, and if they did not find us then they were ordered to go to Portobello, and lay there till they had farther intelligence of us, and he supposed these armadillos to be now there.

We that came overland out of the South Seas, being weary of living among the French, desired Captain Wright to fit up his prize the tartane, and make a man-of-war of her for us, which he at first seemed to decline, because he was settled among the French in Hispaniola, and was very well beloved both by the governor of Petit Guavres, and all the gentry; and they would resent it ill that Captain Wright, who had no occasion of men, should be so unkind to Captain Archembo as to seduce his men from him, he being so meanly manned that he could hardly sail his ship with his Frenchmen. We told him we would no longer remain with Captain Archembo, but would go ashore there and build canoes to transport ourselves down to the Moskitos if he would not entertain us; for privateers are not obliged to any ship, but free to go ashore where they please, or to go into any other ship that will entertain them, only paying for their provision.

When Captain Wright saw our resolutions he agreed with us on condition we should be under his command as one ship's company, to which we unanimously consented.

The Corn Islands, and their inhabitants.

We stayed here about 10 days to see if any more of our fleet would come to us; but there came no more of us to the island but three, namely, Captain Wright, Captain Archembo, and Captain Tucker. Therefore we concluded the rest were bore away either for Boca Toro or Bluefield's River on the Main; and we designed to seek them. We had fine weather while we lay here, only some tornadoes, or thundershowers: but in this isle of San Andreas, there being neither fish, fowl, nor deer, and it being therefore but an ordinary place for us, who had but little provision, we sailed from hence again in quest of our scattered fleet, directing our course for some islands lying near the Main, called by the privateers the Corn Islands; being in hopes to get corn there. These islands I take to be the same which are generally called in the maps the Pearl Islands, lying about the latitude of 12 degrees 10 minutes north. Here we arrived the next day, and went ashore on one of them, but found none of the inhabitants; for here are but a few poor naked Indians that live here; who have been so often plundered by the privateers that they have but little provision; and when they see a sail they hide themselves; otherwise ships that come here would take them, and make slaves of them; and I have seen some of them that have been slaves. They are people of a mean stature, yet strong limbs; they are of a dark copper-colour, black hair, full round faces, small black eyes, their eyebrows hanging over their eyes, low foreheads, short thick noses, not high, but flattish; full lips, and short chins. They have a fashion to cut holes in the lips of the boys when they are young, close to their chin; which they keep open with little pegs till they are 14 or 15 years old: then they wear beards in them, made of turtle or tortoiseshell, in the form you see in the illustration. The little notch at the upper end they put in through the lip, where it remains between the teeth and the lip; the under-part hangs down over their chin. This they commonly wear all day, and when they sleep they take it out. They have likewise holes bored in their ears, both men and women when young; and, by continual stretching them with great pegs, they grow to be as big as a milled five-shilling piece. Herein they wear pieces of wood cut very round and smooth, so that their ear seems to be all wood with a little skin about it. Another ornament the women use is about their legs, which they are very curious in; for from the infancy of the girls their mothers make fast a piece of cotton cloth about the small of their leg, from the ankle to the calf, very hard; which makes them have a very full calf: this the women wear to their dying day. Both men and women go naked, only a clout about their waists; yet they have but little feet, though they go barefoot. Finding no provision here we sailed towards Bluefield's River, where we careened our tartane; and there Captain Archembo and Captain Tucker left us, and went towards Boca Toro.

Bluefield's River, and an account of the manatee there, or sea-cow; with the manner how the Moskito Indians kill them, and tortoise, etc.

This Bluefield's River comes out between the rivers of Nicaragua and Veragna. At its mouth is a fine sandy bay where barks may clean: it is deep at its mouth but a shoal within; so that ships may not enter, yet barks of 60 or 70 tuns may. It had this name from Captain Bluefield, a famous privateer living on Providence Island long before Jamaica was taken. Which island of Providence was settled by the English, and belonged to the Earls of Warwick.

In this river we found a canoe coming down the stream; and though we went with our canoes to seek for inhabitants yet we found none, but saw in two or three places signs that Indians had made on the side of the river. The canoe which we found was but meanly made for want of tools, therefore we concluded these Indians have no commerce with the Spaniards, nor with other Indians that have.

While we lay here, our Moskito men went in their canoe and struck us some manatee, or sea-cow. Besides this Bluefield's River, I have seen of the manatee in the Bay of Campeachy, on the coasts of Boca del Drago, and Boca del Toro, in the river of Darien, and among the South Keys or little islands of Cuba. I have heard of their being found on the north of Jamaica a few, and in the rivers of Surinam in great multitudes, which is a very low land. I have seen of them also at Mindanao, one of the Philippine Islands, and on the coast of New Holland. This creature is about the bigness of a horse, and 10 or 12 foot long. The mouth of it is much like the mouth of a cow, having great thick lips. The eyes are no bigger than a small pea; the ears are only two small holes on each side of the head. The neck is short and thick, bigger than the head. The biggest part of this creature is at the shoulders where it has two large fins, one on each side of its belly. Under each of these fins the female has a small dug to suckle her young. From the shoulders towards the tail it retains its bigness for about a foot, then grows smaller and smaller to the very tail, which is flat, and about 14 inches broad and 20 inches long, and in the middle 4 or 5 inches thick, but about the edges of it not above 2 inches thick. From the head to the tail it is round and smooth without any fin but those two before mentioned. I have heard that some have weighed above 1200 pounds, but I never saw any so large. The manatee delights to live in brackish water; and they are commonly in creeks and rivers near the sea. It is for this reason possibly they are not seen in the South Seas (that ever I could observe) where the coast is generally a bold shore, that is, high land and deep water close home by it, with a high sea or great surges, except in the Bay of Panama; yet even there is no manatee. Whereas the West Indies, being as it were one great bay composed of many smaller, are mostly low land and shoal water, and afford proper pasture (as I may say) for the manatee. Sometimes we find them in salt water, sometimes in fresh; but never far at sea. And those that live in the sea at such places where there is no river nor creek fit for them to enter yet do commonly come once or twice in 24 hours to the mouth of any fresh-water river that is near their place of abode. They live on grass 7 or 8 inches long, and of a narrow blade, which grows in the sea in many places, especially among islands near the Main. This grass grows likewise in creeks, or in great rivers near the sides of them, in such places where there is but little tide or current. They never come ashore, nor into shallower water than where they can swim. Their flesh is white, both the fat and the lean, and extraordinary sweet, wholesome meat. The tail of a young cow is most esteemed; but if old both head and tail are very tough. A calf that sucks is the most delicate meat; privateers commonly roast them; as they do also great pieces cut out of the bellies of the old ones.

The ski n of the manatee is of great use to privateers for they cut them into straps which they make fast on the sides of their canoes, through which they put their oars in rowing, instead of tholes or pegs. The skin of the bull or of the back of the cow is too thick for this use; but of it they make horse-whips, cutting them 2 or 3 foot long: at the handle they leave the full substance of the skin, and from thence cut it away tapering, but very even and square all the four sides. While the thongs are green they wist them and hang them to dry; which in a week's time become as hard as wood. The Moskito men have always a small canoe for their use to strike fish, tortoise, or manatee, which they keep usually to themselves, and very neat and clean. They use no oars but paddles, the broad part of which does not go tapering towards the staff, pole or handle of it, as in the oar; nor do they use it in the same manner by laying it on the side of the vessel; but hold it perpendicular, gripping the staff hard with both hands, and putting back the water by main strength, and very quick strokes. One of the Moskitos (for they go but two in a canoe) sits in the stern, the other kneels down in the head, and both paddle till they come to the place where they expect their game. Then they lie still or paddle very softly, looking well about them; and he that is in the head of the canoe lays down his paddle, and stands up with his striking-staff in his hand. This staff is about 8 foot long, almost as big as a man's arm at the great end, in which there is a hole to place his harpoon in. At the other end of his staff there is a piece of light wood called bob-wood, with a hole in it, through which the small end of the staff comes; and on this piece of bob-wood there is a line of 10 or 12 fathom wound neatly about, and the end of the line made fast to it. The other end of the line is made fast to the harpoon, which is at the great end of the staff, and the

Moskito men keep about a fathom of it loose in his hand. When he strikes, the harpoon presently comes out of the staff, and as the manatee swims away the line runs off from the bob; and although at first both staff and bob may be carried under water, yet as the line runs off it will rise again. Then the Moskito men paddle with all their might to get hold of the bob again, and spend usually a quarter of an hour before they get in. When the Manatee begins to be tired, it lies still, and then the Moskito men paddle to the bob and take it up, and begin to haul in the line. When the manatee feels them he swims away again, with the canoe after him; then he that steers must be nimble to turn the head of the canoe that way that his consort points, who, being in the head of the canoe, and holding the line, both sees and feels which way the manatee is swimming. Thus the canoe is towed with a violent motion, till the manatee's strength decays. Then they gather in the line, which they are often forced to let all go to the very end. At length, when the creature's strength is spent, they haul it up to the canoe's side, and knock it on the head, and tow it to the nearest shore, where they make it fast and seek for another; which having taken, they get on shore with it to put it into their canoe: for it is so heavy that they cannot lift it in, but they haul it up in shoal water, as near the shore as they can, and then overset the canoe, laying one side close to the manatee. Then they roll in, which brings the canoe upright again; and when they have heaved out the water they fasten a line to the other manatee that lies afloat, and tow it after them. I have known two Moskito men for a week every day bring aboard 2 manatee in this manner; the least of which has not weighed less than 600 pound, and that in a very small canoe, that three Englishmen would scarce adventure to go in. When they strike a cow that has a young one they seldom miss the calf, for she commonly takes her young under one of her fins. But if the calf is so big that she cannot carry it, or so frightened that she only minds to save her own life, yet the young never leaves her till the Moskito men have an opportunity to strike her.

The manner of striking manatee and tortoise is much the same; only when they seek for manatee they paddle so gently that they make no noise, and never touch the side of their canoe with their paddle, because it is a creature that hears very well. But they are not so nice when they seek for tortoise, whose eyes are better than his ears. They strike the tortoise with a square sharp iron peg, the other with a harpoon. The Moskito men make their own striking instruments, as harpoons, fishhooks, and tortoise-irons or pegs. These pegs, or tortoise-irons, are made 4-square, sharp at one end, and not much above an inch in length, of such a figure as you see in the illustration. The small spike at the broad end has a line fastened to it, and goes also into a hole at the end of the striking-staff, which when the tortoise is struck flies off, the iron and the end of the line fastened to it going quite within the shell, where it is so buried that the tortoise cannot possibly escape.

When we had cleaned our tartane we sailed from hence, bound for Boca Toro, which is an opening between 2 islands about 10 degrees 10 minutes north latitude between the rivers of Veragne and Chagre. Here we met with Captain Yankes, who told us that there had been a fleet of Spanish armadillos to seek us: that Captain Tristian, having fallen to leeward, was coming to Boca Toro, and fell in amongst them, supposing them to be our fleet: that they fired and chased him, but he rowed and towed, and they supposed he got away: that Captain Pain was likewise chased by them and Captain Williams; and that they had not seen them since they lay within the islands: that

A manatee and calf.

the Spaniards never came in to him; and that Captain Coxon was in at the careening-place.

The savages of Boca Toro.

This Boca Toro is a place that the privateers use to resort to as much as any place on all the coast, because here is plenty of green tortoise, and a good careening place. The Indians here have no commerce with the Spaniards; but are very barbarous and will not be dealt with. They have destroyed many privateers, as they did not long after this some of Captain Pain's men; who, having built a tent ashore to put his goods in while he careened his ship, and some men lying there with their arms, in the night the Indians crept softly into the tent, and cut off the heads of three or four men, and made their escape; nor was this the first time they had served the privateers so. There grow on this coast vinelloes in great quantity, with which chocolate is perfumed. These I shall describe elsewhere.

He touches again at Point Sambalas, and its islands. The groves of sapadilloes there, the soldier's insect, and manchaneel-tree.

Our fleet being thus scattered, there were now no hopes of getting together again; therefore everyone did what they thought most conducing to obtain their ends. Captain Wright, with whom I now was, was resolved to cruise on the coast of Cartagena; and, it being now almost the westerly-wind season, we sailed from hence, and Captain Yankes with us; and we consorted, because Captain Yankes had no commission, and was afraid the French would take away his bark. We passed by Scuda, a small island (where it is said Sir Francis Drake's bowels were buried) and came to a small river to westward of Chagre; where we took two new canoes, and carried them with us into the Samballoes. We had the wind at west, with much rain; which brought us to Point Samballas. Here Captain Wright and Captain Yankes left us in the tartane to fix the canoes, while they went on the coast of Cartagena to seek for provision. We cruised in among the islands, and kept our Moskito men, or strikers-out, who brought aboard some half-grown tortoise; and some of us went ashore every day to hunt for what we could find in the woods: sometimes we got peccary, warree or deer; at other times we light on a drove of large fat monkeys, or quames, curassows (each a large sort of fowl) pigeons, parrots, or turtle-doves. We lived very well on what we got, not staying long in one place; but sometimes we would go on the islands, where there grow great groves of sapadilloes, which is a sort of fruit much like a pear, but more juicy; and under those trees we found plenty of soldiers, a little kind of animals that live in shells and have two great claws like a crab, and are good food. One time our men found a great many large ones, and being sharp-set had them dressed, but most of them were very sick afterwards, being poisoned by them: for on this island were many manchaneel-trees, whose fruit is like a small crab, and smells very well, but they are not wholesome; and we commonly take care of meddling with any animals that eat them. And this we take for a general rule; when we find any fruits that we have not seen before, if we see them pecked by birds, we may freely eat, but if we see no such sign we let them alone; for of this fruit no birds will taste. Many of these islands have of these manchaneel trees growing on them.

Thus, cruising in among these islands, at length we came again to La Sound's Key; and the day before having met with a Jamaica sloop that was come over on the coast to trade, she went with us. It was in the evening when we came to an anchor, and the next morning we fired two guns for the Indians that lived on the Main to come aboard; for by this time we concluded we should hear from our five men that we left in the heart of the country among the Indians, this being about the latter end of August, and it was the beginning of May when we parted from them. According to our expectations the Indians came aboard and brought our friends with them: Mr. Wafer wore a clout about him, and was painted like an Indian; and he was some time aboard before I knew him. One of them, named Richard Cobson, died within three or four days after, and was buried on La Sound's Key.

After this we went to other keys, to the eastward of these, to meet Captain Wright and Captain Yankes, who met with a fleet of periagos laden with Indian corn, hog and fowls, going to Cartagena; being convoyed by a small armadillo of two guns and six patereroes. Her they chased ashore, and most of the periagos; but they got two of them off, and brought them away.

The river of Darien, and the wild Indians near it; monastery of Madre de Popa, Rio Grande, Santa Marta town, and the high mountain there; Rio la Hacha town, Rancho Reys, and pearl fishery there; the Indian inhabitants and country.

Here Captain Wright's and Captain Yankes's barks were cleaned; and we stocked ourselves with corn, and then went towards the coast of Cartagena. In our way thither we passed by the river of Darien; which is very broad at the mouth, but not above 6 foot water on a spring-tide; for the tide rises but little here. Captain Coxon, about 6 months before we came out of the South Seas, went up this river with a party of men: every man carried a small strong bag to put his gold in; expecting great riches there, though they got little or none. They rowed up about 100 leagues before they came to any settlement, and then found some Spaniards, who lived there to truck with the Indians for gold; there being gold scales in every house. The Spaniards admired how they came so far from the mouth of the river, because there are a sort of Indians living between that place and the sea who are very dreadful to the Spaniards, and will not have any commerce with them, nor with any white people. They use trunks about 8 foot long, out of which they blow poisoned darts; and are so silent in their attacks on their enemies, and retreat so nimbly again, that the Spaniards can never find them. Their darts are made of macaw-wood, being about the bigness and length of a knitting-needle; one end is wound about with cotton, the other end is extraordinary sharp and small; and is jagged with notches like a harpoon: so that whatever it strikes into it immediately breaks off by the weight of the biggest end; which it is not of strength to bear (it being made so slender for that purpose) and is very difficult to be got out again by reason of those notches. These Indians have always war with our Darien friendly Indians, and live on both sides this great river 50 or 60 leagues from the sea, but not near the mouth of the river. There are abundance of manatee in this river, and some creeks belonging to it. This relation I had from several men who accompanied Captain Coxon in that discovery; and from Mr. Cook in particular, who was with them, and is a very intelligent person: he is now chief mate of a ship bound to Guinea. To return therefore to the prosecution of our voyage: meeting with nothing of note, we passed by Cartagena; which is a city so well known that I shall say nothing of it. We sailed by in sight of it, for it lies open to the sea: and had a fair view of Madre de Popa, or Nuestra Senora de Popa, a monastery of the Virgin Mary, standing on the top of a very steep hill just behind Cartagena. It is a place of incredible wealth, by reason of the offerings made here continually; and for this reason often in danger of being visited by the privateers, did not the neighbourhood of Cartagena keep them in awe. It is in short the very Loreto of the West Indies: it has innumerable miracles related of it. Any misfortune that befalls the privateers is attributed to this lady's doing; and the Spaniards report that she was aboard that night the Oxford man-of-war was blown up at the isle of Vacca near Hispaniola, and that she came home all wet; as belike she often returns with her clothes dirty and torn with passing through woods and bad ways when she has been out upon any expedition; deserving doubtless a new suit for such eminent pieces of service.

From hence we passed on to the Rio Grande, where we took up fresh water at sea, a league off the mouth of that river. From thence we sailed eastwards passing by Santa Marta, a large town and good harbour belonging to the Spaniards: yet has it within these few years been twice taken by the privateers. It stands close upon the sea, and the hill within land is a very large one, towering up a great height from a vast body of land. I am of opinion that it is higher than the Pike of Tenerife; others also that have seen both think the same; though its bigness makes its height less sensible. I have seen it in passing by, 30 leagues off at sea; others, as they told me, above 60: and several have told me that they have seen at once Jamaica, Hispaniola, and the high land of Santa Marta; and yet the nearest of these two places is distant from it 120 leagues; and Jamaica, which is farthest off, is accounted near 150 leagues; and I question whether any land on either of those two islands may be seen 50 leagues. Its head is generally hid in the clouds; but in clear weather, when the top appears, it looks white; supposed to be covered with snow. Santa Marta lies in the latitude of 12 degrees north.

Being advanced 5 or 6 leagues to the eastward of Santa Marta, we left our ships at anchor and returned back in our canoes to the Rio Grande; entering it by a mouth of it that disembogues itself near Santa Marta: purposing to attempt some towns that lie a pretty way up that river. But, this design meeting with discouragements, we returned to our ships and set sail to the Rio la Hacha. This has been a strong Spanish town, and is well built; but being often taken by the privateers the Spaniards deserted it some time before our arrival. It lies to the westward of a river; and right against the town is a good road for ships, the bottom clean and sandy. The Jamaica sloops used often to come over to trade here: and I am informed that the Spaniards have again settled themselves in it, and made it very strong. We entered the fort and brought two small guns aboard. From thence we went to the Rancho Reys, one or two small Indian villages where the Spaniards keep two barks to fish for pearl. The pearl-banks lie about 4 or 5 leagues off from the shore, as I have been told; thither the fishing barks go and anchor; then the divers go down to the bottom and fill a basket (which is let down before) with oysters; and when they come up others go down, two at a time; this they do till the bark is full, and then go ashore, where the old men, women, and children of the Indians open the oysters, there being a Spanish overseer to look after the pearl. Yet these Indians do very often secure the best pearl for themselves, as many Jamaica men can testify who daily trade with them. The meat they string up, and hang it a-drying. At this place we went ashore, where we found one of the barks, and saw great heaps of oyster-shells, but the people all fled: yet in another place, between this and Rio La Receba, we took some of the Indians, who seem to be a stubborn sort of people: they are long-visaged, black hair, their noses somewhat rising in the middle, and of a stern look.

The Spaniards report them to be a very numerous nation; and that they will not subject themselves to their yoke. Yet they have Spanish priests among them; and by trading have brought them to be somewhat sociable; but cannot keep a severe hand over them. The land is but barren, it being of a light sand near the sea, and most savannah, or champaign; and the grass but thin and coarse, yet they feed plenty of cattle. Every man knows his own and looks after them; but the land is in common, except only their houses or small plantations where they live, which every man maintains with some fence about it. They may remove from one place to another as they please, no man having right to any land but what he possesses. This part of the country is not so subject to rain as to the westward of Santa Marta; yet here are tornadoes, or thundershowers; but neither so violent as on the coast of Portobello, nor so frequent. The westerly winds in the westerly-wind season blow here, though not so strong nor lasting as on the coasts of Cartagena and Portobello.

When we had spent some time here we returned again towards the coast of Cartagena; and, being between Rio Grande and that place, we met with westerly winds, which kept us still to the eastward of Cartagena 3 or 4 days; and then in the morning we descried a sail off at sea, and we chased her at noon: Captain Wright, who sailed best, came up with her, and engaged her; and in half an hour after Captain Yankes, who sailed better than the tartane (the vessel that I was in) came up with her likewise, and laid her aboard, then Captain Wright also; and they took her before we came up. They lost 2 or 3 men, and had 7 or 8 wounded. The prize was a ship of 12 guns and 40 men, who had all good small arms. She was laden with sugar and tobacco, and 8 or 10 tuns of marmalett on board: she came from St. Jago on Cuba, and was bound to Cartagena.

We went back with her to Rio Grande to fix our rigging which was shattered in the fight, and to consider what to do with her; for these were commodities of little use to us, and not worth going into a port with. At the Rio Grande Captain Wright demanded the prize as his due by virtue of his commission: Captain Yankes said it was his due by the law of privateers. Indeed Captain Wright had the most right to her, having by his commission protected Captain Yankes from the French, who would have turned him out because he had no commission; and he likewise began to engage her first. But the company were all afraid that Captain Wright would presently carry her into a port; therefore most of Captain Wright's men stuck to Captain Yankes, and Captain Wright losing his prize burned his own bark, and had Captain Yankes's, it being bigger than his own; the tartane was sold to a Jamaica trader, and Captain Yankes commanded the prize-ship. We went again from hence to Rio la Hacha, and set the prisoners ashore; and it being now the beginning of November we concluded to go to Curacao to sell our sugar, if favoured by westerly winds, which were now come in.

Not driving a bargain for our sugar with the governor of Curacao, we went from thence to Bonaire, another Dutch island, where we met a Dutch sloop come from Europe, laden with Irish beef; which we bought in exchange for some of our sugar.

Isle of Aves, the booby and man-of-war-bird.

From Bonaire we went to the isle of Aves, or Birds; so called from its great plenty of birds, as men-of-war and boobies; but especially boobies. The booby is a waterfowl, somewhat less than a hen, of a light grayish colour. I observed the boobies of this island to be whiter than others. This bird has a strong bill, longer and bigger than a crow's and broader at the end: her feet are flat like a duck's feet. It is a very simple creature and will hardly go out of a man's way. In other places they build their nests on the ground, but here they build on trees; which I never saw anywhere else; though I have seen of them in a great many places. Their flesh is black and eats fishy, but are often eaten by the privateers. Their numbers have been much lessened by the French fleet which was lost here, as I shall give an account.

The man-of-war (as it is called by the English) is about the bigness of a kite, and in shape like it, but black; and the neck is red. It lives on fish, yet never lights on the water, but soars aloft like a kite, and when it sees its prey it flies down head foremost to the water's edge very swiftly, takes its prey out of the sea with its bill, and immediately mounts again as swiftly, and never touching the water with his bill. His wings are very long; his feet are like other land-fowl, and he builds on trees where he finds any; but where they are wanting, on the ground.

This island Aves lies about 8 or 9 leagues to the eastward of the island Bonaire, about 14 or 15 leagues from the Main, and about the latitude of 11 degrees 45 minutes north. It is but small, not above four mile in length, and towards the east end not half a mile broad. On the north side it is low land, commonly overflown with the tide; but on the south side there is a great rocky bank of coral thrown up by the sea. The west end is, for near a mile space, plain even savannah land, without any trees. There are 2 or 3 wells dug by privateers, who often frequent this island, because there is a good harbour about the middle of it on the north side where they may conveniently careen. The reef or bank of rocks on which the French fleet was lost, as I mentioned above, runs along from the east end to the northward about 3 mile, then trends away to the westward, making as it were a half moon. This reef breaks off all the sea, and there is good riding in even sandy ground to the westward of it. There are 2 or 3 small low sandy keys or islands within this reef, about 3 miles from the main island.

The Isles los Roques, the noddy and tropic-bird, mineral water, egg-birds; the mangrove-trees, black, red, and white, Isle of Tortuga, its salt ponds.

The islands Los Roques are a parcel of small uninhabited islands lying about the latitude of 11 degrees 40 minutes about 15 or 16 leagues from the Main, and about 20 leagues north-west by west from Tortuga, and 6 or 7 leagues to the westward of Orchilla, another island lying about the same distance from the Main; which island I have seen, but was never at it. Los Roques stretch themselves east and west about 5 leagues, and their breadth about 3 leagues. The northernmost of these islands is the most remarkable by reason of a high white rocky hill at the west end of it, which may be seen a great way; and on it there are abundance of tropic-birds, men-of-war, booby and noddies, which breed there.

By the sea on the south side of that high hill there's fresh water comes out of the rocks, but so slowly that it yield not above 40 gallons in 24 hours, and it tastes so copperish, or aluminous rather, and rough in the mouth, that it seems very unpleasant at first drinking: but after two or three days any water will seem to have no taste.

The middle of this island is low plain land, overgrown with long grass, where there are multitudes of small grey fowls no bigger than a blackbird, yet lay eggs bigger than a magpie's; and they are therefore by privateers called egg-birds. The east end of the island is overgrown with black mangrove-trees.

The land of this east end is light sand which is sometimes overflown with the sea at spring tides. The road for ships is on the south side against the middle of the island. The rest of the islands of Los Roques are low. The next to this on the south side is but small, flat, and even, without trees, bearing only grass. On the south side of it is a pond of brackish water which sometimes privateers use instead of better; there is likewise good riding by it. About a league from this are two other islands, not 200 yards distant from each other; yet a deep channel for ships to pass through. They are both overgrown with red mangrove-trees; which trees, above any of the mangroves, do flourish best in wet drowned land, such as these two islands are; only the east point of the westermost island is dry sand, without tree or bush. On this point we careened, lying on the south side of it.

After we had filled what water we could from hence we set out again in April 1682 and came to Salt Tortuga, so called to distinguish it from the shoals of Dry Tortugas, near Cape Florida, and from the isle of Tortugas by Hispaniola, which was called formerly French Tortugas; though, not having heard any mention of that name a great while, I am apt to think it is swallowed up in that of Petit Guavres, the chief garrison the French have in those parts. This island we arrived at is pretty large, uninhabited, and abounds with salt. It is in latitude 11 degrees north, and lies west and a little northerly from Margarita, an island inhabited by the Spaniards, strong and wealthy; it is distant from it about 14 leagues, and 17 or 18 from Cape Blanco on the Main: a ship being within these islands a little to the southward may see at once the Main, Magarita and Tortuga when it is clear weather. The east end of Tortuga is full of rugged, bare, broken rocks which stretch themselves a little way out to sea. At the south-east part is an indifferent good road for ships, much frequented in peaceable times by merchant-ships that come thither to lade salt in the months of May, June, July, and August. For at the east end is a large salt pond, within 200 paces of the sea. The salt begins to kern or grain in April, except it is a dry season; for it is observed that rain makes the salt kern. I have seen above 20 sail at a time in this road come to lade salt; and these ships coming from some of the Caribbean Islands are always well stored with rum, sugar and lime-juice to make punch, to hearten their men when they are at work, getting and bringing aboard the salt; and they commonly provide the more, in hopes to meet with privateers who resort hither in the aforesaid months purposely to keep a Christmas, as they call it; being sure to meet with liquor enough to be merry with, and are very liberal to those that treat them. Near the west end of the island, on the south side, there is a small harbour and some fresh water: that end of the island is full of shrubby trees, but the east end is rocky and barren as to trees, producing only coarse grass. There are some goats on it, but not many; and turtle or tortoise come upon the sandy bays to lay their eggs, and from thence the island has its name. There is no riding anywhere but in the roads where the salt ponds are, or in the harbour.

Isle of Blanco; the iguana animal, their variety; and the best sea-tortoise.

At this isle we thought to have sold our sugar among the English ships that come hither for salt; but, failing there, we designed for Trinidad, an island near the Main, inhabited by the Spaniards, tolerably strong and wealthy; but, the current and easterly winds hindering us, we passed through between Margarita and the Main, and went to Blanco, a pretty large island almost north of Margarita; about 30 leagues from the

Main, and in 11 degrees 50 minutes north latitude. It is a flat, even, low, uninhabited island, dry and healthy: most savannah of long grass, and has some trees of lignum-vitae growing in spots, with shrubby bushes of other wood about them. It is plentifully stored with iguanas, which are an animal like a lizard, but much bigger. The body is as big as the small of a man's leg, and from the hindquarter the tail grows tapering to the end, which is very small. If a man takes hold of the tail, except very near the hindquarter, it will part and break off in one of the joints, and the iguana will get away. They lay eggs, as most of those amphibious creatures do, and are very good to eat. Their flesh is much esteemed by privateers, who commonly dress them for their sick men; for they make very good broth. They are of divers colours, as almost black, dark brown, light brown, dark green, light green, yellow and speckled. They all live as well in the water as on land, and some of them are constantly in the water, and among rocks: these are commonly black. Others that live in swampy wet ground are commonly on bushes and trees, these are green. But such as live in dry ground, as here at Blanco, are commonly yellow; yet these also will live in the water, and are sometimes on trees. The road is on the north-west end against a small cove, or little sandy bay. There is no riding anywhere else, for it is deep water, and steep close to the land. There is one small spring on the west side, and there is sandy bays round the island, where turtle or tortoise come up in great abundance, going ashore in the night. These that frequent this island are called green turtle, and they are the best of that sort, both for largeness and sweetness of any in all the West Indies. I would here give a particular description of these and other sorts of turtle in these seas; but because I shall have occasion to mention some other sort of turtle when I come again into the South Seas, that are very different from all these, I shall there give a general account of all these several sorts at once, that the difference between them may be the better discerned. Some of our modern descriptions speak of goats on this island. I know not what there may have been formerly, but there are none now to my certain knowledge; for myself, and many more of our crew, have been all over it.

The coast of Caracas, its remarkable land, and product of the best cocoa-nuts.

We stayed at the isle of Blanco not above ten days, and then went back to Salt Tortuga again, where Captain Yankes parted with us: and from thence, after about four days, all which time our men were drunk and quarrelling, we in Captain Wright's ship went to the coast of Caracas on the mainland. This coast is upon several accounts very remarkable: it is a continued tract of high ridges of hills and small valleys intermixed for about 20 leagues, stretching east and west but in such manner that the ridges of hills and the valleys alternately run pointing upon the shore from south to north: the valleys are some of them about 4 or 5, others not above 1 or 2 furlongs wide, and in length from the sea scarce any of them above 4 or 5 mile at most; there being a long ridge of mountains at that distance from the sea-coast, and in a manner parallel to it, that joins those shorter ridges, and closes up the south end of the valleys, which at the north ends of them lie open to the sea, and make so many little sandy bays that are the only landing-places on the coast. In some of the valleys there's a strong red clay, but in the general they are extremely fertile, well-watered, and inhabited by Spaniards and their Negroes. They have maize and plantains for their support, with Indian fowls and some hogs.

The cocoa described at large, with the husbandry of it.

But the main product of these valleys, and indeed the only commodity it vends, are the cocoa-nuts, of which the chocolate is made. The cocoa-tree grows nowhere in the North Seas but in the Bay of Campeachy, on Costa Rica, between Portobello and Nicaragua, chiefly up Carpenter's River; and on this coast as high as the isle of Trinidad. In the South Seas it grows in the river of Guayaquil, a little to the southward of the Line, and in the valley of Colima, on the south side of the continent of Mexico; both which places I shall hereafter describe. Besides these I am confident there's no places in the world where the cocoa grows, except those in Jamaica, of which there are now but few remaining, of many and large walks or plantations of them found there by the English at their first arrival, and since planted by them; and even these, though there is a great deal of pains and care bestowed on them, yet seldom come to anything, being generally blighted. The nuts of this coast of Caracas, though less than those of Costa Rica, which are large flat nuts, yet are better and fatter, in my opinion, being so very oily that we are forced to use water in rubbing them up; and the Spaniards that live here, instead of parching them to get off the shell before they pound or rub them to make chocolate, do in a manner burn them to dry up the oil; for else, they say, it would fill them too full of blood, drinking chocolate as they do five or six times a day. My worthy consort Mr. Ringrose commends most the Guayaquil nut; I presume because he had little knowledge of the rest; for, being intimately acquainted with him, I know the course of his travels and experience: but I am persuaded, had he known the rest so well as I pretend to have done, who have at several times been long used to, and in a manner lived upon all the several sorts of them above mentioned, he would prefer the Caracas nuts before any other; yet possibly the drying up of these nuts so much by the Spaniards here, as I said, may lessen their esteem with those Europeans that use their chocolate ready rubbed up: so that we always chose to make it up ourselves.

The cocoa-tree has a body about a foot and a half thick (the largest sort) and 7 or 8 foot high, to the branches, which are large and spreading like an oak, with a pretty thick, smooth, dark green leaf, shaped like that of a plum-tree, but larger. The nuts are enclosed in cods as big as both a man's fists put together: at the broad end of which there is a small, tough, limber stalk, by which they hang pendulous from the body of the tree, in all parts of it from top to bottom, scattered at irregular distances, and from the greater branches a little way up; especially at the joints of them or partings, where they hang thickest, but never on the smaller boughs. There may be ordinarily about 20 or 30 of these cods upon a well-bearing tree; and they have two crops of them in a year, one in December, but the best in June. The cod itself or shell is almost half an inch thick; neither spongy nor woody, but of a substance between both, brittle, yet harder than the rind of a lemon; like which its surface is grained or knobbed, but more coarse and unequal. The cods at first are of a dark green, but the side of them next the sun of a muddy red. As they grow ripe, the green turns to a fine bright yellow, and the muddy to a more lively, beautiful red, very pleasant to the eye. They neither ripen nor are gathered at once: but for three weeks or a month when the season is the overseers of the plantations go every day about to see which are turned yellow; cutting at once, it may be, not above one from a tree. The cods thus gathered they lay in several heaps to sweat, and then, bursting the shell with their hands, they pull out the nuts which are the only substance they contain, having no stalk or pith among them, and (excepting that these nuts lie in regular rows) are placed like the grains of maize, but sticking together, and so closely stowed that, after they have been once separated, it would be hard to place them again in so narrow a compass. There are generally near 100 nuts in a cod; in proportion to the greatness of which, for it varies, the nuts are bigger or less. When taken out they dry them in the sun upon mats spread on the ground: after which they need no more care, having a thin hard skin of their own, and much oil, which preserves them. Salt water will not hurt them; for we had our bags rotten, lying in the bottom of our ship, and yet the nuts never the worse. They raise the young trees of nuts set with the great end downward in fine black mould, and in the same places where they are to bear; which they do in 4 or 5 years' time, without the trouble of transplanting. There are ordinarily of these trees from 500 to 2000 and upward in a plantation or cocoa-walk, as they call them; and they shelter the young trees from the weather with plantains set about them for two or three years; destroying all the plantains by such time the cocoa-trees are of a pretty good body and able to endure the heat; which I take to be the most pernicious to them of anything; for, though these valleys lie open to the north winds, unless a little sheltered here and there by some groves of plantain-trees, which are purposely set near the shores of the several bays, yet, by all that I could either observe or learn, the cocoas in this country are never blighted,

as I have often known them to be in other places. Cocoa-nuts
are used as money in the Bay of Campeachy.

Of the sucking fish, or remora.

In our way thither we took several of the sucking-fishes: for
when we see them about the ship, we cast out a line and hook,
and they will take it with any manner of bait, whether fish or
flesh. The sucking-fish is about the bigness of a large whiting,
and much of the same make towards the tail, but the head is
flatter. From the head to the middle of its back there grows a
sort of flesh of a hard gristly substance like that of the limpet (a
shellfish tapering up pyramidically) which sticks to the rocks;
or like the head or mouth of a shell-snail, but harder. This
excrescence is of a flat and oval form, about seven or eight
inches long and five or six broad; and rising about half an
inch high. It is full of small ridges with which it will fasten
itself to anything that it meets with in the sea, just as a snail
does to a wall. When any of them happen to come about a
ship they seldom leave her, for they will feed on such filth as
is daily thrown overboard, or on mere excrements. When it
is fair weather, and but little wind, they will play about the
ship; but in blustering weather, or when the ship sails quick,
they commonly fasten themselves to the ship's bottom, from
whence neither the ship's motion, though never so swift, nor
the most tempestuous sea can remove them. They will likewise
fasten themselves to any other bigger fish; for they never swim
fast themselves if they meet with anything to carry them. I
have found them sticking to a shark after it was hauled in
on the deck, though a shark is so strong and boisterous a
fish, and throws about him so vehemently for half an hour
together, it may be, when caught, that did not the sucking-fish
stick at no ordinary rate, it must needs be cast off by so much
violence. It is usual also to see them sticking to turtle, to any
old trees, planks, or the like, that lie driven at sea. Any knobs
or inequalities at a ship's bottom are a great hindrance to the
swiftness of its sailing; and 10 or 12 of these sticking to it must
needs retard it as much, in a manner, as if its bottom were
foul. So that I am inclined to think that this fish is the remora,

of which the ancients tell such stories; if it be not I know no other that is, and I leave the reader to judge. I have seen of these sucking-fishes in great plenty in the Bay of Campeachy and in all the sea between that and the coast of Caracas, as about those islands particularly I have lately described, Los Roques, Blanco, Tortugas, etc. They have no scales, and are very good meat.

The author's arrival in Virginia.

We met nothing else worth remark in our voyage to Virginia, where we arrived in July 1682. That country is so well known to our nation that I shall say nothing of it, nor shall I detain the reader with the story of my own affairs, and the trouble that befell me during about thirteen months of my stay there; but in the next chapter enter immediately upon my second voyage into the South Seas, and round the globe.

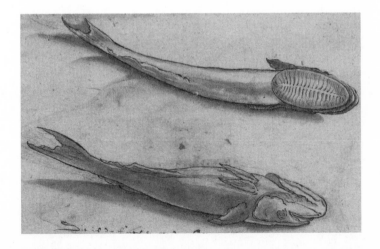

17th century drawing of a remora.

CHAPTER 4

The Castaway of Juan Fernandez

The author's voyage to the isle of Juan Fernandez in the South Seas.

Being now entering upon the relation of a new voyage which makes up the main body of this book, proceeding from Virginia by the way of Tierra del Fuego, and the South Seas, the East Indies, and so on, till my return to England by the way of the Cape of Good Hope, I shall give my reader this short account of my first entrance upon it. Among those who accompanied Captain Sharp into the South Seas in our former expedition, and leaving him there, returned overland, as is said in the Introduction and in the 1st and 2nd chapters there was one Mr. Cook, an English native of St. Christopher's, a Cirole, as we call all born of European parents in the West Indies. He was a sensible man, and had been some years a privateer. At our joining ourselves with those privateers, we met at our coming again to the North Seas; his lot was to be with Captain Yankes, who kept company for some considerable time with Captain Wright, in whose ship I was, and parted with us at our 2nd anchoring at the isle of Tortugas; as I have said in the last chapter. After our parting, this Mr. Cook being quartermaster under Captain Yankes, the second place in the ship according to the law of privateers, laid claim to a ship they took from the Spaniards; and such of Captain Yankes's men as were so disposed, particularly all those who came with us overland, went aboard this prize-ship under the new Captain Cook. This distribution was made at the isle of Vacca, or the isle of Ash, as we call it; and here they parted also such goods as they had taken. But Captain Cook having no commission, as Captain Yankes, Captain Tristian, and some other French commanders had, who lay then at that island, and they grudging the English such a vessel, they all joined together, plundered the English of their ships, goods, and arms, and turned them ashore. Yet Captain Tristian took in about 8 or 10 of these English, and carried them with him to Petit Guavres: of which number Captain Cook was one, and Captain Davis another, who with the rest found means to seize the ship as she lay at anchor in the road, Captain Tristian and many of his men being then ashore: and the English sending ashore such Frenchmen as remained in the ship and were mastered by them, though superior in number, stood away with her immediately for the isle of Vacca before any notice of this surprise could reach the French governor of that isle; so, deceiving him also by a stratagem, they got on board the rest of their countrymen who had been left on that island; and going thence they took a ship newly come from France laden with wines. They also took a ship of good force, in which they resolved to embark themselves, and make a new expedition into the South Seas, to cruise on the coast of Chile and Peru. But first they went for Virginia with their prizes; where they arrived the April after my coming thither. The best of their prizes carried 18 guns; this they fitted up there with sails, and everything necessary for so long a voyage; selling the wines they had taken for such provisions as they wanted. Myself and those of our fellow-travellers over the Isthmus of America who came with me to Virginia the year before this (most of which had since made a short voyage to Carolina, and were again returned to Virginia) resolved to join ourselves to these new adventurers: and as many more engaged in the same design as made our whole crew consist of about 70 men. So, having furnished ourselves with necessary materials, and agreed upon some particular rules, especially of temperance and sobriety, by reason of the length of our intended voyage, we all went on board our ship.

August 23 1683 we sailed from Achamack in Virginia under the command of Captain Cook bound for the South Seas. I shall not trouble the reader with an account of every day's run, but hasten to the less known parts of the world to give a description of them; only relating such memorable accidents

as happened to us and such places as we touched at by the
way.

He arrives at the Isles of Cape Verde.

We met nothing worth observation till we came to the Islands
of Cape Verde, excepting a terrible storm which we could not
escape: this happened in a few days after we left Virginia; with
a south-south-east wind just in our teeth. The storm lasted
above a week: it drenched us all like so many drowned rats,
and was one of the worst storms I ever was in. One I met with
in the East Indies was more violent for the time; but of not
above 24 hours continuance.

The flamingo, and its remarkable nest.

I know not whether there are any other beasts on the island:
there are some wildfowl, but I judge not many. I saw a few
flamingos, which is a sort of large fowl, much like a heron
in shape, but bigger, and of a reddish colour. They delight
to keep together in great companies, and feed in mud or
ponds, or in such places where there is not much water: they
are very shy, therefore it is hard to shoot them. Yet I have
lain obscured in the evening near a place where they resort,
and with two more in my company have killed 14 of them
at once; the first shot being made while they were standing
on the ground, the other two as they rose. They build their
nests in shallow ponds where there is much mud, which
they scrape together, making little hillocks like small islands
appearing out of the water a foot and a half high from the
bottom. They make the foundation of these hillocks broad,
bringing them up tapering to the top, where they leave a
small hollow pit to lay their eggs in; and when they either
lay their eggs or hatch them they stand all the while, not
on the hillock but close by it with their legs on the ground
and in the water, resting themselves against the hillock and
covering the hollow nest upon it with their rumps: for their
legs are very long; and building thus, as they do, upon the

ground, they could neither draw their legs conveniently into their nests, nor sit down upon them otherwise than by resting their whole bodies there, to the prejudice of their eggs or their young, were it not for this admirable contrivance which they have by natural instinct. They never lay more than two eggs and seldom fewer. The young ones cannot fly till they are almost full-grown; but will run prodigiously fast; yet we have taken many of them. The flesh of both young and old is lean and black, yet very good meat, tasting neither fishy nor any way unsavoury. Their tongues are large, having a large knob of fat at the root, which is an excellent bit: a dish of flamingo's tongues being fit for a prince's table.

When many of them are standing together by a pond's side, being half a mile distant from a man, they appear to him like a brick wall; their feathers being of the colour of new red brick: and they commonly stand upright and single, one by one, exactly in a row (except when feeding) and close by each other. The young ones at first are of a light grey; and as their wing-feathers spring out they grow darker; and never come to their right colour, or any beautiful shape, under ten or eleven months old. I have seen flamingoes at Rio la Hacha, and at an island lying near the Main of America, right against Curacao, called by privateers Flamingo Key, from the multitude of these fowls that breed there: and I never saw of their nests and young but here.

There are not above 5 or 6 men on this island of Sal, and a poor governor, as they called him, who came aboard in our boat, and about 3 or 4 poor lean goats for a present to our captain, telling him they were the best that the island did afford. The captain, minding more the poverty of the giver than the value of the present, gave him in requital a coat to clothe him; for he had nothing but a few rags on his back and an old hat not worth three farthings; which yet I believe he wore but seldom, for fear he should want before he might get another; for he told us there had not been a ship in 3 years before. We bought of him about 20 bushels of salt for a few old clothes: and he begged a little powder and shot. We stayed here 3 days; in which time one of these Portuguese offered to some of our men a lump of ambergris in exchange for some clothes, desiring them to keep it secret, for he said if

A flock of flamingos.

the governor should know it he should be hanged. At length one Mr. Coppinger bought for a small matter; yet I believe he gave more than it was worth.

Tornadoes, sharks, flying-fish.

We had but little wind after we got out, and very hot weather with some fierce tornadoes, commonly rising out of the northeast which brought thunder, lightning, and rain. These did not last long; sometimes not a quarter of an hour, and then the wind would shuffle about to the southward again, and fall flat calm; for these tornadoes commonly come against the wind that is then blowing, as our thunder-clouds are often observed to do in England; but the tornadoes I shall describe more largely in my Chapter of Winds, in the Appendix to this book. At this time many of our men were taken with fevers yet we lost but one. While we lay in the calms we caught several great sharks; sometimes two or three in a day, and ate them all, boiling and squeezing them dry, and then stewing them with vinegar, pepper, etc., for we had but little flesh aboard. We took the benefit of every tornado, which came sometimes three or four in a day, and carried what sail we could to get to the southward, for we had but little wind when they were over; and those small winds between the tornadoes were much against us, at south by east and south-south-east till we passed the Equinoctial Line, which we crossed about a degree to the eastward of the meridian of the isle of St. Jago, one of the Cape Verde Islands.

1684.

At first we could scarcely lie south-west but, being got a degree to the southward of the Line, the wind veered most easterly, and then we stemmed south-west by south and as we got farther to the southward, so the wind came about to the eastward and freshened upon us. In the latitude of 3 south we had the wind at south-east. In the latitude of 5 we had it at east south where it stood a considerable time and blew a fresh top-gallant gale. We then made the best use of it, steering on briskly with all the sail we could make; and this wind, by the 18th of January carried us into the latitude of 36 south. In all this time we met with nothing worthy remark; not so much as a fish except flying fish, which have been so often described that I think it needless to do it.

A sea deep and clear, yet pale.

Here we found the sea much changed from its natural greenness to a white or palish colour, which caused us to sound, supposing we might strike ground: for whenever we find the colour of the sea to change we know we are not far from land or shoals which stretch out into the sea, running from some land. But here we found no ground with one hundred fathom line. I was this day at noon by reckoning 48 degrees 50 minutes west from the Lizard, the variation by our morning amplitude 15 degrees 10 minutes east, the variation increasing. The 20th day one of our surgeons died much lamented, because we had but one more for such a dangerous voyage.

Strait le Maire.

Leaving the Sibbel de Ward Islands, as having neither good
anchorage nor water, we sailed on, directing our course for
the Straits of Magellan. But, the winds hanging in the wester-
board and blowing hard, oft put us by our topsails, so that we
could not fetch it. The 6th day of February we fell in with the
Straits Le Maire, which is very high land on both sides, and
the straits very narrow. We had the wind at north-north-west
a fresh gale; and, seeing the opening of the straits, we ran in
with it, till within four mile of the mouth, and then it fell calm,
and we found a strong tide setting out of the straits to the
northward, and like to founder our ship; but whether flood or
ebb I know not; only it made such a short cockling sea as if it
had been in a race, or place where two tides meet; for it ran
every way, sometimes breaking in over our waist, sometimes
over our poop, sometimes over our bow, and the ship tossed
like an eggshell, so that I never felt such uncertain jerks in a
ship. At 8 o'clock in the evening we had a small breeze at west-
north-west and steered away to the eastward, intending to go
round the States Island, the east end of which we reached the
next day by noon, having a fresh breeze all night.

States Island.

The 7th day at noon, being off the east end of States Island, I
had a good observation of the sun, and found myself in latitude
54 degrees 52 minutes south.

At the east end of States Island are three small islands, or
rather rocks, pretty high, and white with the dung of fowls.

Cape Horn in Tierra del Fuego.

Wherefore having observed the sun, we hauled up south,
designing to pass round to the southward of Cape Horne,
which is the southermost Land of Tierra del Fuego. The winds
hung in the western quarter betwixt the north-west and the

west, so that we could not get much to the westward, and we never saw Tierra del Fuego after that evening that we made the Straits Le Maire. I have heard that there have been smokes and fires on Tierra del Fuego, not on the tops of hills, but in plains and valleys, seen by those who have sailed through the Straits of Magellan; supposed to be made by the natives.

We did not see the sun at rising or setting in order to make an amplitude after we left the Sibbel de Wards till we got into the South Sea: therefore I know not whether the variation increased any more or no. Indeed I had an observation of the sun at noon in latitude 59 degrees 30 minutes and we were then standing to the southward with the wind at west by north, and that night the wind came about more to the southward of the west and we tacked. I was then in latitude 60 by reckoning, which was the farthest south latitude that ever I was in.

The 14th day of February, being in latitude 57 and to the west of Cape Horne, we had a violent storm, which held us to the 3rd day of March, blowing commonly south-west and south-west by west and west-south-west, thick weather all the time with small drizzling rain, but not hard. We made a shift however to save 23 barrels of rainwater besides what we dressed our victuals withal.

March the 3rd the wind shifted at once, and came about at south, blowing a fierce gale of wind; soon after it came about to the eastward, and we stood into the South Seas.

The 9th day, having an observation of the sun, not having seen it of late, we found ourselves in latitude 47 degrees 10 minutes and the variation to be but 15 degrees 30 minutes east.

The wind stood at south-east, we had fair weather, and a moderate gale, and the 17th day we were in latitude 36 by observation, and then found the variation to be but 8 degrees east.

Their meeting with Captain Eaton in the South Seas, and their going together to the Isle of Juan Fernandez.

The 19th day when we looked out in the morning we saw a ship to the southward of us, coming with all the sail she could

An early map of the Islands of Juan Fernandez.

Venant du côté de l'Est Nord Est

Baye de Cumberland   Baye de l'Ouest

Pointe de l'Ouest
22
Baye du Pain de Sucre
ou de l'Ouest

34 Baye de l'Ouest

56   Fond de Sable fin
Baye de Cumberland
32   44   55
52
La Crique
40
39   Sable gris fin
30
19
26   Banc de Roches
sous l'eau
27
25
Caye du
Singe
Pointe de l'Est

Tome 16 in 8º. Page 285.

make after us: we lay muzzled to let her come up with us, for we supposed her to be a Spanish ship come from Valdivia bound to Lima: we being now to the northward of Valdivia and this being the time of the year when ships that trade thence to Valdivia return home. They had the same opinion of us, and therefore made sure to take us, but coming nearer we both found our mistakes. This proved to be one Captain Eaton in a ship sent purposely from London to the South Seas. We hailed each other, and the captain came on board, and told us of his actions on the coast of Brazil, and in the river of Plate.

He met Captain Swan (one that came from England to trade here) at the east entrance into the Straits of Magellan, and they accompanied each other through the straits, and were separated after they were through by the storm before-mentioned. Both we and Captain Eaton being bound for Juan Fernandez Isle, we kept company, and we spared him bread and beef, and he spared us water, which he took in as he passed through the straits.

Of a Moskito man left there alone three years: his art and sagacity; with that of other Indians.

March the 22nd 1684, we came in sight of the island, and the next day got in and anchored in a bay at the south end of the island, and 25 fathom water, not two cables' length from the shore. We presently got out our canoe, and went ashore to see for a Moskito Indian whom we left here when we were chased hence by three Spanish ships in the year 1681, a little before we went to Arica; Captain Watling being then our commander, after Captain Sharp was turned out.

This Indian lived here alone above three years and, although he was several times sought after by the Spaniards, who knew he was left on the island, yet they could never find him. He was in the woods hunting for goats when Captain Watling drew off his men, and the ship was under sail before he came back to shore. He had with him his gun and a knife, with a small horn of powder and a few shot; which, being spent, he contrived a way by notching his knife to saw the barrel of his gun into small pieces wherewith he made harpoons, lances, hooks, and a long knife, heating the pieces first in the fire, which he struck with his gunflint, and a piece of the barrel of his gun, which he hardened; having learnt to do that among the English. The hot pieces of iron he would hammer out and bend as he pleased with stones, and saw them with his jagged knife; or grind them to an edge by long labour, and harden them to a good temper as there was occasion. All this may seem strange to those that are not acquainted with the sagacity of the Indians; but it is no more than these Moskito men are accustomed to in their own country, where they make their own fishing and striking-instruments, without either forge or anvil; though they spend a great deal of time about them.

Other wild Indians who have not the use of iron, which the Moskito men have from the English, make hatchets of a very hard stone, with which they will cut down trees (the cotton-tree especially, which is a soft tender wood) to build their houses or make canoes; and, though in working their canoes hollow, they cannot dig them so neat and thin, yet they will make them fit for their service. This their digging or hatchet-work they help out by fire; whether for the felling of trees or for the making the inside of their canoe hollow. These contrivances are used particularly by the savage Indians of Bluefield's River, described in the 3rd chapter, whose canoes and stone hatchets I have seen. These stone hatchets are about 10 inches long, 4 broad, and three inches thick in the middle. They are ground away flat and sharp at both ends: right in the midst and clear round it they make a notch, so wide and deep that a man might place his finger along it and, taking a stick or withe about 4 foot long, they bind it round the hatchet head, in that notch, and so, twisting it hard, use it as a handle or helve; the head being held by it very fast. Nor are other wild Indians less ingenious. Those of Patagonia particularly head their arrows with flint, cut or ground; which I have seen and admired. But to return to our Moskito man on the isle of Juan Fernandez. With such instruments as he made in that manner, he got such provision as the island afforded; either goats or fish. He told us that at first he was forced to eat seal, which is very ordinary meat, before he had made hooks: but afterwards he never killed any seals but to make lines, cutting their skins into thongs. He had a little house or hut half a mile from the sea, which was lined with goat's skin; his couch or barbecue of sticks lying along about two foot distant from the ground, was spread with the same, and was all his bedding. He had no clothes left, having worn out those he brought from Watling's ship, but only a skin about his waist. He saw our ship the day before we came to an anchor, and did believe we were English, and therefore killed three goats in the morning before we came to an anchor, and dressed them with cabbage, to treat us when we came ashore. He came then to the seaside to congratulate our safe arrival. And when we landed a Moskito Indian named Robin first leapt ashore and, running to his brother Moskito man, threw himself flat on his face at his feet, who helping him up, and embracing him, fell flat with his face on the ground at Robin's feet, and was by him taken up also. We stood with pleasure to behold the surprise, and tenderness, and solemnity of this interview, which was exceedingly affectionate on both sides; and when their ceremonies of civility were over we also that stood gazing at them drew near, each of us embracing him we had found here, who was overjoyed to see so many of his old friends come hither, as he thought purposely to fetch him. He was named Will, as the other was Robin. These were names given them by the English, for they had no names among themselves; and they take it as a great favour to be named by any of us; and will complain for want of it if we do not appoint them some name when they are with us: saying of themselves they are poor men, and have no name.

Seals. Sea-lions.

Seals swarm as thick about this island as if they had no other place in the world to live in; for there is not a bay nor rock that one can get ashore on but is full of them. Sea-lions are here in great companies, and fish, particularly snapper and rock-fish, are so plentiful that two men in an hour's time will take with hook and line as many as will serve 100 men.

The seals are a sort of creatures pretty well known, yet it may not be amiss to describe them. They are as big as calves, the head of them like a dog, therefore called by the Dutch the sea-hounds. Under each shoulder grows a long thick fin: these

serve them to swim with when in the sea, and are instead of
legs to them when on the land for raising their bodies up on
end, by the help of these fins or stumps, and so having their
tail-parts drawn close under them, they rebound as it were, and
throw their bodies forward, drawing their hinder parts after
them; and then again rising up, and springing forward with
their fore parts alternately, they lie tumbling thus up and down
all the while they are moving on land. From their shoulders
to their tails they grow tapering like fish, and have two small
fins on each side the rump; which is commonly covered with
their fins. These fins serve instead of a tail in the sea; and on
land they sit on them when they give suck to their young. Their
hair is of divers colours, as black, grey, dun, spotted, looking
very sleek and pleasant when they come first out of the sea:
for these at Juan Fernandez have fine thick short fur; the like I
have not taken notice of anywhere but in these seas. Here are
always thousands, I might say possibly millions of them, either
sitting on the bays, or going and coming in the sea round the
island; which is covered with them (as they lie at the top of
the water playing and sunning themselves) for a mile or two
from the shore. When they come out of the sea they bleat like
sheep for their young; and, though they pass through hundreds
of others' young ones before they come to their own, yet they
will not suffer any of them to suck. The young ones are like
puppies, and lie much ashore; but when beaten by any of us,
they, as well as the old ones, will make towards the sea, and
swim very swift and nimble; though on shore they lie very
sluggishly and will not go out of our ways unless we beat them,
but snap at us. A blow on the nose soon kills them. Large ships
might here load themselves with seal-skins, and train-oil; for
they are extraordinary fat. Seals are found as well in cold as
hot climates; and in the cold places they love to get on lumps
of ice, where they will lie and sun themselves, as here on the
land: they are frequent in the northern parts of Europe and
America, and in the southern parts of Africa, as about the Cape
of Good Hope and at the Straits of Magellan: and though I
never saw any in the West Indies but in the Bay of Campeachy,
at certain islands called the Alceranes, and at others called the
Desarts; yet they are over all the American coast of the South
Seas, from Tierra del Fuego up to the Equinoctial Line; but

to the north of the Equinox again, in these seas, I never saw any till as far as 21 north latitude. Nor did I ever see any in the East Indies. In general they seem to resort where there is plenty of fish, for that is their food; and fish, such as they feed on, as cods, groupers, etc., are most plentiful on rocky coasts: and such is mostly this western coast of the South America; as I shall further relate.

The sea-lion is a large creature about 12 or 14 foot long. The biggest part of his body is as big as a bull: it is shaped like a seal, but six times as big. The head is like a lion's head; it has a broad face with many long hairs growing about its lips like a cat. It has a great goggle eye, the teeth three inches long, about the bigness of a man's thumb: in Captain Sharp's time, some of our men made dice with them. They have no hair on their bodies like the seal; they are of a dun colour, and are all extraordinary fat; one of them being cut up and boiled will yield a hogshead of oil which is very sweet and wholesome to fry meat withal. The lean flesh is black, and of a coarse grain; yet indifferent good food. They will lie a week at a time ashore if not disturbed. Where 3 or 4 or more of them come ashore together they huddle one on another like swine, and grunt like them, making a hideous noise. They eat fish, which I believe is their common food.

CHAPTER 5

The Galapagos Islands

The author departs from Juan Fernandez.
Of the Pacific Sea.

The 8th of April 1684 we sailed from the isle of Juan Fernandez with the wind at south-east. We were now two ships in company: Captain Cook's, whose ship I was in, and who here took the sickness of which he died a while after, and Captain Eaton's. Our passage lay now along the Pacific Sea, properly so called. For though it be usual with our map-makers to give that name to this whole ocean, calling it Mare Australe, Mal del Zur, or Mare Pacificum; yet in my opinion the name of the Pacific Sea ought not to be extended from south to north farther than from 30 to about 4 degrees south latitude, and from the American shore westward indefinitely, with respect to my observation; who have been in these parts 250 leagues or more from land, and still had the sea very quiet from winds. For in all this tract of water of which I have spoken there are no dark rainy clouds, though often a thick horizon so as to hinder an observation of the sun with the quadrant; and in the morning hazy weather frequently, and thick mists, but scarce able to wet one. Nor are there in this sea any winds but the trade-wind, no tempests, no tornadoes or hurricanes (though north of the Equator they are met with as well in this ocean as in the Atlantic) yet the sea itself at the new and full of the moon runs with high, large, long surges, but such as never break out at sea and so are safe enough; unless that where they fall in and break upon the shore they make it bad landing.

Of the Andes, or high mountains in Peru and Chile.

In this sea we made the best of our way toward the Line till in the latitude of 24 south where we fell in with the mainland of the South America. All this course of the land, both of Chile and Peru, is vastly high; therefore we kept 12 or 14 leagues off from shore, being unwilling to be seen by the Spaniards dwelling there. The land (especially beyond this, from 24 degrees south latitude 17, and from 14 to 10) is of a most prodigious height. It lies generally in ridges parallel to the shore, and 3 or 4 ridges one with another, each surpassing other in height; and those that are farthest within land are much higher than others. They always appear blue when seen at sea: sometimes they are obscured with clouds, but not so often as the high lands in other parts of the world, for here are seldom or never any rains on these hills, any more than in the sea near it; neither are they subject to fogs. These are the highest mountains that ever I saw, far surpassing the Pike of Tenerife or Santa Marta and, I believe, any mountains in the world.

I have seen very high land in the latitude of 30 south, but not so high as in the latitudes before described. In Sir John Narborough's voyage also to Valdivia (a city on this coast) mention is made of very high land seen near Valdivia: and the Spaniards with whom I have discoursed have told me that there is a very high land all the way between Coquimbo (which lies in about 30 degrees south latitude) and Valdivia, which is in 40 south; so that by all likelihood these ridges of mountains do run in a continued chain from one end of Peru and Chile to the other, all along this South Sea coast, called usually the Andes, or Sierra Nevada des Andes. The excessive height of these mountains may possibly be the reason that there are no rivers of note that fall into these seas. Some small rivers indeed there are, but very few of them, for in some places there is not one that comes out into the sea in 150 or 200 leagues, and where they are thickest they are 30, 40, or 50 leagues asunder, and too little and shallow to be navigable. Besides, some of these do not constantly run, but are dry at certain seasons of the year; as the river of Ylo runs flush with a quick current at the latter end of January, and so continues till June, and then it decreases by degrees, growing less, and running slow till the latter end of September, when it fails wholly, and runs no more till January again: this I have seen at both seasons in two former voyages I made hither, and have been informed by the Spaniards that other rivers on this coast are of the like nature, being rather torrents or land-floods caused by their rains at certain seasons far within land than perennial streams.

A prize taken.

We kept still along in sight of this coast but at a good distance from it, encountering with nothing of note till in the latitude of 9 degrees 40 minutes south. On the 3rd of May we descried a sail to the northward of us. She was plying to windward, we chased her, and Captain Eaton being ahead soon took her: she came from Guayaquil about a month before, laden with timber, and was bound to Lima. Three days before we took her she came from Santa, whither she had gone for water, and where they had news of our being in these seas by an express from Valdivia, for, as we afterwards heard, Captain Swan had been at Valdivia to seek a trade there; and he having met Captain Eaton in the Straits of Magellan, the Spaniards of Valdivia were doubtless informed of us by him, suspecting him also to be one of us, though he was not. Upon this news the viceroy of Lima sent expresses to all the sea ports, that they might provide themselves against our assaults.

Isle of Lobos: penguins and other birds there.

We immediately steered away for the island Lobos which lies in latitude 6 degrees 24 minutes south latitude (I took the elevation of it ashore with an astrolabe) and it is 5 leagues from the Main. It is called Lobos de la Mar, to distinguish it from another that is not far from it, and extremely like it, called Lobos de la Terra, for it lies nearer the main. Lobos, or Lovos, is the Spanish name for a seal, of which there are great plenty about these and several other islands in these seas that go by this name.

The 9th of May we arrived at this isle of Lobos de la Mar and came to an anchor with our prize. This Lobos consists indeed of two little islands, each about a mile round, of an indifferent height, a small channel between, fit for boats only; and several rocks lying on the north side of the islands, a little way from shore. There is a small cove or sandy bay sheltered from the winds at the west end of the eastermost island, where ships may careen: the rest of the shore, as well round the two islands as between them, is a rocky coast consisting of small cliffs. Within land they are both of them partly rocky, and partly sandy, barren, without any fresh water, tree, shrub, grass, or herbs; or any land animals (for the seals and sea-lions come ashore here) but fowls, of which there are great multitudes; as boobies, but mostly penguins, which I have seen plentifully all over the South Seas, on the coast of Newfoundland, and of the Cape of Good Hope. They are a sea-fowl, about as big as a duck, and such feet; but a sharp bill, feeding on fish. They do not fly, but flutter, having rather stumps like a young gosling's than wings: and these are instead of fins to them in the water. Their feathers are downy. Their flesh is but ordinary food but their eggs are good meat. There is another sort of small black fowl that makes holes in the sand for their night habitations whose flesh is good sweet meat. I never saw any of them but here and at Juan Fernandez.

There is good riding between the eastermost island and the rocks in ten, twelve, or fourteen fathom, for the wind is commonly at south or south-south-east, and the eastermost island lying east and west, shelters that road.

Here we scrubbed our ships and, being in a readiness to sail, the prisoners were examined to know if any of them could conduct us to some town where we might make some attempt; for they had before informed us that we were descried by the Spaniards, and by that we knew that they would send no riches by sea so long as we were here. Many towns were considered on, as Guayaquil, Zana, Truxillo, and others: at last Truxillo was pitched on as the most important, therefore the likeliest to make us a voyage if we could conquer it: which we did not much question though we knew it to be a very populous city.

But the greatest difficulty was in landing; for Guanchaquo, which is the nearest sea port to it, but six miles off, is an ill place to land, since sometimes the very fishermen that live there are not able to go in three or four days.

The Islands Galapagos: the dildoe-tree, burton-wood, mammee-trees, iguanas, land-tortoise, their several kind; green snakes, turtle-doves, tortoise, or turtle-grass.

It was the 31st day of May when we first had sight of the islands Galapagos: some of them appeared on our weather bow, some on our lee bow, others right ahead. We at first sight trimmed our sails and steered as nigh the wind as we could, striving to get to the southermost of them but, our prizes being deep laden, their sails but small and thin, and a very small gale, they could not keep up with us; therefore we likewise edged away again a point from the wind to keep near them; and in the evening the ship that I was in and Captain Eaton anchored on the east side of one of the eastermost islands, a mile from the shore, in sixteen fathom water, clean, white, hard sand.

The Galapagos Islands are a great number of uninhabited islands lying under and on both sides of the Equator. The eastermost of them are about 110 leagues from the Main. They are laid down in the longitude of 181, reaching to the westward as far as 176, therefore their longitude from England westward is about 68 degrees. But I believe our hydrographers do not place them far enough to the westward. The Spaniards who first discovered them, and in whose charts alone they are laid down, report them to be a great number stretching north-west from the Line, as far as 5 degrees north, but we saw not above 14 or 15. They are some of them 7 or 8 leagues long, and 3 or 4 broad. They are of a good height, most of them flat and even on the top; 4 or 5 of the eastermost are rocky, barren and hilly, producing neither tree, herb, nor grass, but a few dildoe-trees, except by the seaside. The dildoe-tree is a green prickly shrub that grows about 10 or 12 foot high, without either leaf or fruit. It is as big as a man's leg, from the root to the top, and it is full of sharp prickles growing in thick rows from top to bottom;

this shrub is fit for no use, not so much as to burn. Close by the sea there grows in some places bushes of burton-wood, which is very good firing. This sort of wood grows in many places in the West Indies, especially in the Bay of Campeachy and the Samballoes. I did never see any in these seas but here. There is water on these barren islands in ponds and holes among the rocks. Some other of these islands are mostly plain and low, and the land more fertile, producing trees of divers sorts unknown to us. Some of the westermost of these islands are nine or ten leagues long and six or seven broad; the mould deep and black. These produce trees of great and tall bodies, especially mammee-trees, which grow here in great groves. In these large islands there are some pretty big rivers; and in many of the other lesser islands there are brooks of good water. The Spaniards when they first discovered these islands found multitudes of iguanas, and land-turtle or tortoise, and named them the Galapagos Islands. I do believe there is no place in the world that is so plentifully stored with those animals. The iguanas here are fat and large as any that I ever saw; they are so tame that a man may knock down twenty in an hour's time with a club. The land-turtle are here so numerous that 5 or 600 men might subsist on them alone for several months without any other sort of provision: they are extraordinary large and fat; and so sweet that no pullet eats more pleasantly. One of the largest of these creatures will weigh 150 or 200 weight, and some of them are 2 foot, or 2 foot 6 inches over the challapee or belly. I did never see any but at this place that will weigh above 30 pound weight. I have heard that at the isle of St. Lawrence or Madagascar, and at the English Forest, an island near it called also Don Mascarin and now possessed by the French, there are very large ones, but whether so big, fat, and sweet as these, I know not. There are 3 or 4 sorts of these creatures in the West Indies. One is called by the Spaniards hecatee; these live most in fresh-water ponds, and seldom come on land. They weigh about 10 or 15 pound; they have small legs and flat feet, and small long necks. Another sort is called tenapen; these are a great deal less than the hecatee; the shell on their backs is all carved naturally, finely wrought, and well clouded: the backs of these are rounder than those before mentioned; they are otherwise much of the same form: these delight to live in wet swampy places, or on the land near such places. Both these sorts are very good meat. They are in great plenty on the isles of Pines near Cuba: there the Spanish hunters when they meet them in the woods bring them home to their huts, and mark them by notching their shells, then let them go; this they do to have them at hand, for they never ramble far from thence. When these hunters return to Cuba, after about a month or six weeks' stay, they carry with them 3 or 400 or more of these creatures to sell; for they are very good meat, and every man knows his own by their marks. These tortoise in the Galapagos are more like the hecatee except that, as I said before, they are much bigger; and they have very long small necks and little heads. There are some green snakes on these islands, but no other land animal that I did ever see. There are great plenty of turtle-doves so tame that a man may kill 5 or 6 dozen in a forenoon with a stick. They are somewhat less than a pigeon, and are very good meat, and commonly fat.

There are good wide channels between these islands fit for ships to pass, and in some places shoal water where there grows plenty of turtle-grass; therefore these islands are plentifully stored with sea-turtle of that sort which is called the green turtle. I have hitherto deferred the description of these creatures therefore I shall give it here.

Sea-turtle, their several kinds.

There are 4 sorts of sea-turtle, namely, the trunk-turtle, the loggerhead, the hawksbill, and the green turtle. The trunk-turtle is commonly bigger than the other, their backs are higher and rounder, and their flesh rank and not wholesome. The loggerhead is so called because it has a great head, much bigger than the other sorts; their flesh is likewise very rank, and seldom eaten but in case of necessity: they feed on moss that grows about rocks. The hawksbill-turtle is the least kind, they are so called because their mouths are long and small, somewhat resembling the bill of a hawk: on the backs of these hawksbill turtle grows that shell which is so much esteemed for making cabinets, combs, and other things. The largest of them may have 3 pound and a half of shell; I have taken some that have had 3 pound 10 ounces: but they commonly have a pound and a half or two pound; some not so much. These are but ordinary food, but generally sweeter than the loggerhead: yet these hawksbills in some places are unwholesome, causing them that eat them to purge and vomit excessively, especially those between the Samballoes and Portobello. We meet with other fish in the West Indies of the same malignant nature: but I shall describe them in the Appendix. These hawksbill-turtles are better or worse according to their feeding. In some places they feed on grass, as the green tortoise also does; in other places they keep among rocks and feed on moss or seaweeds; but these are not so sweet as those that eat grass, neither is their shell so clear; for they are commonly overgrown with barnacles which spoil the shell; and their flesh is commonly yellow, especially the fat.

Hawksbill-turtle are in many places of the West Indies: they have islands and places peculiar to themselves where they lay their eggs, and seldom come among any other turtle. These and all other turtle lay eggs in the sand; their time of laying is in May, June, July. Some begin sooner, some later. They lay 3 times in a season, and at each time 80 or 90 eggs. Their eggs are as big as a hen's egg, and very round, covered only with a white tough skin. There are some bays on the north side of Jamaica where these hawksbills resort to lay. In the Bay of Honduras are islands which they likewise make their breeding-places, and many places along all the coast on the Main of the West Indies from Trinidad de La Vera Cruz in the Bay of Nova Hispania. When a sea-turtle turns out of the sea to lay she is at least an hour before she returns again, for she is to go above high-water mark, and if it be low-water when she comes ashore, she must rest once or twice, being heavy, before she comes to the place where she lays. When she has found a place for her purpose she makes a great hole with her fins in the sand, wherein she lays her eggs, then covers them 2 foot deep with the same sand which she threw out of the hole, and so returns. Sometimes they come up the night before they intend to lay, and take a view of the place, and so having made a tour, or semicircular march, they return to the sea again, and they never fail to come ashore the next night to lay near that place. All sorts of turtle use the same methods in laying. I knew a man in Jamaica that

made 8 pound Sterling of the shell of these hawksbill turtle
which he got in one season and in one small bay, not half a
mile long. The manner of taking them is to watch the bay by
walking from one part to the other all night, making no noise,
nor keeping any sort of light. When the turtle comes ashore
the man that watches for them turns them on their backs, then
hauls them above high-water mark, and leaves them till the
morning. A large green turtle, with her weight and struggling,
will puzzle 2 men to turn her. The hawksbill-turtle are not only
found in the West Indies but on the coast of Guinea, and in the
East Indies. I never saw any in the South Seas.

The green turtle are so called because their shell is greener
than any other. It is very thin and clear and better clouded than
the hawksbill; but it is used only for inlays, being extraordinary
thin. These turtles are generally larger than the hawksbill; one
will weigh 2 or 3 hundred pound. Their backs are flatter than
the hawksbill, their heads round and small. Green turtle are
the sweetest of all the kinds: but there are degrees of them
both in respect to their flesh and their bigness. I have observed
that at Blanco in the West Indies the green turtle (which is the
only kind there) are larger than any other in the North Seas.
There they will commonly weigh 280 or 300 pound: their fat
is yellow, and the lean white, and their flesh extraordinary
sweet. At Boca Toro, west of Portobello, they are not so large,
their flesh not so white, nor the fat so yellow. Those in the
Bay of Honduras and Campeachy are somewhat smaller still;
their fat is green, and the lean of a darker colour than those
at Boca Toro. I heard of a monstrous green turtle once taken
at Port Royal in the Bay of Campeachy that was four foot
deep from the back to the belly, and the belly six foot broad;
Captain Roch's son, of about nine or ten years of age, went in
it as in a boat on board his father's ship, about a quarter of a
mile from the shore. The leaves of fat afforded eight gallons of
oil. The turtle that live among the keys or small islands on the
south side of Cuba are a mixed sort, some bigger, some less;
and so their flesh is of a mixed colour, some green, some dark,
some yellowish. With these Port Royal in Jamaica is constantly
supplied by sloops that come hither with nets to take them.
They carry them alive to Jamaica where the turtles have wires
made with stakes in the sea to preserve them alive; and the

market is every day plentifully stored with turtle, it being the common food there, chiefly for the ordinary sort of people.

Green turtle live on grass which grows in the sea in 3, 4, 5, or 6 fathom water, at most of the places before mentioned. This grass is different from manatee-grass, for that is a small blade; but this a quarter of an inch broad and six inches long. The turtle of these islands Galapagos are a sort of a bastard green turtle; for their shell is thicker than other green turtle in the West or East Indies, and their flesh is not so sweet. They are larger than any other green turtle; for it is common for these to be two or three foot deep, and their callapees or bellies five foot wide: but there are other green turtle in the South Seas that are not so big as the smallest hawksbill. These are seen at the island Plata, and other places thereabouts: they feed on moss and are very rank but fat.

Both these sorts are different from any others, for both he's and she's come ashore in the daytime and lie in the sun; but in other places none but the she's go ashore, and that in the night only to lay their eggs. The best feeding for turtle in the South Seas is among these Galapagos Islands, for here is plenty of grass.

There is another sort of green turtle in the South Seas which are but small, yet pretty sweet: these lie westward on the coast of Mexico. One thing is very strange and remarkable in these creatures; that at the breeding time they leave for two or three months their common haunts, where they feed most of the year, and resort to other places only to lay their eggs: and it is not thought that they eat anything during this season: so that both he's and she's grow very lean; but the he's to that degree that none will eat them. The most remarkable places that I did ever hear of for their breeding is at an island in the West Indies called Caymans, and the isle Ascension in the Western Ocean: and when the breeding time is past there are none remaining. Doubtless they swim some hundreds of leagues to come to those two places: for it has been often observed that at Cayman, at the breeding time, there are found all those sort of turtle before described. The South Keys of Cuba are above 40 leagues from thence, which is the nearest place that these creatures can come from; and it is most certain that there could not live so many there as come here in one season.

Those that go to lay at Ascension must needs travel much farther; for there is no land nearer it than 300 leagues: and it is certain that these creatures live always near the shore. In the South Sea likewise the Galapagos is the place where they live the biggest part of the year; yet they go from thence at their season over to the Main to lay their eggs; which is 100 leagues the nearest place. Although multitudes of these turtles go from their common places of feeding and abode to those laying-places, yet they do not all go: and at the time when the turtle resort to these places to lay their eggs they are accompanied with abundance of fish, especially sharks; the places which the turtle then leave being at that time destitute of fish, which follow the turtle.

When the she's go thus to their places to lay the male accompany them, and never leave them till they return: both male and female are fat the beginning of the season; but before they return the male, as I said, are so lean that they are not fit to eat, but the female are good to the very last; yet not so fat as at the beginning of the season. It is reported of these creatures that they are nine days engendering, and in the water, the male on the female's back. It is observable that the male, while engendering, do not easily forsake their female: for I have gone and taken hold of the male when engendering: and a very bad striker may strike them then, for the male is not shy at all: but the female, seeing a boat when they rise to blow, would make her escape, but that the male grasps her with his two fore fins, and holds her fast. When they are thus coupled it is best to strike the female first, then you are sure of the male also. These creatures are thought to live to a great age; and it is observed by the Jamaica turtlers that they are many years before they come to their full growth.

A sea turtle.

Some of the islands described, their soil, etc.

The next island of the Galapagos that we came to is but two leagues from this: it is rocky and barren like this; it is about five or six leagues long and four broad. We anchored in the afternoon at the north side of the island, a quarter of a mile from the shore in 16 fathom water. It is steep all round this island and no anchoring only at this place. Here it is but ordinary riding; for the ground is so steep that if an anchor starts it never holds again; and the wind is commonly off from the land except in the night when the land-wind comes more from the west, for there it blows right along the shore, though but faintly. Here is no water but in ponds and holes of the rocks.

That which we first anchored at has water on the north end falling down in a stream from high steep rocks upon the sandy bay, where it may be taken up. As soon as we came to an anchor, we made a tent ashore for Captain Cook who was sick. Here we found the sea-turtle lying ashore on the sand; this is not customary in the West Indies. We turned them on their backs that they might not get away. The next day more came up, when we found it to be their custom to lie in the sun: so we never took care to turn them afterwards; but sent ashore the cook every morning, who killed as many as served for the day. This custom we observed all the time we lay here, feeding sometimes on land-turtle, sometimes on sea-turtle, there being plenty of either sort. Captain Davis came hither again a second time; and then he went to other islands on the west side of these. There he found such plenty of land-turtle that he and his men ate nothing else for three months that he stayed there. They were so fat that he saved sixty jars of oil out of those that he spent: this oil served instead of butter to eat with doughboys or dumplings, in his return out of these seas. He found very convenient places to careen, and good channels between the islands; and very good anchoring in many places. There he found also plenty of brooks of good fresh water, and firewood enough, there being plenty of trees fit for many uses. Captain Harris, one that we shall speak of hereafter, came thither likewise, and found some islands that had plenty of mammee-trees, and pretty large rivers. The sea about these islands is plentifully stored with fish such as are at Juan Fernandez. They are both large and fat and as plentiful here as at Juan Fernandez. Here are particularly abundance of sharks. The north part of this second isle we anchored at lies 28 minutes north of the Equator. I took the height of the sun with an astrolabe. These isles of the Galapagos have plenty of salt. We stayed here but 12 days in which time we put ashore 5000 packs of flour for a reserve if we should have occasion of any before we left these seas. Here one of our Indian prisoners informed us that he was born at Realejo, and that he would engage to carry us thither. He being examined of the strength and riches of it satisfied the company so well that they were resolved to go thither.

Having thus concluded; the 12th of June we sailed from hence, designing to touch at the island Cocos, as well to put ashore some flour there as to see the island, because it was in our way to Realejo. We steered north till in latitude 4 degrees 40 minutes, intending then to steer west by north, for we expected to have had the wind at south by east or south-south-east as we had on the south side of the Equator. Thus I had formerly found the winds near the shore in these latitudes; but when we first parted from the Galapagos we had the wind at south, and as we sailed farther north we had the winds at south by west then at south-south-west, winds which we did not expect. We thought at first that the wind would come about again to the south; but when we came to sail off west to the island Cocos we had the wind at south-west by south and could lie but west by north. Yet we stood that course till we were in the latitude 5 degrees 40 minutes north and then despairing, as the winds were, to find the island Cocos, we steered over to the Main; for had we seen the island then, we could not have fetched it, being so far to the north of it.

Captain Cook dies.

Captain Cook, who was then sick at Juan Fernandez, continued so till we came within 2 or 3 leagues of Cape Blanco, and then died of a sudden; though he seemed that morning to be as likely to live, as he had been some weeks before; but it is usual with sick men coming from the sea, where they have nothing but the sea air, to die off as soon as ever they come within the view of the land. About four hours after we all came to an anchor (namely the ship that I was in, Captain Eaton, and the great meal prize) a league within the cape, right against the brook of fresh water, in 14 fathom clean hard sand. Presently after we came to an anchor Captain Cook was carried ashore to be buried, twelve men carried their arms to guard those that were ordered to dig the grave: for although we saw no appearance of inhabitants, yet we did not know but the country might be thick inhabited. And before Captain Cook was interred three Spanish Indians came to the place where our men were digging the grave and demanded what they were, and from whence they came? To whom our men answered they came from Lima and were bound to Realejo, but that the captain of one of the ships dying at sea, obliged them to come into this place to give him Christian burial. The three Spanish Indians who were very shy at first began to be very bold and, drawing near, asked many silly questions; and our men did not stick to soothe them up with as many falsehoods, purposely to draw them into their clutches. Our men often laughed at their temerity; and asked them if they never saw any Spaniards before? They told them that they themselves were Spaniards and that they lived among Spaniards, and that although they were born there yet they had never seen 3 ships there before: our men told them that neither now might they have seen so many if it had not been on an urgent occasion. At length they drilled them by discourse so near that our men laid hold on all three at once; but before Captain Cook was buried one of them made his escape, the other two were brought off aboard our ship. Captain Eaton immediately came aboard and examined them; they confessed that they came purposely to view our ship and if possible to inform themselves what we were; for the president of Panama not long before sent a letter of advice to Nicoya, informing the magistrates thereof that some enemies were come into these seas, and that therefore it behoved them to be careful of themselves. Nicoya is a small Mulatto town about 12 or 14 leagues east from hence, standing on the banks of a river of that name. It is a place very fit for building ships, therefore most of the inhabitants are carpenters who are commonly employed in building new or repairing old ships. It was here that Captain Sharp (just after I left him in the year 1681) got carpenters to fix his ship before he returned to England: and for that reason it behoved the Spaniards to be careful (according to the governor of Panama's advice) lest any men at other times wanting such necessaries as that place afforded might again be supplied there.

A *narrow escape of twelve men.*

I was minded to return aboard, and endeavoured to persuade them all to go with me, but some would not, therefore I returned with 12, which was half, and left the other 12 behind. At this place I saw three or four tun of the redwood; which I take to be that sort of wood, called in Jamaica blood-wood, or Nicaragua-wood. We who returned aboard met no one to oppose us, and the next day we expected our consorts that we left ashore, but none came; therefore at four o'clock in the afternoon ten men went in our canoe to see what was become of them: when they came to the bay where we landed to go to the estancia they found our men all on a small rock, half a mile from the shore, standing in the water up to their waists. These men had slept ashore in the house and turned out betimes in the morning to pen the cattle; 2 or 3 went one way and as many another way to get the cattle to the pen, and others stood at the pen to drive them in. When they were thus scattered about 40 or 50 armed Spaniards came in among them. Our men immediately called to each other and drew together in a body before the Spaniards could attack them; and marched to their boat, which was hauled up dry on the sand. But when they came to the sandy bay they found their boat all in flames. This was a very unpleasing sight for they knew not how to get aboard unless they marched by land to the place where Captain Cook was buried, which was near a league. The greatest part of the way was thick woods, where the Spaniards might easily lay an ambush for them, at which they are very expert. On the other side, the Spaniards now thought them secure; and therefore came to them, and asked them if they would be pleased to walk to their plantations, with many other such flouts; but our men answered never a word. It was about half ebb when one of our men took notice of a rock a good distance from the shore, just appearing above water; he showed it to his consorts, and told them it would be a good castle for them if they could get thither. They all wished themselves there; for the Spaniards, who lay as yet at a good distance from them behind the bushes, as secure of their prey, began to whistle now and then a shot among them. Having therefore well considered the place together with the danger they were in, they proposed to send one of the tallest men to try if the sea between them and the rock were fordable. This counsel they presently put in execution and found it according to their desire. So they all marched over to the rock, where they remained till the canoe came to them; which was about seven hours. It was the latter part of the ebb when they first went over, and then the rock was dry; but when the tide of flood returned again the rock was covered, and the water still flowing; so that if our canoe had stayed but one hour longer they might have been in as great danger of their lives from the sea as before from the Spaniards; for the tide rises here about eight foot. The Spaniards remained on the shore, expecting to see them destroyed, but never came from behind the bushes where they first planted themselves; they having not above 3 or 4 hand-guns, the rest of them being armed with lances. The Spaniards in these parts are very expert in heaving or darting the lance; with which upon occasion, they will do great feats, especially in ambuscades: and by their good will, they care not for fighting otherwise, but content themselves with standing aloof, threatening and calling names, at which they are as expert as the other; so that if their tongues be quiet, we always take it for granted they have laid some ambush. Before night our canoe came aboard, and brought our men all safe. The next day two canoes were sent to the bottom of the bay to seek for a large canoe, which we were informed was there. The Spaniards have neither ships nor barks here, and but a few canoes, which they seldom use: neither are there any fishermen here, as I judge, because fish is very scarce; for I never saw any here, neither could any of our men ever take any; and yet wherever we come to an anchor we always send out our strikers, and put our hooks and lines overboard, to try for fish. The next day our men returned out of the bay and brought the canoe with them, which they were sent for, and three or four days afterwards the two canoes were sent out again for another, which they likewise brought aboard. These canoes were fitted with thwarts or benches, straps and oars fit for service; and one of these Captain Eaton had for his share, and we the other, which we fixed for landing men when occasion required.

Other islands in the Gulf of Amapalla.

There are a great many more islands in this bay, but none inhabited as these. There is one pretty large island belonging to a nunnery, as the Indians told us, this was stocked with bulls and cows; there were 3 or 4 Indians lived there to look after the cattle, for the sake of which we often frequented this island while we lay in the bay: they are all low islands except Amapalla and Mangera. There are two channels to come into this gulf, one between Point Casivina and Mangera, the other between Mangera and Amapalla: the latter is the best. The riding-place is on the east side of Amapalla, right against a spot of low ground; for all the island except this one place is high land. Running in farther ships may anchor near the Main, on the north-east side of the island Amapalla. This is the place most frequented by Spaniards: it is called the Port of Martin Lopez. This gulf or lake runs in some leagues beyond all the islands; but it is shoal water and not capable of ships.

It was into this gulf that Captain Davis was gone with the two canoes to endeavour for a prisoner, to gain intelligence, if possible, before our ships came in: he came the first night to Mangera, but for want of a pilot did not know where to look for the town. In the morning he found a great many canoes hauled up on the bay; and from that bay found a path which led him and his company to the town. The Indians saw our ships in the evening coming towards the island, and, being before informed of enemies in the sea, they kept scouts out all night for fear: who, seeing Captain Davis coming, ran into the town, and alarmed all the people. When Captain Davis came thither they all run into the woods. The friar happened to be there at this time; who, being unable to ramble into the woods, fell into Captain Davis's hands: there were two Indian boys with him who were likewise taken. Captain Davis went only to get a prisoner, therefore was well satisfied with the friar, and immediately came down to the seaside. He went from thence to the island Amapalla, carrying the friar and the two Indian boys with him. These were his pilots to conduct him to the landing-place, where they arrived about noon. They made no stay here, but left three or four men to look after the canoes, and Captain Davis with the rest marched to the town, taking the friar with them. The town, as is before noted, is about a mile from the landing-place, standing in a plain on the top of a hill, having a very steep ascent to go to it. All the Indians stood on the top of the hill waiting Captain Davis's coming.

The secretary, mentioned before, had no great kindness for the Spaniards. It was he that persuaded the Indians to wait Captain Davis's coming; for they were all running into the woods; but he told them that if any of the Spaniard's enemies came thither it was not to hurt them, but the Spaniards whose slaves they were; and that their poverty would protect them. This man with the casica stood more forward than the rest, at the bank of the hill, when Captain Davis with his company appeared beneath. They called out therefore in Spanish, demanding of our men what they were, and from whence they came? To whom Captain Davis and his men replied they were Biscayers, and that they were sent thither by the king of Spain to clear those seas from enemies; that their ships were coming into the gulf to careen, and that they came thither before the ships to seek a convenient place for it, as also to desire the Indian's assistance. The secretary, who, as I said before, was the only man that could speak Spanish, told them that they were welcome, for he had a great respect for any Old Spain men, especially for the Biscayers, of whom he had heard a very honourable report; therefore he desired them to come up to their town. Captain Davis and his men immediately ascending the hill, the friar going before; and they were received with a great deal of affection by the Indians. The casica and secretary embraced Captain Davis, and the other Indians received his men with the like ceremony. These salutations being ended, they all marched towards the church, for that is the place of all public meetings, and all plays and pastimes are acted there also; therefore in the churches belonging to Indian towns they have all sorts of vizards, and strange antick dresses both for men and women, and abundance of musical hautboys and strumstrums. The strumstrum is made somewhat like a sittern; most of those that the Indians use are made of a large gourd cut in the midst, and a thin board laid over the hollow, and which is fastened to the sides; this serves for the belly; over which the strings are placed. The nights before any holidays, or the nights ensuing, are the times when they all meet to make merry. Their mirth consists in singing, dancing, and sporting in those antick habits, and using as many antick gestures. If the moon shine they use but few torches, if not, the church is full of light. There meet at these times all sorts of both sexes. All the Indians that I have been acquainted with who are under the Spaniards seem to be more melancholy than other Indians that are free; and at these public meetings, when they are in the greatest of their jollity, their mirth seems to be rather forced than real. Their songs are very melancholy and doleful; so is their music: but whether it be natural to the Indians to be thus melancholy, or the effect of their slavery, I am not certain: but I have always been prone to believe that they are then only condoling their misfortunes, the loss of their country and liberties: which although these that are now living do not know, nor remember what it was to be free, yet there seems to be a deep impression of the thoughts of the slavery which the Spaniards have brought them under, increased probably by some traditions of their ancient freedom.

Captain Davis intended when they were all in the church to shut the doors and then make a bargain with them, letting them know what he was, and so draw them afterwards by fair means to our assistance: the friar being with him, who had also promised to engage them to it: but before they were all in the church, one of Captain Davis's men pushed one of the Indians to hasten him into the church. The Indian immediately ran away, and all the rest taking the alarm sprang out of the church like deer; it was hard to say which was first: and Captain Davis, who knew nothing of what happened, was left in the church only with the friar. When they were all fled, Captain Davis's men fired and killed the secretary; and thus our hopes perished by the indiscretion of one foolish fellow.

Captain Eaton and Captain Davis careen their ships here, and afterwards part.

In the afternoon the ships came into the gulf between Point Casivina and Mangera, and anchored near the island Amapalla on the east side in 10 fathom water, clean hard sand. In the evening Captain Davis and his company came aboard, and brought the friar with them; who told Captain Davis that if the secretary had not been killed he could have sent him a letter by one of the Indians that was taken at Mangera, and persuaded him to come to us; but now the only way was to send one of those Indians to seek the casica, and that himself would instruct him what to say, and did not question but the casica would come in on his word. The next day we sent ashore one of the Indians, who before night returned with the casica and six other Indians, who remained with us all the time that we stayed here. These Indians did us good service; especially in piloting us to an island where we killed beef whenever we wanted; and for this their service we satisfied them to their hearts' content. It was at this island Amapalla that a party of Englishmen and Frenchmen came afterwards, and stayed a great while, and at last landed on the Main, and marched overland to the Cape River, which disembogues into the North Seas near Cape Gracias a Dios, and is therefore called the Cape River: near the head of this river they made bark-logs (which I shall describe in the next chapter) and so went into the North Seas. This was the way that Captain Sharp had proposed to go if he had been put to it; for this way was partly known by privateers by the discovery that was made into the country about 30 years since, by a party of Englishmen that went up that river in canoes, about as far as the place where these Frenchmen made their bark-logs: there they landed and marched to a town called Segovia in the country. They were near a month getting up the river, for there were many cataracts where they were often forced to leave the river and haul their canoes ashore over the land till they were past the cataracts, and then launch their canoes again into the river. I have discoursed several men that were in that expedition, and if I mistake not Captain Sharp was one of them. But to return to our voyage in hand; when both our ships were clean and our water filled Captain Davis and Captain Eaton broke off consortships. Captain Eaton took aboard of his ship 400 packs of flour, and sailed out of the gulf the second day of September.

CHAPTER 6

Plata, Payta, Lobos de la Mar

Point Santa Helena.

Point Santa Helena bears south from the island Plata. It lies in latitude 2 degrees 15 minutes south. The point is pretty high, flat, and even at top, overgrown with many great thistles, but no sort of tree; at a distance it appears like an island because the land within it is very low.

This point strikes out west into the sea, making a pretty large bay on the north side. A mile within the point on the sandy bay close by the sea there is a poor small Indian village called Santa Helena; the land about it is low, sandy and barren, there are no trees nor grass growing near it; neither do the Indians produce any fruit, grain, or plant but watermelons only, which are large and very sweet. There is no fresh water at this place nor near it; therefore the inhabitants are obliged to fetch all their water from the river Colanche, which is in the bottom of the bay, about 4 leagues from it.

Algatrane, a sort of tar.

Not far from this town, on the bay close by the sea, about 5 paces from high-water mark, there is a sort of bituminous matter boils out of a little hole in the earth; it is like thin tar: the Spaniards call it algatrane. By much boiling it becomes hard like pitch. It is frequently used by the Spaniards instead of pitch; and the Indians that inhabit here save it in jars. It boils up most at high water; and then the Indians are ready to receive it. These Indians are fishermen and go out to sea on bark-logs. Their chief subsistence is maize, most of which they get from ships that come hither from Algatrane. There is good anchoring to leeward of the point right against the village: but on the west side of the point it is deep water and no anchoring.

A Spanish wreck.

The Spaniards do report that there was once a very rich ship driven ashore here in calm for want of wind to work her. As soon as ever she struck she heeled off to sea, 7 or 8 fathom water, where she lies to this day; none having attempted to fish for her, because she lies deep, and there falls in here a great high sea.

Cruisings.

When we were abreast of this point, we sent away our canoes in the night to take the Indian village. They landed in the morning betimes close by the town and took some prisoners. They took likewise a small bark which the Indians had set on fire, but our men quenched it and took the Indians that did it; who being asked wherefore he set the bark on fire said that there was an order from the viceroy lately set out commanding all seamen to burn their vessels if attacked by us, and betake themselves to their boats. There was another bark in a small cove a mile from the village, thither our men went, thinking to take her, but the seamen that were aboard set her in flames and fled: in the evening our men came aboard and brought the small bark with them, the fire of which they had quenched; and then we returned again towards Plata; where we arrived the 26th day of September.

Manta, near Cape san Lorenzo.

In the evening we sent out some men in our bark lately taken, and canoes, to an Indian village called Manta, two or three leagues to the westward of Cape San Lorenzo; hoping there to get other prisoners, for we could not learn from those we took at Point Santa Helena the reason why the viceroy should give such orders to burn the ships. They had a fresh sea-breeze till about 12 o'clock at night, and then it proved calm; wherefore they rowed away with their canoes as near to the town as they thought convenient, and lay still till day.

Monte Christo.

On the back of the town, a pretty way up in the country, there is a very high mountain, towering up like a sugar-loaf, called Monte Christo. It is a very good sea-mark, for there is none like it on all the coast. The body of this mountain bears due south from Manta. About a mile and a half from the shore, right against the village, there is a rock, which is very dangerous, because it never appears above water; neither does the sea break on it, because there is seldom any great sea; yet it is now so well known that all ships bound to this place do easily avoid it. A mile within this rock there is good anchoring in 6, 8, or 10 fathom water, good hard sand and clear ground. And a mile from the road on the west side there is a shoal running out a mile into the sea. From Manta to Cape San Lorenzo the land is plain and even, of an indifferent height.

Cruisings.

As soon as ever the day appeared our men landed, and marched towards the village, which was about a mile and a half from their landing-place: some of the Indians who were stirring saw them coming and alarmed their neighbours; so that all that were able got away. They took only two old women who both said that it was reported that a great many enemies were come overland through the country of Darien into the South Seas, and that they were at present in canoes and periagos: and that the viceroy upon this news had set out the forementioned order for burning their own ships. Our men found no sort of provision here; the viceroy having likewise sent orders to all sea ports to keep no provision, but to just supply themselves.

These women also said that the Manta Indians were sent over to the island Plata to destroy all the goats there; which they performed about a month agone. With this news our men returned again, and arrived at Plata the next day.

We lay still at the island Plata, being not resolved what to do; till the 2nd day of October, and then Captain Swan in the Cygnet of London arrived there. He was fitted out by very eminent merchants of that city, on a design only to trade with the Spaniards or Indians, having a very considerable cargo well sorted for these parts of the world; but meeting with divers disappointments and, being out of hopes to obtain a trade in these seas, his men forced him to entertain a company of privateers which he met with near Nicoya, a town whither he was going to seek a trade, and these privateers were bound thither in boats to get a ship. These were the men that we had heard of at Manta; they came overland under the command of Captain Peter Harris, nephew to that Captain Harris who was killed before Panama. Captain Swan was still commander of his own ship, and Captain Harris commanded a small bark under Captain Swan. There was much joy on all sides when they arrived; and immediately hereupon Captain Davis and Captain Swan consorted, wishing for Captain Eaton again. Our little bark, which was taken at Santa Helena, was immediately sent out to cruise, while the ships were fitting; for Captain Swan's ship being full of goods was not fit to entertain his new guest till the goods were disposed of; therefore he by the consent of the supercargo got up all his goods on deck, and sold to anyone that would buy upon trust: the rest was thrown overboard into the sea except fine goods, as silks, muslins, stockings, etc., and except the iron, whereof he had a good quantity, both wrought and in bars: this was saved for ballast.

The third day after our bark was sent to cruise she brought in a prize of 400 tuns, laden with timber: they took her in the Bay of Guayaquil; she came from a town of that name and was bound to Lima. The commander of this prize said that it was generally reported and believed at Guayaquil that the viceroy was fitting out 10 sail of frigates to drive us out of these seas. This news made our unsettled crew wish that they had been persuaded to accept of Captain Eaton's company on reasonable terms. Captain Davis and Captain Swan had some discourse concerning Captain Eaton; they at last concluded to send our small bark towards the coast of Lima, as far as the island Lobos, to seek Captain Eaton. This being approved by all hands she was cleaned the next day and sent away, manned with twenty men, ten of Captain Davis's, and ten of Swan's men, and Captain Swan writ a letter directed to Captain Eaton, desiring his company, and the isle of Plata was appointed for the general rendezvous. When this bark was gone we turned another bark which we had into a fire-ship; having six or seven carpenters who soon fixed her; and while the carpenters were at work about the fire-ship we scrubbed and cleaned our men-of-war as well as time and place would permit.

The 19th day of October we finished our business, and the 20th day we sailed towards the island Lobos, where our bark was ordered to stay for us, or meet us again at Plata. We had but little wind, therefore it was the 23rd day before we passed by Point Santa Helena. The 25th day we crossed over the Bay of Guayaquil.

Cape Blanco.

The 30th day we doubled Cape Blanco. This cape is in latitude 3 degrees 45 minutes. It is counted the worst cape in all the South Seas to double, passing to the southward; for in all other places ships may stand off to sea 20 or 30 leagues off if they find they cannot get anything under the shore; but here they dare not do it: for, by relation of the Spaniards, they find a current setting north-west which will carry a ship off more in two hours than they can run in again in five. Besides, setting to the northward they lose ground: therefore they always beat up in under the shore, which ofttimes they find very difficult because the wind commonly blows very strong at south-south-west or south by west without altering; for here are never any land-winds. This cape is of an indifferent height: it is fenced with white rocks to the sea; for which reason, I believe, it has this name. The land in the country seems to be full of high, steep, rugged and barren rocks.

Payta.

The 2nd day of November we got as high as Payta: we lay about six leagues off shore all the day, that the Spaniards might not see us; and in the evening sent our canoes ashore to take it, manned with 110 men.

Payta is a small Spanish sea port town in the latitude of 5 degrees 15 minutes. It is built on the sand, close by the sea, in a nook, elbow, or small bay, under a pretty high hill. There are not above 75 or 80 houses and two churches. The houses are but low and ill built.

The road of Payta.

The road of Payta is one of the best on the coast of Peru. It is sheltered from the south-west by a point of land which makes a large bay and smooth water for ships to ride in. There is room enough for a good fleet of ships, and good anchoring in any depth, from 6 fathom water to 20 fathom. Right against the town, the nearer the town, the shallower the water and the smoother the riding, it is clean sand all over the bay. Most ships passing either to the north or the south touch at this place for water, for, though here is none at the town, yet those Indian fishermen of Colan will, and do, supply all ships very reasonably; and good water is much prized on all this coast through the scarcity of it.

November the 3rd at 6 o'clock in the morning our men landed about 4 miles to the south of the town and took some prisoners that were sent thither to watch for fear of us; and these prisoners said that the governor of Piura came with 100 armed men to Payta the night before, purposely to oppose our landing there if we should attempt it.

Our men marched directly to the fort on the hill, and took it without the loss of one man. Hereupon the governor of Piura with all his men and the inhabitants of the town ran away as fast as they could. Then our men entered the town and found it emptied both of money and goods; there was not so much as a meal of victuals left for them.

The prisoners told us a ship had been here a little before and burnt a great ship in the road, but did not land their men; and that here they put ashore all their prisoners and pilots. We knew this must be Captain Eaton's ship which had done this, and by these circumstances we supposed he was gone to the East Indies, it being always designed by him. The prisoners told us also that, since Captain Eaton was here, a small bark had been off the harbour and taken a pair of bark-logs a-fishing, and made the fishermen bring aboard 20 or 30 jars of fresh water. This we supposed was our bark that was sent to the Lobos to seek Captain Eaton.

In the evening we came in with our ships and anchored before the town in 10 fathom water, near a mile from the shore. Here we stayed till the sixth day, in hopes to get a ransom from the town. Our captains demanded 300 packs of flour, 3000 pound of Sugar, 25 jars of wine, and 1000 jars of water to be brought off to us; but we got nothing of it. Therefore Captain Swan ordered the town to be fired, which was presently done. Then all our men came aboard, and Captain Swan ordered the bark which Captain Harris commanded to be burnt because she did not sail well.

At night, when the land-wind came off, we sailed from hence towards Lobos. The 10th day in the evening we saw a sail bearing north-west by north as far as we could well discern her on our deck. We immediately chased, separating ourselves the better to meet her in the night; but we missed her. Therefore the next morning we again trimmed sharp and made the best of our way to Lobos de la Mar.

Lobos de Terra.

The 14th day we had sight of the island Lobos de Terra: it bore east from us; we stood in towards it, and betwixt 7 and 8 o'clock in the night came to an anchor at the north-east end of the island, in 4 fathom water. This island at sea is of an indifferent height, and appears like Lobos de la Mar. About a quarter of a mile from the north end there is a great hollow rock, and a good channel between, where there is 7 fathom water. The 15th day we went ashore and found abundance of penguins and boobies, and seal in great quantities. We sent aboard of all these to be dressed, for we had not tasted any flesh in a great while before; therefore some of us did eat very heartily. Captain Swan, to encourage his men to eat this coarse flesh, would commend it for extraordinary food, comparing the seal to a roasted pig, the boobies to hens, and the penguins to ducks: this he did to train them to live contentedly on coarse meat, not knowing but we might be forced to make use of such food before we departed out of these seas; for it is generally seen among privateers that nothing emboldens them sooner to mutiny than want, which we could not well suffer in a place where there are such quantities of these animals to be had if men could be persuaded to be content with them.

They come again to Lobos de la Mar.

In the afternoon we sailed from Lobos de Terra with the wind at south by east and arrived at Lobos de la Mar on the 19th day. Here we found a letter, left by our bark that was sent to seek Captain Eaton, by which we understood that Captain Eaton had been there but was gone before they arrived, and had left no letter to advise us which way he was gone; and that our bark was again returned to Plata in hopes to find us there, or meet us by the way, else resolving to stay for us there. We were sorry to hear that Captain Eaton was gone, for now we did not expect to meet with him any more in these seas.

The 21st day we sent out our Moskito strikers for turtle, who brought aboard enough to serve both ships' companies; and this they did all the time that we abode here. While we lay at this island Captain Swan made new yards, squarer than those he had before, and made his sails larger, and our ship's company in the meantime split plank for firewood, and put aboard as many planks as we could conveniently stow for other uses: here being plank enough of all sorts which we had brought hither in the first prize that we took and left here.

The 26th day in the evening we saw a small bark about 3 leagues north-north-west from the island, but, we supposing her to be our own bark, did not go after her. The next morning she was two leagues south of the island, standing off to sea; but we did not now chase her neither, although we knew she was not our bark; for, being to windward of us, she could have made her escape if we had chased her. This bark, as we were afterwards informed, was sent out purposely to see if we were at this island. Her orders were not to come too near, only to appear in sight; they supposing that if we were here we should soon be after her; as indeed it was a wonder we had not chased her: but our not doing so, and lying close under the island undiscerned by them, was a great occasion of our coming upon Puna afterwards unexpectedly, they being now without fear of any enemy so near them.

The Bay of Guayaquil.

The 28th day we scrubbed our ship's bottom, intending to sail the next day towards Guayaquil; it being concluded upon to attempt that town before we returned again to Plata. Accordingly, on the 29th day in the morning, we loosed from hence, steering directly for the Bay of Guayaquil. This bay runs in between Cape Blanco on the south side, and Point Chandy on the north.

Isle of Santa Clara.

About 25 leagues from Cape Blanco, near the bottom of the bay, there is a small island called Santa Clara, which lies east and west: it is of an indifferent length, and it appears like a dead man stretched out in a shroud. The east end represents the head, and the west end the feet. Ships that are bound into the river of Guayaquil pass on the south side to avoid the shoals which lie on the north side of it; whereon formerly ships have been lost.

A rich Spanish wreck there.

It is reported by the Spaniards that there is a very rich wreck lies on the north side of that island, not far from it; and that some of the plate has been taken up by one who came from Old Spain, with a patent from the king to fish in those seas for wrecks; but he dying, the project ceased, and the wreck still remains as he left it; only the Indians by stealth do sometimes take up some of it; and they might have taken up much more if it were not for the cat-fish which swarms hereabouts.

Catfish.

The cat-fish is much like a whiting, but the head is flatter and bigger. It has a great wide mouth, and certain small strings pointing out from each side of it, like cat's whiskers; and for that reason it is called a cat-fish. It has three fins; one growing on the top of his back, and one on either side. Each of these fins has a stiff sharp bone which is very venomous if it strikes into a man's flesh; therefore it is dangerous diving where many of these fish are. The Indians that adventured to search this wreck have to their sorrow experienced it; some having lost their lives, others the use of their limbs by it: this we were informed of by an Indian who himself had been fishing on it by stealth. I myself have known some white men that have lost the use of their hands only by a small prick with the fin of these fish: therefore when we catch them with a hook we tread on them to take the hook out of their mouths, or otherwise, in flurting about (as all fish will when first taken) they might accidentally strike their sharp fins into the hands of those that caught them. Some of the fish are seven or eight pound weight: some again, in some particular places, are none of them bigger than a man's thumb, but their fins are all alike venomous. They use to be at the mouths of rivers, or where there is much mud and oaze, and they are found all over the American coast, both in the North and South Sea, at least in the hot countries, as also in the East Indies: where, sailing with Captain Minchin among certain islands near the Straits of Malacca, he pointed to an island at which he told me he lost the use of his hand by one of these only in going to take the hook out of its mouth. The wound was scarce visible yet his hand was much swollen, and the pain lasted about 9 weeks; during most part of which the raging heat of it was almost ready to distract him. However, though the bony fins of these fish are so venomous, yet the bones in their bodies are not so; at least we never perceived any such effect in eating the fish; and their flesh is very sweet, delicious and wholesome meat.

CHAPTER 7

In Pursuit of Spanish Treasure

The cabbage-tree.

As the cotton is the biggest tree in the woods, so the cabbage-tree is the tallest: the body is not very big, but very high and straight. I have measured one in the Bay of Campeachy 120 feet long as it lay on the ground, and there are some much higher. It has no limbs nor boughs, but at the head there are many branches bigger than a man's arm. These branches are not covered but flat with sharp edges; they are 12 or 14 foot long. About two foot from the trunk the branches shoot forth small long leaves about an inch broad, which grow so regularly on both sides of the branch that the whole branch seems to be but one leaf made up of many small ones. The cabbage-fruit shoots out in the midst of these branches from the top of the tree; it is invested with many young leaves or branches which are ready to spread abroad as the old branches drop and fall down. The cabbage itself, when it is taken out of the leaves which it seems to be folded in, is as big as the small of a man's leg and a foot long; it is as white as milk and as sweet as a nut if eaten raw, and it is very sweet and wholesome if boiled. Besides the cabbage itself there grow out between the cabbage and the large branches small twigs, as of a shrub, about two foot long from their stump. At the end of those twigs (which grow very thick together) there hang berries hard and round and as big as a cherry. These the trees shed every year, and they are very good for hogs: for this reason the Spaniards fine any who shall cut down any of these in their woods. The body of the tree is full of rings round it, half a foot asunder from the bottom to the top. The bark is thin and brittle; the wood is black and very hard, the heart or middle of the tree is white pith. They do not climb to get the cabbage but cut them down; for should they gather it off the tree as it stands, yet its head being gone it soon dies. These trees are much used by planters in Jamaica to board the sides of the houses, for it is but splitting the trunk into four parts with an axe, and there are so many planks. Those trees appear very pleasant, and they beautify the whole wood, spreading their green branches above all other trees.

All this country is subject to very great rains, so that this part of Peru pays for the dry weather which they have about Lima and all that coast. I believe that is one reason why the Spaniards have made such small discoveries in this and other rivers on this coast. Another reason may be because it lies not so directly in their way; for they do not coast it along in going from Panama to Lima, but first go westward as far as to the keys or isles of Cobaya, for a westerly wind, and from thence stand over towards Cape San Francisco, not touching anywhere usually till they come to Manta near Cape San Lorenzo. In their return indeed from Lima to Panama they may keep along the coast hereabouts; but then their ships are always laden; whereas the light ships that go from Panama are most at leisure to make discoveries. A third reason may be the wildness and enmity of all the natives on this coast, who are naturally fortified by their rivers and vast woods, from whence with their arrows they can easily annoy any that shall land there to assault them. At this river particularly there are no Indians live within 6 leagues of the sea, and all the country so far is full of impassable woods; so that to get at the Indians, or the mines and mountains, there is no way but by rowing up the river; and if any who are enemies to the natives attempt this (as the Spaniards are always hated by them) they must all the way be exposed to the arrows of those who would lie purposely in ambush in the woods for them. These wild Indians have small plantations of maize and good plantain-gardens; for plantains are their chiefest food. They have also a few fowls and hogs.

The Isle of Gallo.

Gallo is a small uninhabited island lying in between two and three degrees north latitude. It lies in a wide bay about three leagues from the mouth of the river Tomaco; and four leagues and a half from a small Indian village called Tomaco: the island Gallo is of an indifferent height; it is clothed with very good timber-trees, and is therefore often visited with barks from Guayaquil and other places: for most of the timber carried from Guayaquil to Lima is first fetched from Gallo. There is a spring of good water at the north-east end: at that place there is a fine small sandy bay, where there is good landing. The road for ships is against this bay, where there is good secure riding in six or seven fathom water; and here ships may careen. It is but shoal water all about this island; yet there is a channel to come in at, where there is no less than four fathom water: you must go in with the tide of flood and come out with ebb, sounding all the way.

Tomaco is a large river that takes its name from an Indian village so called: it is reported to spring from the rich mountains about Quito. It is thick inhabited with Indians; and there are some Spaniards that live there who traffic with the Indians for gold. It is shoal at the mouth of the river yet barks may enter.

The river and village of Tomaco.

This village Tomaco is but small, and is seated not far from the mouth of the river. It is a place to entertain the Spanish merchants that come to Gallo to load timber, or to traffic with the Indians for gold. At this place one Doleman, with seven or eight men more, once of Captain Sharp's crew, were killed in the year 1680. From the branch of the river St. Jago, where we now lay, to Tomaco is about five leagues; the land low and full of creeks so that canoes may pass within land through those creeks, and from thence into Tomaco River.

The 28th day we left the river of St. Jago, crossing some creeks in our way with our canoes; and came to an Indian house where we took the man and all his family. We stayed here till the afternoon, and then rowed towards Tomaco, with the man of this house for our guide. We arrived at Tomaco about 12 o'clock at night. Here we took all the inhabitants of the village and a Spanish knight called Don Diego de Pinas.

This knight came in a ship from Lima to lade timber. The ship was riding in a creek about a mile off, and there were only one Spaniard and 8 Indians aboard. We went in a canoe with 7 men and took her; she had no goods but 12 or 13 jars of good wine, which we took out, and the next day let the ship go. Here an Indian canoe came aboard with three men in her. These men could not speak Spanish, neither could they distinguish us from Spaniards; the wild Indians usually thinking all white men to be Spaniards. We gave them 3 Or 4 calabashes of wine, which they freely drank. They were straight-bodied and well-limbed men of a mean height; their hair black, long-visaged, small noses and eyes; and were thin-faced, ill-looked men, of a very dark copper colour. A little before night Captain Swan and all of us returned to Tomaco and left the vessel to the seamen. The 31st day two of our canoes who had been up the river of Tomaco returned back again to the village. They had rowed seven or eight leagues up and found but one Spanish house, which they were told did belong to a lady who lived at Lima; she had servants here that traded with the Indians for gold; but they seeing our men coming ran away: yet our men found there several ounces of gold in calabashes.

1685.

The first day of January 1685 we went from Tomaco towards Gallo. We carried the knight with us and two small canoes which we took there, and while we were rowing over one of our canoes took a packet-boat that was sent from Panama to Lima. The Spaniards threw the packet of letters overboard with a line and a buoy to it, but our men seeing it took it up, and brought the letters and all the prisoners aboard our ships that were then at an anchor at Gallo. Here we stayed till the 6th day, reading the letters, by which we understood that the armada from Old Spain was come to Portobello: and that the president of Panama had sent this packet on purpose to hasten the Plate fleet thither from Lima.

We were very joyful of this news, and therefore sent away the packet-boat with all her letters; and we altered our former resolutions of going to Lavelia. We now concluded to careen our ships as speedily as we could, that we might be ready to intercept this fleet. The properest place that we could think on for doing it was among the King's Islands or Pearl Keys, because they are near Panama and all ships bound to Panama from the coast of Lima pass by them; so that being there we could not possibly miss the fleet. According to these resolutions we sailed the next morning, in order to execute what we designed. We were two ships and three barks in company, namely, Captain Davis, Captain Swan, a fire-ship, and two small barks as tenders; one on Captain Davis's ship, the other on Captain Swan's. We weighed before day and got out all but Captain Swan's tender, which never budged; for the men were all asleep when we went out and, the tide of flood coming on before they waked, we were forced to stay for them till the next day.

The 8th day in the morning we descried a sail to the west of us; the wind was at south and we chased her and before noon took her. She was a ship of about 90 tun laden with flour; she came from Truxillo and was bound to Panama. This ship came very opportunely to us for flour began to grow scarce, and Captain Davis's men grudged at what was given to Captain Swan; who, as I said before, had none but what he had from Captain Davis.

We jogged on after this with a gentle gale towards Gorgona, an island lying about 25 leagues from the island Gallo. The 9th day we anchored at Gorgona, on the west side of the island in 38 fathom clean ground, not two cables' length from the shore. Gorgona is an uninhabited island in latitude about three degrees north: it is a pretty high island, and very remarkable by reason of two saddles, or risings and fallings on the top. It is about 2 leagues long and a league broad; and it is four leagues from the Main: at the west end is another small island. The land against the anchoring-place is low; there is a small sandy bay and good landing. The soil or mould of it is black and deep in the low ground, but on the side of the high land it is a kind of a red clay. This island is very well clothed with large trees of several sorts that are flourishing and green all the year. It's very well watered with small brooks that issue from the high land. Here are a great many little black monkeys, some Indian conies, and a few snakes, which are all the land animals that I know there. It is reported of this island that it rains on every day in the year more or less; but that I can disprove: however, it is a very wet coast, and it rains abundantly here all the year long. There are but few fair days; for there is little difference in the seasons of the year between the wet and dry; only in that season which should be the dry time the rains are less frequent and more moderate than in the wet season, for then it pours as out of a sieve. It is deep water and no anchoring anywhere about this island, only at the west side: the tide rises and falls seven or eight foot up and down. Here are a great many periwinkles and mussels to be had at low water. Then the monkeys come down by the seaside and catch them; digging them out of their shells with their claws.

Here are pearl-oysters in great plenty: they grow to the loose rocks in 4, 5, or 6 fathom water by beards, or little small roots, as a mussel: these oysters are commonly flatter and thinner than other oysters; otherwise much alike in shape. The fish is not sweet nor very wholesome; it is as slimy as a shell-snail; they taste very copperish if eaten raw, and are best boiled. The Indians who gather them for the Spaniards hang the meat of them on strings like jews-ears, and dry them before they eat them. The pearl is found at the head of the oyster lying between the meat and the shell. Some will have 20 or 30 small seed-pearl, some none at all, and some will have one or two pretty large ones. The inside of the shell is more glorious than the pearl itself. I did never see any in the South Seas but here. It is reported there are some at the south end of California. In the West Indies, the Rancho Reys, or Rancheria, spoken of in Chapter 3, is the place where they are found most plentifully. It is said there are some at the island Margarita, near St. Augustin, a town in the Gulf of Florida, etc. In the East Indies the island Ainam, near the south end of China, is said to have plenty of these oysters, more productive of large round pearl than those in other places. They are found also in other parts of the East Indies, and on the Persian coast.

Isle of Gorgona, the pearl-oysters there and in other parts.

At this island Gorgona we rummaged our prize and found a few boxes of marmalade and three or four jars of brandy, which were equally shared between Captain Davis and Captain Swan and their men. Here we filled all our water and Captain Swan furnished himself with flour: afterward we turned ashore a great many prisoners but kept the chiefest to put them ashore in a better place.

The 13th day we sailed from hence towards the King's Islands. We were now six sail, two men-of-war, two tenders, a fire-ship, and the prize. We had but little wind but what we had was the common trade at south.

The course the armada takes; with an incidental account of the first inducements that made the privateers undertake the passage over the isthmus of Darien into the south seas, and of the particular beginning of their correspondence with the Indians that inhabit that isthmus.

Now I am on this subject I think it will not be amiss to give the reader an account of the progress of the armada from Old Spain, which comes thus every three years into the Indies. Its first arrival is at Cartagena, from whence, as I have been told, an express is immediately sent overland to Lima, through the southern continent, and another by sea to Portobello with two packets of letters, one for the viceroy of Lima, the other for the viceroy of Mexico. I know not which way that of Mexico goes after its arrival at Portobello, whether by land or sea: but I believe by sea to La Vera Cruz. That for Lima is sent by land to Panama and from thence by sea to Lima.

Upon mention of these packets I shall digress yet a little further and acquaint my reader that before my first going over into the South Seas with Captain Sharp (and indeed before any privateers, at least since Drake and Oxenham had gone that way which we afterwards went, except La Sound, a French captain, who by Captain Wright's instructions had ventured as far as Cheapo Town with a body of men but was driven back again) I being then on board Captain Coxon, in company with three or four more privateers, about four leagues to the east of Portobello, we took the packets bound thither from

Cartagena. We opened a great quantity of the merchants' letters and found the contents of many of them to be very surprising, the merchants of several parts of Old Spain thereby informing their correspondents of Panama and elsewhere of a certain prophecy that went about Spain that year, the tenor of which was THAT THERE WOULD BE ENGLISH PRIVATEERS THAT YEAR IN THE WEST INDIES, WHO WOULD MAKE SUCH GREAT DISCOVERIES AS TO OPEN A DOOR INTO THE SOUTH SEAS; which they supposed was fastest shut: and the letters were accordingly full of cautions to their friends to be very watchful and careful of their coasts.

This door they spoke of we all concluded must be the passage overland through the country of the Indians of Darien, who were a little before this become our friends, and had lately fallen out with the Spaniards, breaking off the intercourse which for some time they had with them: and upon calling also to mind the frequent invitations we had from those Indians a little before this time to pass through their country and fall upon the Spaniards in the South Seas, we from henceforward began to entertain such thoughts in earnest, and soon came to a resolution to make those attempts which we afterwards did with Captain Sharp, Coxon, etc., so that the taking these letters gave the first life to those bold undertakings: and we took the advantage of the fears the Spaniards were in from that prophecy, or probable conjecture, or whatever it were; for we sealed up most of the letters again, and sent them ashore to Portobello.

The occasion of this our late friendship with those Indians was thus: about 15 years before this time, Captain Wright being cruising near that coast and going in among the Samballoes Isles to strike fish and turtle, took there a young Indian lad as he was paddling about in a canoe. He brought him aboard his ship and gave him the name of John Gret, clothing him and intending to breed him among the English. But his Moskito strikers, taking a fancy to the boy, begged him of Captain Wright, and took him with them at their return into their own country, where they taught him their art, and he married a wife among them and learnt their language, as he had done some broken English while he was with Captain Wright, which he improved among the Moskitos, who, corresponding so much with us, do all of them smatter English after a sort; but his own language he had almost forgot. Thus he lived among them for many years; till, about six or eight months before our taking these letters, Captain Wright being again among the Samballoes, took thence another Indian boy about 10 or 12 years old, the son of a man of some account among those Indians; and, wanting a striker, he went away to the Moskito's country, where he took John Gret, who was now very expert at it. John Gret was much pleased to see a lad there of his own country, and it came into his mind to persuade Captain Wright upon this occasion to endeavour a friendship with those Indians; a thing our privateers had long coveted but never durst attempt, having such dreadful apprehensions of their numbers and fierceness: but John Gret offered the captain that he would go ashore and negotiate the matter; who accordingly sent him in his canoe till he was near the shore, which of a sudden was covered with Indians standing ready with their bows and arrows. John Gret, who had only a clout about his middle as the fashion of the Indians is, leapt then out of the boat and swam, the boat retiring a little way back; and the Indians ashore, seeing him in that habit and hearing him call to them in their own tongue (which he had recovered by conversing with the boy lately taken) suffered him quietly to land, and gathered all about to hear how it was with him. He told them particularly that he was one of their countrymen, and how he had been taken many years ago by the English, who had used him very kindly; that they were mistaken in being so much afraid of that nation who were not enemies to them but to the Spaniards: to confirm this he told them how well the English treated another young lad of theirs they had lately taken, such a one's son; for this he had learnt of the youth, and his father was one of the company that was got together on the shore. He persuaded them therefore to make a league with these friendly people, by whose help they might be able to quell the Spaniards; assuring also the father of the boy that, if he would but go with him to the ship which they saw at anchor at an island there (it was Golden Island, the eastermost of the Samballoes, a place where there is good striking for turtle) he should have his son restored to him and they might all expect a very kind reception. Upon these assurances 20 or 30 of them went off presently in two or three canoes laden with plantains, bananas, fowls, etc. And, Captain Wright having treated them on board, went ashore with them, and was entertained by them, and presents were made on each side. Captain Wright gave the boy to his father in a very handsome English dress which he had caused to be made purposely for him; and an agreement was immediately struck up between the English and these Indians who invited the English through their country into the South Seas.

Pursuant to this agreement the English, when they came upon any such design, or for traffic with them, were to give a certain signal which they pitched upon, whereby they might be known. But it happened that Mr. La Sound, the French captain spoken of a little before, being then one of Captain Wright's men, learnt this signal, and, staying ashore at Petit Guavres upon Captain Wright's going thither soon after, who had his commission from thence, he gave the other French there such an account of the agreement before mentioned, and the easiness of entering the South Seas thereupon, that he got at the head of about 120 of them who made that unsuccessful attempt upon Cheapo, as I said; making use of the signal they had learnt for passing the Indians' country, who at that time could not distinguish so well between the several nations of the Europeans as they can since.

From such small beginnings arose those great stirs that have been since made over the South Seas, namely, from the letters we took, and from the friendship contracted with these Indians by means of John Gret. Yet this friendship had like to have been stifled in its infancy; for within a few months after an English trading sloop came on this coast from Jamaica, and John Gret, who by this time had advanced himself as a grandee among these Indians, together with five or six more of that quality, went off to the sloop in their long gowns, as the custom is for such to wear among them. Being received aboard they expected to find everything friendly, and John Gret talked to them in English; but these Englishmen, having no knowledge at all of what had happened, endeavoured to make them slaves (as is commonly done) for upon carrying them to Jamaica they could have sold them for 10 or 12 pound apiece. But John Gret and the rest perceiving this, leapt all overboard, and were by the others killed every one of them in the water. The Indians on shore never came to the knowledge of it; if they had it would have endangered our correspondence. Several times after, upon our conversing with them, they enquired of us what was become of their countrymen: but we told them we knew not, as indeed it was a great while after that we heard this story; so they concluded the Spaniards had met with them and killed or taken them.

But to return to the account of the progress of the armada which we left at Cartagena. After an appointed stay there of about 60 days, as I take it, it goes thence to Portobello, where it lies 30 days and no longer. Therefore the viceroy of Lima, on notice of the armada's arrival at Cartagena, immediately sends away the King's treasure to Panama, where it is landed and lies ready to be sent to Portobello upon the first news of the armada's arrival there. This is the reason partly of their sending expresses so early to Lima, that upon the armada's first coming to Portobello, the treasure and goods may lie ready at Panama to be sent away upon the mules, and it requires some time for the Lima fleet to unlade, because the ships ride not at Panama but at Perica, which are three small islands 2 leagues from thence. The King's treasure is said to amount commonly to about 24,000,000 of pieces-of-eight: besides abundance of merchants' money. All this treasure is carried on mules, and there are large stables at both places to lodge them. Sometimes the merchants to steal the custom pack up money among goods and send it to Venta de Cruzes on the river Chagre; from thence down the river, and afterwards by sea to Portobello; in which passage I have known a whole fleet of periagos and canoes taken. The merchants who are not ready to sail by the thirteenth day after the armada's arrival are in danger to be left behind, for the ships all weigh the 30th day precisely, and go to the harbour's mouth: yet sometimes, on great importunity, the admiral may stay a week longer; for it is impossible that all the merchants should get ready, for want of men. When the armada departs from Portobello it returns again to Cartagena, by which time all the King's revenue which comes out of the country is got ready there. Here also meets them again a great ship called the Pattache, one of the Spanish galleons, which before their first arrival at Cartagena goes from the rest of the armada on purpose to gather the tribute of the coast, touching at the Margaritas and other places in her way thence to Cartagena, as Punta de Guaira Moracaybo, Rio de la Hacha, and Santa Marta; and at all these places takes in treasure for the king. After the set stay at Cartagena the armada goes away to the Havana in the isle of Cuba, to meet there the flota, which is a small number of ships that go to La Vera Cruz, and there takes in the effects of the city and country of Mexico, and what is brought thither in the ship which comes thither every year from the Philippine Islands; and, having joined the rest at the Havana, the whole armada sets sail for Spain through the Gulf of Florida. The ships in the South Seas lie a great deal longer at Panama before they return to Lima. The merchants and gentlemen which come from Lima stay as little time as they can at Portobello, which is at the best but a sickly place, and at this time is very full of men from all parts. But Panama, as it is not overcharged with men so unreasonably as the other, though very full, so it enjoys a good air, lying open to the sea-wind which rises commonly about 10 or 11 o'clock in the morning, and continues till 8 or 9 o'clock at night: then the land-wind comes and blows till 8 or 9 in the morning.

The Isles of Perico.

The 20th day we went and anchored within a league of the islands Perico (which are only 3 little barren rocky islands) in expectation of the president of Panama's answer to the letter I said we sent him by Don Diego, treating about exchange of prisoners; this being the day on which he had given us his parole to return with an answer. The 21st day we took another bark laden with hogs, fowls, salt-beef and molasses; she came from Lavelia, and was going to Panama. In the afternoon we sent another letter ashore by a young Mestizo (a mixed brood of Indians and Europeans) directed to the president, and 3 or 4 copies of it to be dispersed abroad among the common people. This letter, which was full of threats, together with the young man's managing the business, wrought so powerfully among the common people that the city was in an uproar. The president immediately sent a gentleman aboard, who demanded the flour-prize that we took off of Gallo and all the prisoners for the ransom of our two men: but our captains told him they would exchange man for man. The gentleman said he had not orders for that, but if we would stay till the next day he would bring the governors' answer. The next day he brought aboard our two men and had about 40 prisoners in exchange.

Tabago, a pleasant island.

The 24th day we ran over to the island Tabago. Tabago is in the bay and about six leagues south of Panama. It is about 3 mile long and 2 broad, a high mountainous island. On the north side it declines with a gentle descent to the sea. The land by the sea is of a black mould and deep; but towards the top of the mountain it is strong and dry. The north side of this island makes a very pleasant show, it seems to be a garden of fruit enclosed with many high trees; the chiefest fruits are plantains and bananas. They thrive very well from the foot to the middle of it; but those near the top are but small, as wanting moisture. Close by the sea there are many coconut-trees, which make a very pleasant sight.

The mammee-tree.

Within the coconut-trees there grow many mammee-trees. The mammee is a large, tall, and straight-bodied tree, clean without knots or limbs for 60 or 70 foot or more. The head spreads abroad into many small limbs which grow pretty thick and close together. The bark is of a dark grey colour, thick and rough, full of large chops. The fruit is bigger than a quince; it is round and covered with a thick rind of a grey colour: when the fruit is ripe the rind is yellow and tough; and it will then peel off like leather; but before it is ripe it is brittle: the juice is then white and clammy; but when ripe not so. The ripe fruit under the rind is yellow as a carrot, and in the middle are two large rough stones, flat, and each of them much bigger than an almond. The fruit smells very well and the taste is answerable to the smell. The south-west end of the island has never been cleared but is full of firewood and trees of divers sorts. There is a very fine small brook of fresh water that springs out of the side of the mountain and, gliding through the grove of fruit-trees, falls into the sea on the north side.

The village Tabago.

There was a small town standing by the sea with a church at one end, but now the biggest part of it is destroyed by the privateers. There is good anchoring right against the town about a mile from the shore, where you may have 16 or 18 fathom water, soft oazy ground. There is a small island close by the north-west end of this called Tabogilla, with a small channel to pass between. There is another woody island about a mile on the north-east side of Tabago, and a good channel between them: this island has no name that ever I heard.

A Spanish stratagem or two of Captain Bond their engineer.

While we lay at Tabago we had like to have had a scurvy trick played us by a pretended merchant from Panama, who came as by stealth to traffic with us privately; a thing common enough with the Spanish merchants, both in the North and South Seas, notwithstanding the severe prohibition of the governors; who yet sometimes connive at it and will even trade with the privateers themselves.

Our merchant was by agreement to bring out his bark laden with goods in the night, and we to go and anchor at the south of Perico. Out he came, with a fire-ship instead of a bark, and approached very near, hailing us with the watch-word we had agreed upon. We, suspecting the worst, called to them to come to an anchor, and upon their not doing so fired at them; when immediately their men, going out into the canoes, set fire to their ship, which blew up, and burnt close by us so that we were forced to cut our cables in all haste and scamper away as well as we could.

The Spaniard was not altogether so politick in appointing to meet us at Perico for there we had sea-room; whereas, had he come thus upon us at Tabago, the land-wind bearing hard upon us as it did, we must either have been burnt by the fire-ship or, upon loosing our cables, have been driven ashore: but I suppose they chose Perico rather for the scene of their enterprise, partly because they might there best skulk among the islands, and partly because, if their exploit failed, they could thence escape best from our canoes to Panama, but two leagues off.

During this exploit Captain Swan (whose ship was less than ours, and so not so much aimed at by the Spaniards) lay about a mile off, with a canoe at the buoy of his anchor, as fearing some treachery from our pretended merchant; and a little before the bark blew up he saw a small float on the water and, as it appeared, a man on it making towards his ship; but the man dived and disappeared of a sudden, as thinking probably that he was discovered.

This was supposed to be one coming with some combustible matter to have stuck about the rudder. For such a trick Captain Sharp was served at Coquimbo, and his ship had like to have been burnt by it if, by mere accident, it had not been discovered: I was then aboard Captain Sharp's ship. Captain Swan, seeing the blaze by us, cut his cables as we did, his bark did the like; so we kept under sail all the night, being more scared than hurt. The bark that was on fire drove burning towards Tabago; but after the first blast she did not burn clear, only made a smother, for she was not well made, though Captain Bond had the framing and management of it.

This Captain Bond was he of whom I made mention in my 4th chapter. He, after his being at the isles of Cape Verde, stood away for the South Seas at the instigation of one Richard Morton who had been with Captain Sharp in the South Seas. In his way he met with Captain Eaton and they two consorted a day or two: at last Morton went aboard Captain Eaton and persuaded him to lose Captain Bond in the night, which Captain Eaton did, Morton continuing aboard of Captain Eaton, as finding his the better ship. Captain Bond thus losing both his consort Eaton, and Morton his pilot, and his ship being but an ordinary sailer, he despaired of getting into the South Seas; and had played such tricks among the Caribbean Isles, as I have been told, that he did not dare to appear at any of the English islands. Therefore he persuaded his men to go to the Spaniards and they consented to anything that he should propose: so he presently steered away into the West Indies and the first place where we came to an anchor was at Portobello. He presently declared to the governor that there were English ships coming into the South Seas, and that if they questioned it, he offered to be kept a prisoner till time should discover the truth of what he said; but they believed him and sent him away to Panama where he was in great esteem. This several prisoners told us.

The ignorance of the Spaniards of these parts in sea-affairs.

The Spaniards of Panama could not have fitted out their fire-ship without this Captain Bond's assistance; for it is strange to say how grossly ignorant the Spaniards in the West Indies, but especially in the South Seas, are of sea-affairs. They build indeed good ships, but this is a small matter: for any ship of a good bottom will serve for these seas on the south coast. They rig their ships but untowardly, have no guns but in 3 or 4 of the king's ships, and are meanly furnished with warlike provisions, and much at a loss for the making any fire-ships

The sinking of a Spanish ship.

or other less useful machines. Nay, they have not the sense to have their guns run within the sides upon their discharge, but have platforms without for the men to stand on to charge them; so that when we come near we can fetch them down with small shot out of our boats. A main reason of this is that the native Spaniards are too proud to be seamen, but use the Indians for all those offices: one Spaniard, it may be, going in the ship to command it, and himself of little more knowledge than those poor ignorant creatures: nor can they gain much experience, seldom going far off to sea, but coasting along the shores.

A party of French privateers arrive from overland.

But to proceed: in the morning when it was light we came again to anchor close by our buoys and strove to get our anchors again; but our buoy-ropes, being rotten, broke. While we were puzzling about our anchors we saw a great many canoes full of men pass between Tabago and the other island. This put us into a new consternation: we lay still some time till we saw that they came directly towards us, then we weighed and stood towards them: and when we came within hail we found that they were English and French privateers come out of the North Seas through the Isthmus of Darien. They were 280 men in 28 canoes; 200 of them French, the rest English. They were commanded by Captain Gronet and Captain Lequie. We presently came to an anchor again and all the canoes came aboard. These men told us that there were 180 English men more, under the command of Captain Townley, in the country of Darien, making canoes (as these men had been) to bring them into these seas. All the Englishmen that came over in this party were immediately entertained by Captain Davis and Captain Swan in their own ships, and the French men were ordered to have our flour-prize to carry them, and Captain Gronet being the eldest commander was to command them there; and thus they were all disposed of to their hearts' content. Captain Gronet, to retaliate this kindness, offered Captain Davis and Captain Swan each of them a new commission from the governor of Petit Guavres.

Of the commissions that are given out by the French governour of Petit Guavres.

It has been usual for many years past for the governor of Petit Guavres to send blank commissions to sea by many of his captains with orders to dispose of them to whom they saw convenient. Those of Petit Guavres by this means making themselves the sanctuary and asylum of all people of desperate fortunes; and increasing their own wealth and the strength and reputation of their party thereby. Captain Davis accepted of one, having before only an old commission, which fell to him by inheritance at the decease of Captain Cook; who took it from Captain Tristian, together with his bark, as is before mentioned. But Captain Swan refused it, saying he had an order from the Duke of York neither to give offence to the Spaniards nor to receive any affront from them; and that he had been injured by them at Valdivia, where they had killed some of his men and wounded several more; so that he thought he had a lawful commission of his own to right himself. I never read any of these French commissions while I was in these seas, nor did I then know the import of them; but I have learnt since that the tenor of them is to give a liberty to fish, fowl, and hunt. The occasion of this is that the island Hispaniola, where the garrison of Petit Guavres is, belongs partly to the French and partly to the Spaniards; and in time of peace these commissions are given as a warrant to those of each side to protect them from the adverse party: but in effect the French do not restrain them to Hispaniola, but make them a pretence for a general ravage in any part of America, by sea or land.

Of the Gulf of St. Michael, and the rivers of Congos, Sambo, and Santa Maria: and an error of the common maps, in the placing Point Garachina and Cape san Lorenzo, corrected.

Having thus disposed of our associates we intended to sail toward the Gulf of St. Michael to seek Captain Townley; who by this time we thought might be entering into these seas. Accordingly the second day of March 1685 we sailed from hence towards the Gulf of St. Michael. This gulf lies near 30 leagues from Panama towards the south-east. The way thither from Panama is to pass between the King's Islands and the Main. It is a place where many great rivers having finished their courses are swallowed up in the sea. It is bounded on the south with Point Garachina, which lies in north latitude 6 degrees 40 minutes, and on the north side with Cape San Lorenzo. Where, by the way, I must correct a gross error in our common maps; which, giving no name at all to the south cape which yet is the most considerable, and is the true Point Garachina, do give that name to the north cape, which is of small remark only for those whose business is into the gulf; and the name San Lorenzo, which is the true name of this northern point, is by them wholly omitted; the name of the other point being substituted into its place. The chief rivers which run into this Gulf of St. Michael are Santa Maria, Sambo, and Congos. The river Congos (which is the river I would have persuaded our men to have gone up as their nearest way in our journey overland, mentioned Chapter 1) comes directly out of the country, and swallows up many small streams that fall into it from both sides; and at last loses itself on the north side of the gulf, a league within Cape San Lorenzo. It is not very wide, but deep, and navigable some leagues within land. There are sands without it; but a channel for ships. It is not made use of by the Spaniards because of the neighbourhood of Santa Maria River; where they have most business on account of the mines.

The River of Sambo seems to be a great River for there is a great tide at its mouth; but I can say nothing more of it, having never been in it.

This river falls into the sea on the south side of the gulf near Point Garachina. Between the mouths of these two rivers on either side the gulf runs in towards the land somewhat narrower; and makes five or six small islands which are clothed with great trees, green and flourishing all the year, and good channels between the islands. Beyond which, further in still, the shore on each side closes so near with two points of low mangrove land as to make a narrow or strait, scarce half a mile wide. This serves as a mouth or entrance to the inner part of the gulf, which is a deep bay two or three leagues over every way, and about the east end thereof are the mouths of several rivers, the chief of which is that of Santa Maria. There are many outlets or creeks besides this narrow place I have described, but none navigable besides that. For this reason the Spanish guard-ship mentioned in Chapter 1 chose to lie between these two points as the only passage they could imagine we should attempt; since this is the way that the privateers have generally taken as the nearest between the North and South Seas. The river of Santa Maria is the largest of all the rivers of this gulf. It is navigable eight or nine leagues up; for so high the tide flows. Beyond that place the river is divided into many branches which are only fit for canoes. The tide rises and falls in this river about 18 foot.

Of the town and gold-mines of Santa Maria; and the town of Scuchadero.

About six leagues from the river's mouth, on the south side of it, the Spaniards about 20 years ago, upon their first discovery of the gold-mines here, built the town Santa Maria, of the same name with the river. This town was taken by Captain Coxon, Captain Harris and Captain Sharp, at their entrance into these seas; it being then but newly built. Since that time it is grown considerable; for when Captain Harris, the nephew of the former, took it (as is said in Chapter 6) he found in it all sorts of tradesmen, with a great deal of flour, and wine, and abundance of iron crows and pickaxes. These were instruments for the slaves to work in the gold-mines; for besides what gold and sand they take up together, they often find great lumps wedged between the rocks, as if it naturally grew there. I have seen a lump as big as a hen's egg, brought by Captain Harris from thence (who took 120 pound there) and he told me that there were lumps a great deal bigger: but these they were forced to beat in pieces that they might divide them. These lumps are not so solid, but that they have crevices and pores full of earth and dust. This town is not far from the mines, where the Spaniards keep a great many slaves to work in the dry time of the year: but in the rainy season when the rivers do overflow they cannot work so well. Yet the mines are so nigh the mountains that, as the rivers soon rise, so they are soon down again; and presently after the rain is the best searching for gold in the sands. for the violent rains do wash down the gold into the rivers, where much of it settles to the bottom and remains. Then the native Indians who live hereabouts get most; and of them the Spaniards buy more gold than their slaves get by working. I have been fold that they get the value of five shillings a day, one with another. The Spaniards withdraw most of them with their slaves during the wet season to Panama. At this town of St. Maria Captain Townley was lying with his party, making canoes, when Captain Gronet came into these seas; for it was then abandoned by the Spaniards.

There is another small new town at the mouth of the river called the Scuchadero: it stands on the north side of the open place, at the mouth of the river of Santa Maria, where there is more air than at the mines, or at Santa Maria Town, where they are in a manner stifled with heat for want of air.

All about these rivers, especially near the sea, the land is low, it is deep black earth, and the trees it produces are extraordinary large and high. Thus much concerning the Gulf of St. Michael, whither we were bound.

The second day of March, as is said before, we weighed from Perico, and the same night we anchored again at Pacheca. The third day we sailed from thence steering towards the Gulf. Captain Swan undertook to fetch off Captain Townley and his men: therefore he kept near the Main; but the rest of the ships stood nearer the King's Islands. Captain Swan desired this office because he intended to send letters overland by the Indians to Jamaica, which he did; ordering the Indians to deliver his letters to any English vessel in the other seas. At two o'clock we were again near the place where we cleaned our ships. There we saw two ships coming out who proved to be Captain Townley and his men. They were coming out of the river in the night and took 2 barks bound for Panama: the one was laden with flour, the other with wine, brandy, sugar, and oil. The prisoners that he took declared that the Lima fleet was ready to sail.

Captain Townley's arrival with some more English privateers overland.

We went and anchored among the King's Islands, and the next day Captain Swan returned out of the river of Santa Maria, being informed by the Indians that Captain Townley was come over to the King's Islands. At this place Captain Townley put out a great deal of his goods to make room for his men.

Jars of Pisco-wine.

He distributed his wine and brandy some to every ship that it might be drank out, because he wanted the jars to carry water in. The Spaniards in these seas carry all their wine, brandy, and oil in jars that hold 7 or 8 gallons. When they lade at Pisco (a place about 40 leagues to the southward of Lima, and famous for wine) they bring nothing else but jars of wine, and they stow one tier at the top of another so artificially that we could hardly do the like without breaking them: yet they often carry in this manner 1500 or 2000 or more in a ship, and seldom break one. The 10th day we took a small bark that came from Guayaquil: she had nothing in her but ballast. The 12th day there came an Indian canoe out of the river of Santa Maria and told us that there were 300 English and Frenchmen more coming overland from the North Seas.

A bark of Captain Knight's joins them.

The 15th day we met a bark with five or six Englishmen in her that belonged to Captain Knight, who had been in the South Seas five or six months, and was now on the Mexican coast. There he had espied this bark; but, not being able to come up with her in his ship, he detached these five or six men in a canoe, who took her, but, when they had done, could not recover their own ship again, losing company with her in the night, therefore they came into the Bay of Panama intending to go overland back into the North Seas, but that they luckily met with us: for the Isthmus of Darien was now become a common road for privateers to pass between the North and South Seas at their pleasure. This bark of Captain Knight's had in her 40 or 50 jars of brandy: she was now commanded by Mr. Henry More; but Captain Swan, intending to promote Captain Harris, caused Mr. More to be turned out, alleging that it was very likely these men were run away from their commander. Mr. More willingly resigned her, and went aboard of Captain Swan and became one of his men.

It was now the latter end of the dry season here; and the water at the King's, or Pearl Islands, of which there was plenty when we first came hither, was now dried away. Therefore we were forced to go to Point Garachina, thinking to water our ships there.

Point Garachina again.

Captain Harris, being now commander of the new bark, was sent into the river of Santa Maria to see for those men that the Indians told us of, whilst the rest of the ships sailed towards Point Garachina; where we arrived the 21st day, and anchored two mile from the point, and found a strong tide running out of the river Sambo. The next day we ran within the point and anchored in four fathom at low water. The tide rises here eight or nine foot: the flood sets north-north-east, the ebb south-south-west. The Indians that inhabit in the river Sambo came to us in canoes and brought plantains and bananas. They could not speak nor understand Spanish; therefore I believe they have no commerce with the Spaniards. We found no fresh water here neither; so we went from hence to Port Pinas, which is seven leagues south by west from hence.

Porto de Pinas.

Porto Pinas lies in latitude 7 degrees north. It is so called because there are many pine-trees growing there. The land is pretty high, rising gently as it runs into the country. This country near the sea is all covered with pretty high woods: the land that bounds the harbour is low in the middle, but high and rocky on both sides. At the mouth of the harbour there are two small high islands, or rather barren rocks. The Spaniards in their pilot-books commend this for a good harbour; but it lies all open to the south-west winds, which frequently blow here in the wet season: beside, the harbour within the islands is a place of but small extent, and has a very narrow going in; what depth of water there is in the harbour I know not.

The 25th day we arrived at this Harbour of Pines but did not go in with our ship, finding it but an ordinary place to lie at. We sent in our boats to search it, and they found a stream of good water running into the sea; but there were such great swelling surges came into the harbour that we could not conveniently fill our water there. The 26th day we returned to Point Garachina again. In our way we took a small vessel laden with cocoa: she came from Guayaquil. The 29th day we arrived at Point Garachina: there we found Captain Harris, who had been in the river of Santa Maria; but he did not meet the men that he went for: yet he was informed again by the Indians that they were making canoes in one of the branches of the river of Santa Maria. Here we shared our cocoa lately taken.

Because we could not fill our water here we designed to go to Tabago again, where we were sure to be supplied. Accordingly on the 30th day we set sail, being now nine ships in company; and had a small wind at south-south-east. The first day of April, being in the channel between the King's Islands and the Main, we had much Thunder, lightning, and some rain: this evening we anchored at the island Pacheca, and immediately sent four canoes before us to the island Tabago to take some prisoners for information, and we followed the next day. The 3rd day in the evening we anchored by Perica, and the next morning went to Tabago where we found our four canoes. They arrived there in the night, and took a canoe that came (as is usual) from Panama for plantains. There were in the canoe four Indians and a Mulatto. The Mulatto, because he said he was in the fire-ship that came to burn us in the night, was immediately hanged. These prisoners confirmed that one Captain Bond, an Englishman, did command her.

Here we filled our water and cut firewood; and from hence we sent four canoes over to the Main with one of the Indians lately taken to guide them to a sugar-work: for now we had cocoa we wanted sugar to make chocolate. But the chiefest of their business was to get coppers, for, each ship having now so many men, our pots would not boil victuals fast enough though we kept them boiling all the day. About two or three days after they returned aboard with three coppers.

Isle of Otoque.

While we lay here Captain Davis's bark went to the island Otoque. This is another inhabited island in the Bay of Panama; not so big as Tabago, yet there are good plantain-walks on it, and some Negroes to look after them. These Negroes rear fowls and hogs for their masters, who live at Panama; as at the King's Islands.

The packet from Lima taken. Other English and French privateers arrive.

It was for some fowls or hogs that our men went thither; but by accident they met also with an express that was sent to Panama with an account that the Lima fleet was at sea. Most of the letters were thrown overboard and lost; yet we found some that said positively that the fleet was coming with all the strength that they could make in the kingdom of Peru; yet were ordered not to fight us except they were forced to it: (though afterwards they chose to fight us, having first landed their treasure at Lavelia) and that the pilots of Lima had been in consultation what course to steer to miss us.

For the satisfaction of those who may be curious to know I have here inserted the resolutions taken by the Committee of Pilots, as one of our company translated them out of the Spanish of two of the letters we took. The first letter as follows:

Sir,
Having been with his Excellency, and heard the letter of Captain Michael Sanches de Tena read; wherein he says there should be a meeting of the pilots of Panama in the said city, they say it is not

time, putting for objection the Galapagos: to which I answered that
it was fear of the enemy, and that they might well go that way, I told
this to his Excellency, who was pleased to command me to write
this course, which is as follows.

The day for sailing being come, go forth to the west-south-west;
from that to the west till you are forty leagues off at sea; then keep
at the same distance to the north-west till you come under the Line:
from whence the pilot must shape his course for Moro de Porco,
and for the coast of Lavelia and Natta: where you may speak with
the people, and according to the information they give, you may
keep the same course for Otoque, from thence to Tabago, and so
to Panama: this is what offers as to the course.

The letter is obscure: but the reader must make what he can of
it. The directions in the other letter were to this effect:

The surest course to be observed going forth from Malabrigo is
thus: you must sail west by south that you may avoid the sight
of the islands of Lobos; and if you should chance to see them, by
reason of the breezes, and should fall to leeward of the latitude of
Malabrigo, keep on a wind as near as you can and, if necessary,
go about and stand in for the shore; then tack and stand off, and
be sure keep your latitude; and when you are 40 leagues to the
westward of the island Lobos keep that distance till you come under
the Line; and then, if the general wind follow you farther, you must
sail north-north-east till you come into 3 degrees north. And if in
this latitude you should find the breezes, make it your business
to keep the coast, and so sail for Panama. If in your course you
should come in sight of the land before you are abreast of Cape
San Francisco, be sure to stretch off again out of sight of land, that
you may not be discovered by the enemy.

The last letter supposes the fleet's setting out from Malabrigo
in about 8 degrees South latitude (as the other does its
going immediately from Lima, 4 degrees further south) and
from hence is that caution given of avoiding Lobos, as near
Malabrigo, in their usual way to Panama, and hardly to be kept
out of sight, as the winds are thereabouts; yet to be avoided
by the Spanish fleet at this time, because, as they had twice
before heard of the privateers lying at Lobos de la Mar, they

knew not but at that time we might be there in expectation of them.

The 10th day we sailed from Tabago towards the King's Islands again because our pilots told us that the king's ships did always come this way. The 11th day we anchored at the place where we careened. Here we found Captain Harris, who had gone a second time into the river of Santa Maria, and fetched the body of men that last came overland, as the Indians had informed us: but they fell short of the number they told us of. The 29th day we sent 250 men in 15 canoes to the river Cheapo to take the town of Cheapo. The 21st day all our ships but Captain Harris, who stayed to clean his ships, followed after.

Chepelio, one of the sweetest islands in the world.

The 22nd day we arrived at the island Chepelio.

Chepelio is the pleasantest island in the Bay of Panama: it is but seven leagues from the city of Panama and a league from the Main. This island is about a mile long and almost so broad; it is low on the north side, and rises by a small ascent towards the south side. The soil is yellow, a kind of clay. The high side is stony; the low land is planted with all sorts of delicate fruits, namely, sapadillos, avocado-pears, mammees, mammee-sapotas, star-apples, etc. The midst of the island is planted with plantain-trees, which are not very large, but the fruit extraordinary sweet.

The sapadillo, avocado-pear, mammee-sapota.

The sapadillo-tree is as big as a large pear-tree, the fruit much like a bergamot-pear both in colour, shape and size; but on some trees the fruit is a little longer. When it is green or first gathered, the juice is white and clammy, and it will stick like glue; then the fruit is hard, but after it has been gathered two or three days, it grows soft and juicy, and then the juice is clear as spring-water and very sweet; in the midst of the fruit are two or three black stones or seeds, about the bigness of a pumpkin-seed: this is an excellent fruit.

The avocado-pear-tree is as big as most pear-trees, and is commonly pretty high; the skin or bark black, and pretty smooth; the leaves large, of an oval shape, and the fruit as big as a large lemon. It is of a green colour till it is ripe, and then it is a little yellowish. They are seldom fit to eat till they have been gathered two or three days; then they become soft and the skin or rind will peel off. The substance in the inside is green, or a little yellowish, and as soft as butter. Within the substance there is a stone as big as a horse-plum. This fruit has no taste of itself, and therefore it is usually mixed with sugar and lime-juice and beaten together in a plate; and this is an excellent dish. The ordinary way is to eat it with a little salt and a roasted plantain; and thus a man that's hungry may make a good meal of it. It is very wholesome eaten any way. It is reported that this fruit provokes to lust, and therefore is said to be much esteemed by the Spaniards: and I do believe they are much esteemed by them, for I have met with plenty of them in many places in the North Seas where the Spaniards are settled, as in the Bay of Campeachy, on the coast of Cartagena, and the coast of Caracas; and there are some in Jamaica, which were planted by the Spaniards when they possessed that island.

Some traversings in the Bay of Panama; and an account of the strength of the Spanish fleet, and of the privateers, and the engagement between them.

The 4th of May we sailed hence again bound for the King's Islands; and there we continued cruising from one end of these islands to the other: till on the 22nd day, Captain Davis and Captain Gronet went to Pacheca, leaving the rest of the fleet at anchor at St. Paul's Island. From Pacheca we sent two canoes to the island Chepelio, in hopes to get a prisoner there. The 25th day our canoes returned from Chepelio with three prisoners which they took there: they were seamen belonging to Panama, who said that provision was so scarce and dear there that the poor were almost starved, being hindered by us from those common and daily supplies of plantains, which they did formerly enjoy from the islands; especially from those two of

Chepelio and Tabago that the president of Panama had strictly ordered, that none should adventure to any of the islands for plantains: but necessity had obliged them to trespass against the president's order. They farther reported that the fleet from Lima was expected every day; for it was generally talked that they were come from Lima: and that the report at Panama was that King Charles II of England was dead, and that the Duke of York was crowned King. The 27th day Captain Swan and Captain Townley also came to Pacheca, where we lay, but Captain Swan's bark was gone in among the King's Islands for plantains. The island Pacheca, as I have before related, is the northermost of the King's Islands. It is a small low island about a league round. On the south side of it there are two or three small islands, neither of them half a mile round. Between Pacheca and these islands is a small channel not above six or seven paces wide. and about a mile long. Through this Captain Townley made a bold run, being pressed hard by the Spaniards in the fight I am going to speak of, though he was ignorant whether there was a sufficient depth of water or not. On the east side of this channel all our fleet lay waiting for the Lima fleet, which we were in hopes would come this way.

The 28th day we had a very wet morning, for the rains were come in, as they do usually in May, or June, sooner or later; so that May is here a very uncertain month. Hitherto, till within a few days, we had good fair weather and the wind at north-north-east, but now the weather was altered and the wind at south-south-west.

However about eleven o'clock it cleared up, and we saw the Spanish fleet about three leagues west-north-west from the island Pacheca, standing close on a wind to the eastward; but they could not fetch the island by a league. We were riding a league south-east from the island between it and the Main; only Captain Gronet was about a mile to the northward of us near the island: he weighed so soon as they came in sight and stood over for the Main; and we lay still, expecting when he would tack and come to us: but he took care to keep himself out of harm's way.

Captain Swan and Townley came aboard of Captain Davis to order how to engage the enemy, who we saw came purposely to fight us, they being in all 14 sail, besides periagos rowing with 12 and 14 oars apiece. Six sail of them were ships of good force: first the admiral 48 guns, 450 men; the vice-admiral 40 guns, 400 men; the rear-admiral 36 guns, 360 men; a ship of 24 guns, 300 men; one of 18 guns, 250 men; and one of eight guns, 200 men; two great fire-ships, six ships only with small arms having 800 men on board them all; besides 2 or 3 hundred men in periagos. This account of their strength we had afterwards from Captain Knight who, being to the windward on the coast of Peru, took prisoners, of whom he had this information, being what they brought from Lima. Besides these men they had also some hundreds of Old Spain men that came from Portobello, and met them at Lavelia, from whence they now came: and their strength of men from Lima was 3000 men, being all the strength they could make in that kingdom; and for greater security they had first landed their treasure at Lavelia.

Our fleet consisted of ten sail: first Captain Davis 36 guns, 156 men, most English; Captain Swan 16 guns, 140 men, all English: these were the only ships of force that we had; the rest having none but small arms. Captain Townley had 110 men, all English. Captain Gronet 308 men, all French. Captain Harris 100 men, most English. Captain Branly 36 men, some English, some French; Davis's tender eight men; Swan's tender eight men; Townley's bark 80 men; and a small bark of 30 tuns made a fire-ship, with a canoe's crew in her. We had in all 960 men. But Captain Gronet came not to us till all was over, yet we were not discouraged at it, but resolved to fight them, for, being to windward of the enemy, we had it at our choice whether we would fight or not. It was three o'clock in the afternoon when we weighed, and being all under sail we bore down right afore the wind on our enemies, who kept close on a wind to come to us; but night came on without anything beside the exchanging of a few shot on each side. When it grew dark the Spanish admiral put out a light as a signal for his fleet to come to an anchor. We saw the light in the admiral's top, which continued about half an hour, and then it was taken down. In a short time after we saw the light again and, being to windward, we kept under sail, supposing the light had been in the admiral's top; but as it proved this was only a stratagem of theirs; for this light was put out the second time at one of their bark's topmast-head, and then she was sent to leeward; which deceived us: for we thought still the light was in the admiral's top, and by that means thought ourselves to windward of them.

In the morning therefore, contrary to our expectation, we found they had got the weather-gage of us, and were coming upon us with full sail; so we ran for it and, after a running fight all day, and having taken a turn almost round the Bay of Panama, we came to an anchor again at the isle of Pacheca, in the very same place from whence we set out in the morning.

Thus ended this day's work, and with it all that we had been projecting for five or six months; when, instead of making ourselves masters of the Spanish fleet and treasure, we were glad to escape them; and owed that too, in a great measure, to their want of courage to pursue their advantage.

The 30th day in the morning when we looked out we saw the Spanish fleet all together three leagues to leeward of us at an anchor. It was but little wind till 10 o'clock, and then sprung up a small breeze at south, and the Spanish fleet went away to Panama. What loss they had I know not; we lost but one man: and, having held a consult, we resolved to go to the keys of Quibo or Cobaya, to seek Captain Harris, who was forced away from us in the fight; that being the place appointed for our rendezvous upon any such accident. As for Gronet, he said his men would not suffer him to join us in the fight: but we were not satisfied with that excuse; so we suffered him to go with us to the isles of Quibo, and there cashiered our cowardly companion. Some were for taking from him the ship which we had given him: but at length he was suffered to keep it with his men, and we sent them away in it to some other place.

CHAPTER 8

Realejo

Canoes how made.

The manner of making a canoe is, after cutting down a large long tree, and squaring the uppermost side, and then turning it upon the flat side, to shape the opposite side for the bottom. Then again they turn her, and dig the inside; boring also three holes in the bottom, one before, one in the middle, and one abaft, thereby to gauge the thickness of the bottom; for otherwise we might cut the bottom thinner than is convenient. We left the bottoms commonly about three inches thick, and the sides two inches thick below and one and a half at the top. One or both of the ends we sharpen to a point.

Captain Davis made two very large canoes; one was 36 foot long and five or six feet wide; the other 32 foot long and near as wide as the other. In a month's time we finished our business and were ready to sail. Here Captain Harris went to lay his ship aground to clean her, but she being old and rotten fell in pieces: and therefore he and all his men went aboard of Captain Davis and Captain Swan. While we lay here we struck turtle every day, for they were now very plentiful: but from August to March here are not many. The 18th day of July John Rose, a Frenchman, and 14 men more belonging to Captain Gronet, having made a new canoe, came in her to Captain Davis, and desired to serve under him; and Captain Davis accepted of them because they had a canoe of their own.

Tornadoes, and the sea rough. Realejo harbour.

We had fair weather and little wind till two o'clock in the afternoon, then we had a tornado from the shore, with much thunder, lightning and rain, and such a gust of wind that we were all like to be foundered. In this extremity we put right afore the wind, every canoe's crew making what shift they could to avoid the threatening danger. The small canoes, being most light and buoyant, mounted nimbly over the surges, but the great heavy canoes lay like logs in the sea, ready to be swallowed by every foaming billow. Some of our canoes were half full of water yet kept two men constantly heaving it out. The fierceness of the wind continued about half an hour and abated by degrees; and as the wind died away so the fury of the sea abated: for in all hot countries, as I have observed, the sea is soon raised by the wind, and as soon down again when the wind is gone, and therefore it is a proverb among the seamen: Up wind, up sea, down wind, down sea. At seven o'clock in the evening it was quite calm, and the sea as smooth as a mill-pond. Then we tugged to get in to the shore, but, finding we could not do it before day, we rowed off again to keep ourselves out of sight. By that time it was day we were five leagues from the land, which we thought was far enough off shore. Here we intended to lie till the evening, but at three o'clock in the afternoon we had another tornado, more fierce than that which we had the day before. This put us in greater peril of our lives, but did not last so long. As soon as the violence of the tornado was over we rowed in for the shore and entered the harbour in the night: the creek which leads towards Leon lies on the south-east side of the harbour. Our pilot, being very well acquainted here, carried us into the mouth of it, but could carry us no farther till day because it is but a small creek, and there are other creeks like it. The next morning as soon as it was light we rowed into the creek, which is very narrow; the land on both sides lying so low that every tide it is overflown with the sea. This sort of land produces red mangrove-trees, which are here so plentiful and thick that there is no passing through them. Beyond these mangroves, on the firm land close by the side of the river, the Spaniards have built a breast-work, purposely to hinder an enemy from the landing. When we came in sight of the breast-work we rowed as fast as we could to get ashore: the noise of our oars alarmed the Indians who were set to watch, and presently they ran away towards the city of Leon to give notice of our approach. We landed as soon as we could and marched after them: 470 men were drawn out to march to the town, and I was left with 59 men more to stay and guard the canoes till their return.

The city of Leon taken and burnt.

The city of Leon is 20 mile up in the country: the way to it plain and even through a champion country of long grassy savannahs and spots of high woods. About five mile from the landing-place there is a sugar-work, three mile farther there is another, and two mile beyond that there is a fine river to ford, which is not very deep, besides which there is no water in all the way till you come to an Indian town which is two miles before you come to the city, and from thence it is a pleasant straight sandy way to Leon. This city stands in a plain not far from a high peaked mountain which oftentimes casts forth fire and smoke from its top. It may be seen at sea and it is called the volcano of Leon. The houses of Leon are not high built but strong and large, with gardens about them. The walls are stone and the covering of pan-tile: there are three churches and a cathedral which is the head church in these parts. Our countryman Mr. Gage, who travelled in these parts, recommends it to the world as the pleasantest place in all America, and calls it the Paradise of the Indies. Indeed if we consider the advantage of its situation we may find it surpassing most places for health and pleasure in America, for the country about it is of a sandy soil which soon drinks up all the rain that falls, to which these parts are much subject. It is encompassed with savannahs; so that they have the benefit of the breezes coming from any quarter; all which makes it a very healthy place. It is a place of no great trade and therefore not rich in money. Their wealth lies in their pastures, and cattle, and plantations of sugar. It is said that they make cordage here of hemp, but if they have any such manufactory it is at some distance from the town, for here is no sign of any such thing.

Thither our men were now marching; they went from the canoes about eight o'clock. Captain Townley, with 80 of the briskest men, marched before, Captain Swan with 100 men marched next, and Captain Davis with 170 men marched next, and Captain Knight brought up the rear. Captain Townley, who was near two mile ahead of the rest, met about 70 horsemen four miles before he came to the city, but they never stood him. About three o'clock Captain Townley, only with his 80 men, entered the town, and was briskly charged in a broad street with 170 or 200 Spanish horsemen, but, two or three of their leaders being knocked down, the rest fled. Their foot consisted of about 500 men, which were drawn up in the parade; for the Spaniards in these parts make a large square in every town, though the town itself be small. The square is called the parade: commonly the church makes one side of it, and the gentlemen's houses, with their galleries about them, the other. But the foot also seeing their horse retire left an empty city to Captain Townley; beginning to save themselves by flight. Captain Swan came in about four o'clock, Captain Davis with his men about five, and Captain Knight with as many men as he could encourage to march came in about six, but he left many men tired on the road; these, as is usual, came dropping in one or two at a time, as they were able. The next morning the Spaniards killed one of our tired men; he was a stout old grey-headed man, aged about 84, who had served under Oliver in the time of the Irish rebellion; after which he was at Jamaica, and had followed privateering ever since. He would not accept of the offer our men made him to tarry ashore but said he would venture as far as the best of them: and when surrounded by the Spaniards he refused to take quarter, but discharged his gun amongst them, keeping a pistol still charged, so they shot him dead at a distance. His name was Swan; he was a very merry hearty old man and always used to declare he would never take quarter: but they took Mr. Smith who was tired also; he was a merchant belonging to Captain Swan and, being carried before the governor of Leon, was known by a Mulatta woman that waited on him. Mr. Smith had lived many years in the Canaries and could speak and write very good Spanish, and it was there this Mulatta woman remembered him. He being examined how many men we were said 1000 at the city, and 500 at the canoes, which made well for us at the canoes, who straggling about every day might easily have been destroyed. But this so daunted the governor that he did never offer to molest our men, although he had with him above 1000 men, as Mr. Smith guessed. He sent in a flag of truce about noon, pretending to ransom the town rather than let it be burnt, but our captains demanded 300,000 pieces-of-eight for its ransom, and as much provision as would victual 1000 men four months, and Mr. Smith to be ransomed for some of their prisoners; but the Spaniards did not intend to ransom the town, but only capitulated day after day to prolong time, till they had got more men. Our captains therefore, considering the distance that they were from the canoes, resolved to be marching down. The 14th day in the morning they ordered the city to be set on fire, which was presently done, and then they came away: but they took more time in coming down than in going up. The 15th day in the morning the Spaniards sent in Mr. Smith and had a gentlewoman in exchange.

Realejo creek; the town and commodities; the guava-fruit, and prickly-pear.

Then our captains sent a letter to the governor to acquaint him that they intended next to visit Realejo, and desired to meet him there: they also released a gentleman on his promise of paying 150 beefs for his ransom, and to deliver them to us at Realejo; and the same day our men came to their canoes: where, having stayed all night, the next morning we all entered our canoes and came to the harbour of Realejo, and in the afternoon our ships came thither to an anchor.

The creek that leads to Realejo lies from the north-west part of the harbour and it runs in northerly. It is about two leagues from the island in the harbour's mouth to the town; two thirds of the way it is broad, then you enter a narrow deep creek, bordered on both sides with red mangrove trees whose limbs reach almost from one side to the other. A mile from the mouth of the creek it turns away west. There the Spaniards have made a very strong breast-work fronting towards the mouth of the creek, in which were placed 100 soldiers to hinder us from landing: and 20 yards below that breast-work there was a chain of great trees placed cross the creek so that 10 men could have kept off 500 or 1000.

When we came in sight of the breast-work we fired but two guns and they all ran away: and we were afterwards near half an hour cutting the boom or chain. Here we landed and marched to the town of Realejo, or Rea Lejo, which is about a mile from hence. This town stands on a plain by a small river. It is a pretty large town with three churches and a hospital that has a fine garden belonging to it: besides many large fair houses, they all stand at a good distance one from another, with yards about them. This is a very sickly place and I believe has need enough of a hospital; for it is seated so nigh the creeks and swamps that it is never free from a noisome smell. The land about it is a strong yellow clay: yet where the town stands it seems to be sand. Here are several sorts of fruits, as guavas, pineapples, melons, and prickly-pears. The pineapple and melon are well known.

A ransom paid honourably upon parole: the town burnt.

There are many sugar-works in the country, and estancias or beef farms: there is also a great deal of pitch, tar and cordage, made in the country, which is the chief of their trade. This town we approached without any opposition, and found nothing but empty houses; besides such things as they could not, or would not carry away, which were chiefly about 500 packs of flour, brought hither in the great ship that we left at Amapalla, and some pitch, tar and cordage. These things we wanted and therefore we sent them all aboard. Here we received 150 beefs, promised by the gentleman that was released coming from Leon; besides, we visited the beef-farms every day, and the sugar-works, going in small companies of 20 or 30 men, and brought away every man his load; for we found no horses, which if we had, yet the ways were so wet and dirty that they would not have been serviceable to us. We stayed here from the 17th till the 24th day, and then some of our destructive crew set fire to the houses: I know not by whose order, but we marched away and left them burning; at the breast-work we embarked into our canoes and returned aboard our ships.

Captain Davis and others go off for the south coast.

The 25th day Captain Davis and Captain Swan broke off consortship; for Captain Davis was minded to return again on the coast of Peru but Captain Swan desired to go farther to the westward. I had till this time been with Captain Davis, but now left him, and went aboard of Captain Swan. It was not from any dislike to my old Captain, but to get some knowledge of the northern parts of this continent of Mexico: and I knew that Captain Swan determined to coast it as far north as he thought convenient, and then pass over for the East Indies; which was a way very agreeable to my inclination. Captain Townley, with his two barks, was resolved to keep us company; but Captain Knight and Captain Harris followed Captain Davis. The 27th day in the morning Captain Davis with his ships went out of the harbour, having a fresh land wind. They were in company, Captain Davis's ship with Captain Harris in her; Captain Davis's bark and fire-ship, and Captain Knight in his own ship, in all four sail. Captain Swan took his last farewell of him by firing fifteen guns, and he fired eleven in return of the civility.

A contagious sickness at Realejo.

We stayed here some time afterwards to fill our water and cut firewood; but our men, who had been very healthy till now, began to fall down apace in fevers. Whether it was the badness of the water or the unhealthiness of the town was the cause of it we did not know; but of the two I rather believe it was a distemper we got at Realejo; for it was reported that they had been visited with a malignant fever in that town, which had occasioned many people to abandon it; and although this visitation was over with them, yet their houses and goods might still retain somewhat of the infection and communicate the same to us.

I the rather believe this because it afterwards raged very much, not only among us, but also among Captain Davis and his men, as he told me himself since when I met him in England: himself had like to have died, as did several of his and our men. The 3rd day of September we turned ashore all our prisoners and pilots, they being unacquainted further to the west, which was the coast that we designed to visit: for the Spaniards have a very little trade by sea beyond the river Lempa, a little to the north-west of this place.

About 10 o'clock in the morning the same day we went from hence, steering westward, being in company four sail, as well as they who left us, namely, Captain Swan and his bark, and Captain Townley and his bark, and about 340 men.

The vinello-plant and fruit.

The vinello is a little cod full of small black seeds; it is four or five inches long, about the bigness of the stem of a tobacco leaf, and when dried much resembling it: so that our privateers at first have often thrown them away when they took any, wondering why the Spaniards should lay up tobacco stems. This cod grows on a small vine which climbs about and supports itself by the neighbouring trees: it first bears a yellow flower from whence the cod afterwards proceeds. It is first green, but when ripe it turns yellow; then the Indians (whose manufacture it is, and who sell it cheap to the Spaniards) gather it, and lay it in the sun, which makes it soft; then it changes to a chestnut-colour. Then they frequently press it between their fingers, which makes it flat. If the Indians do anything to them beside I know not; but I have seen the Spaniards sleek them with oil.

These vines grow plentifully at Boca Toro, where I have gathered and tried to cure them, but could not: which makes me think that the Indians have some secret that I know not of to cure them. I have often asked the Spaniards how they were cured, but I never could meet with any could tell me. One Mr. Cree also, a very curious person who spoke Spanish well and had been a privateer all his life, and seven years a prisoner among the Spaniards at Portobello and Cartagena, yet upon all his enquiry could not find any of them that understood it. Could we have learnt the art of it several of us would have gone to Boca Toro yearly at the dry season and cured them, and freighted our vessel. We there might have had turtle enough for food, and store of vinelloes. Mr. Cree first showed me those at Boca Toro. At or near a town also, called Caihooca in the Bay of Campeachy, these cods are found. They are commonly sold for three pence a cod among the Spaniards in the West Indies, and are sold by the druggist, for they are much used among chocolate to perfume it. Some will use them among tobacco for it gives a delicate scent. I never heard of any vinelloes but here in this country, about Caihooca, and at Boca Toro.

The Indians of this village could speak but little Spanish. They seemed to be a poor innocent people: and by them we understood that there are very few Spaniards in these parts; yet all the Indians hereabout are under them. The land from the sea to their houses is black earth mixed with some stones and rocks; all the way full of very high trees.

The 10th day we sent four canoes to the westward who were ordered to lie for us at Port Angels; where we were in hopes that by some means or other they might get prisoners that might give us a better account of the country than at present we could have; and we followed them with our ships, all our men being now pretty well recovered of the fever which had raged amongst as ever since we departed from Realejo.

CHAPTER 9

A Series of Disappointments

They set out from Guatulco.

It was the 12th of October 1685 when we set out of the harbour with our ships. The land here lies along west and a little southerly for about 20 or 30 leagues, and the sea-winds are commonly at west-south-west, sometimes at south-west, the land-winds at north. We had now fair weather and but little wind.

The isle Sacrificio.

We coasted along to the westward, keeping as near the shore as we could for the benefit of the land-winds, for the sea-winds were right against us; and we found a current setting to the eastward which kept us back and obliged us to anchor at the island Sacrificio, which is a small green island about half a mile long. It lies about a league to the west of Guatulco and about half a mile from the Main. There seems to be a fine bay to the west of the island; but it is full of rocks. The best riding is between the island and the Main: there you will have five or six fathom water. Here runs a pretty strong tide; the sea rises and falls five or six foot up and down.

The 18th day we sailed from hence, coasting to the westward after our canoes. We kept near the shore, which was all sandy bays, the country pretty high and woody, and a great sea tumbling in upon the shore. The 22nd day two of our canoes came aboard and told us they had been a great way to the westward, but could not find Port Angels. They had attempted to land the day before at a place where they saw a great many bulls and cows feeding, in hopes to get some of them; but the sea ran so high that they overset both canoes, and wet all their arms, and lost four guns, and had one man drowned, and with much ado got off again. They could give no account of the other two canoes for they lost company the first night that they went from Guatulco and had not seen them since.

Port Angels.

We were now abreast of Port Angels, though our men in the canoes did not know it; therefore we went in and anchored there. This is a broad open bay with two or three rocks at the west side. Here is good anchoring all over the bay in 30 or 20 or 12 fathom water; but you must ride open to all winds except the land-winds till you come into 12 or 13 fathom water; then you are sheltered from the west-south-west which are the common trade winds. The tide rises here about five foot; the flood sets to the north-east and the ebb to the south-west. The landing in this bay is bad; the place of landing is close by the west side behind a few rocks; here always goes a great swell. The Spaniards compare this harbour for goodness to Guatulco, but there is a great difference between them. For Guatulco is almost landlocked and this an open road, and no one would easily know it by their character of it, but by its marks and its latitude, which is 15 degrees north. For this reason our canoes, which were sent from Guatulco and ordered to tarry here for us, did not know it (not thinking this to be that fine harbour) and therefore went farther; two of them, as I said before, returned again, but the other two were not yet come to us. The land that bounds this harbour is pretty high, the earth sandy and yellow, in some places red; it is partly woodland, partly savannahs. The trees in the woods are large and tall and the savannahs are plentifully stored with very kindly grass. Two leagues to the east of this place is a beef farm belonging to Don Diego de la Rosa.

The 23rd day we landed about 100 men and marched thither where we found plenty of fat bulls and cows feeding in the savannahs, and in the house good store of salt and maize; and some hogs, and cocks and hens: but the owners or overseers were gone. We lay here two or three days feasting on fresh provision, but could not contrive to carry any quantity aboard because the way was so long and our men but weak, and a great wide river to ford. Therefore we returned again from thence the 26th day and brought everyone a little beef or pork for the men that stayed aboard.

Jackals.

The two nights that we stayed ashore at this place we heard great droves of jackals, as we supposed them to be, barking all night long not far from us. None of us saw these; but I do verily believe they were jackals; though I did never see these creatures in America, nor hear any but at this time. We could not think that there were less than 30 or 40 in a company. We got aboard in the evening; but did not yet hear any news of our two canoes.

The 27th day in the morning we sailed from hence with the land-wind at north by west. The sea-wind came about noon at west-south-west, and in the evening we anchored in 16 fathom water by a small rocky island which lies about half a mile from the Main and six leagues westward from Port Angels. The Spaniards give no account of this island in their pilot-book. The 28th day we sailed again with the land-wind: in the afternoon the sea-breeze blew hard and we sprung our main-top-mast. This coast is full of small hills and valleys, and a great sea falls in upon the shore. In the night we met with the other two of our canoes that went from us at Guatulco. They had been as far as Acapulco to seek Port Angels. Coming back from thence they went into a river to get water and were encountered by 150 Spaniards, yet they filled their water in spite of them, but had one man shot through the thigh. Afterward they went into a lagoon, or lake of salt water, where they found much dried fish and brought some aboard. We being now abreast of that place sent in a canoe manned with twelve men for more fish. The mouth of this lagoon is not pistol-shot wide, and on both sides are pretty high rocks, so conveniently placed by nature that many men may abscond behind; and within the rocks and lagoon opens wide on both sides.

A *narrow escape.*

The Spaniards, being alarmed by our two canoes that had been there two or three days before, came armed to this place to secure their fish; and seeing our canoe coming, they lay snug behind the rocks, and suffered the canoe to pass in, then they fired their volley and wounded five of our men. Our people were a little surprised at this sudden adventure, yet fired their guns and rowed farther into the lagoon, for they durst not adventure to come out again through the narrow entrance which was near a quarter of a mile in length. Therefore they rowed into the middle of the lagoon where they lay out of gun-shot and looked about to see if there was not another passage to get out at, broader than that by which they entered, but could see none. So they lay still two days and three nights, in hopes that we should come to seek them; but we lay off at sea about three leagues distant, waiting for their return, supposing by their long absence that they had made some greater discovery and were gone farther than the fish-range; because it is usual with privateers when they enter upon such designs to search farther than they proposed if they meet any encouragement. But Captain Townley and his bark being nearer the shore heard some guns fired in the lagoon. So he manned his canoe and went towards the shore, and, beating the Spaniards away from the rocks, made a free passage for our men to come out of their pound, where else they must have been starved or knocked on the head by the Spaniards. They came aboard their ships again the 31st of October. This lagoon is about the latitude of 16 degrees 40 minutes north.

The rock *Algatross, and the neighbouring coast.*

From hence we made sail again, coasting to the westward, having fair weather and a current setting to the west. The second day of November we passed by a rock called by the Spaniards the Algatross. The land hereabout is of an indifferent height and woody, and more within the country mountainous. Here are seven or eight white cliffs by the sea, which are very remarkable because there are none so white and so thick together on all the coast. They are five or six mile to the west of the Algatross Rock. There is a dangerous shoal lies south by west from these cliffs, four or five mile off at sea. Two leagues to the west of these cliffs there is a pretty large river which forms a small island at its mouth. The channel on the east side is but shoal and sandy, but the west channel is deep enough for canoes to enter. On the banks of this channel the Spaniards have made a breast-work to hinder an enemy from landing or filling water.

The 3rd day we anchored abreast of this river in 14 fathom water about a mile and a half off shore. The next morning we manned our canoes and went ashore to the breast-work with little resistance, although there were about 200 men to keep us off. They fired about twenty or thirty guns at us but seeing we were resolved to land they quitted the place; one chief reason why the Spaniards are so frequently routed by us, although many times much our superiors in numbers, and in many places fortified with breast-works, is their want of small firearms, for they have but few on all the sea coasts unless near their larger garrisons. Here we found a great deal of salt, brought hither, as I judge, for to salt fish, which they take in the lagoons.

The town of Acapulco.

We marched two or three leagues into the country and met with but one house, where we took a Mulatto prisoner who informed us of a ship that was lately arrived at Acapulco; she came from Lima. Captain Townley, wanting a good ship, thought now he had an opportunity of getting one if he could persuade his men to venture with him into the harbour of Acapulco and fetch this Lima ship out. Therefore he immediately proposed it and found not only all his own men willing to assist him but many of Captain Swan's men also. Captain Swan opposed it because, provision being scarce with us, he thought our time might be much better employed in first providing ourselves with food, and here was plenty of maize in the river where we now were, as we were informed by the same prisoner who offered to conduct us to the place where it was.

Of the trade it drives with the Philippine Islands.

But neither the present necessity nor Captain Swan's persuasion availed anything, no nor yet their own interest; for the great design we had then in hand was to lie and wait for a rich ship which comes to Acapulco every year richly laden from the Philippine Islands. But it was necessary we should be well stored with provisions to enable us to cruise about and wait the time of her coming. However, Townley's party prevailing, we only filled our water here and made ready to be gone. So the 5th day in the afternoon we sailed again, coasting to the westward towards Acapulco.

Acapulco today.

The haven of Acapulco.

The 7th day in the afternoon, being about twelve leagues from the shore, we saw the high land of Acapulco, which is very remarkable: for there is a round hill standing between two other hills; the westermost of which is the biggest and highest, and has two hillocks like two paps on its top: the eastermost hill is higher and sharper than the middlemost. From the middle hill the land declines toward the sea, ending in a high round point. There is no land shaped like this on all the coast. In the evening Captain Townley went away from the ships with 140 men in twelve canoes to try to get the Lima ship out of Acapulco Harbour.

Acapulco is a pretty large town, 17 degrees north of the Equator. It is the sea-port for the city of Mexico on the west side of the continent; as La Vera Cruz, or St. John d'Ulloa in the Bay of Nova Hispania is on the north side. This town is the only place of trade on all this coast; for there is little or no traffic by sea on all the north-west part of this vast kingdom, here being, as I have said, neither boats, barks, nor ships (that I could ever see) unless only what come hither from other parts, and some boats near the south-east end of California; as I guess, by the intercourse between that and the Main, for pearl-fishing.

The ships that trade hither are only three, two that constantly go once a year between this and Manila in Luconia, one of the Philippine Islands, and one ship more every year to and from Lima. This from Lima commonly arrives a little before Christmas; she brings them quicksilver, cocoa, and pieces-of-eight. Here she stays till the Manila ships arrive, and then takes in a cargo of spices, silks, calicoes, and muslins, and other East India commodities, for the use of Peru, and then returns to Lima. This is but a small vessel of twenty guns, but the two Manila ships are each said to be above 1000 tun. These make their voyages alternately so that one or other of them is always at the Manilas. When either of them sets out from Acapulco it is at the latter end of March or the beginning of April; she always touches to refresh at Guam, one of the Ladrone Islands, in about sixty days space after she sets out. There she stays but two or three days and then prosecutes her voyage to Manila where she commonly arrives some time in June. By that time the other is ready to sail from thence laden with East India commodities. She stretches away to the north as far as 36, or sometimes into 40 degrees of north latitude before she gets a wind to stand over to the American shore. She falls in first with the coast of California, and then coasts along the shore to the south again, and never misses a wind to bring her away from thence quite to Acapulco. When she gets the length of Cape San Lucas, which is the southermost point of California, she stretches over to Cape Corrientes, which is in about the 20th degree of north latitude. From thence she coasts along till she comes to Sallagua, and there she sets ashore passengers that are bound to the city of Mexico: from thence she makes her best way, coasting still along shore, till she arrives at Acapulco, which is commonly about Christmas, never more than eight or ten days before or after. Upon the return of this ship to the Manila the other which stays there till her arrival takes her turn back to Acapulco. Sir John Narborough therefore was imposed on by the Spaniards who told him that there were eight sail, or more, that used this trade.

The Port of Acapulco is very commodious for the reception of ships, and so large that some hundreds may safely ride there without damnifying each other. There is a small low island crossing the mouth of the harbour; it is about a mile and a half long and half a mile broad, stretching east and west. It leaves a good wide deep channel at each end where ships may safely go in or come out, taking the advantage of the winds; they must enter with the sea-wind, and go out with the land-wind, for these winds seldom or never fail to succeed each other alternately in their proper season of the day or night. The westermost channel is the narrowest, but so deep there is no anchoring, and the Manila ships pass in that way, but the ships from Lima enter on the south-west channel. This harbour runs in north about three miles then, growing very narrow, it turns short about to the west and runs about a mile farther, where it ends. The town stands on the north-west side at the mouth of this narrow passage, close by the sea, and at the end of the town there is a platform with a great many guns. Opposite to the town, on the east side, stands a high strong castle, said to have forty guns of a very great bore. Ships commonly ride near the bottom of the harbour, under the command both of the castle and the platform.

A tornado.

Captain Townley, who, as I said before, with 140 men, left our ships on a design to fetch the Lima ship out of the harbour, had not rowed above three or four leagues before the voyage was like to end with all their lives; for on a sudden they were encountered with a violent tornado from the shore, which had like to have foundered all the canoes: but they escaped that danger and the second night got safe into Port Marquis.

Port Marquis. Captain Townley makes a fruitless attempt.

Port Marquis is a very good harbour a league to the east of Acapulco Harbour. Here they stayed all the next day to dry themselves, their clothes, their arms and ammunition, and the next night they rowed softly into Acapulco Harbour; and because they would not be heard they hauled in their oars, and paddled as softly as if they had been seeking manatee. They paddled close to the castle; then struck over to the town, and found the ship riding between the breast-work and the fort, within about a hundred yards of each. When they had well viewed her and considered the danger of the design they thought it not possible to accomplish it; therefore they paddled softly back again till they were out of command of the forts, and then they went to land, and fell in among a company of Spanish soldiers (for the Spaniards, having seen them the day before, had set guards along the coast) who immediately fired at them but did them no damage, only made them retire farther from the shore. They lay afterwards at the mouth of the harbour till it was day to take a view of the town and castle, and then returned aboard again, being tired, hungry, and sorry for their disappointment.

A long sandy bay, but very rough seas.

The 11th day we made sail again further on to the westward
with the land-wind, which is commonly at north-east, but the
sea-winds are at south-west. We passed by a long sandy bay
of above twenty leagues. All the way along it the sea falls with
such force on the shore that it is impossible to come near it
with boat or canoe; yet it is good clean ground, and good
anchoring a mile or two from the shore. The land by the sea
is low and indifferent fertile, producing many sorts of trees,
especially the spreading palm, which grows in spots from one
end of the bay to the other.

The hill of Petaplan.

The land in the country is full of small peaked barren hills,
making as many little valleys, which appear flourishing and
green. At the west end of this bay is the hill of Petaplan, in
latitude 17 degrees 30 minutes north. This is a round point
stretching out into the sea: at a distance it seems to be an
island. A little to the west of this hill are several round rocks,
which we left without us, steering in between them and the
round point, where we had eleven fathom water. We came to
an anchor on the north-west side of the hill and went ashore,
about 170 men of us, and marched into the country twelve
or fourteen miles.

A poor Indian village.

There we came to a poor Indian village that did not afford us
a meal of victuals. The people all fled, only a Mulatta woman
and three or four small children, who were taken and brought
aboard. She told us that a carrier (one who drives a caravan
of mules) was going to Acapulco, laden with flour and other
goods, but stopped in the road for fear of us, a little to the west
of this village (for he had heard of our being on this coast)
and she thought he still remained there: and therefore it was

we kept the woman to be our guide to carry us to that place. At this place where we now lay our Moskito men struck some small turtle and many small jewfish.

Jew-fish.

The jew-fish is a very good fish, and I judge so called by the English because it has scales and fins, therefore a clean fish, according to the Levitical law, and the Jews at Jamaica buy them and eat them very freely. It is a very large fish, shaped much like a cod but a great deal bigger; one will weigh three, or four, or five hundredweight. It has a large head, with great fins and scales, as big as an half-crown, answerable to the bigness of his body. It is very sweet meat, and commonly fat. This fish lives among the rocks; there are plenty of them in the West Indies, about Jamaica and the coast of Caracas; but chiefly in these seas, especially more westward.

Chequetan, a good harbour.

We went from hence with our ships the 18th [sic] day, and steered west about two leagues farther to a place called Chequetan. A mile and a half from the shore there is a small key, and within it is a very good harbour where ships may careen; there is also a small river of fresh water, and wood enough.

Estapa; mussels there.

The 14th day in the morning we went with 95 men in six canoes to seek for the carrier, taking the Mulatto woman for our guide; but Captain Townley would not go with us. Before day we landed at a place called Estapa, a league to the west of Chequetan. The woman was well acquainted here, having been often at this place for mussels as she told us; for here are great plenty of them. They seem in all respects like our English mussels.

A *caravan of mules taken.*

She carried us through the pathless wood by the side of a river for about a league: then we came into a savannah full of bulls and cows; and here the carrier before mentioned was lying at the estancia-house with his mules, not having dared to advance all this while, as not knowing where we lay; so his own fear made him, his mules, and all his goods, become a prey to us. He had 40 packs of flour, some chocolate, a great many small cheeses, and abundance of earthenware. The eatables we brought away, but the earthen vessels we had no occasion for and therefore left them. The mules were about 60: we brought our prize with them to the shore, and so turned them away. Here we also killed some cows and brought with us to our canoes. In the afternoon our ships came to an anchor half a mile from the place where we landed; and then we went aboard. Captain Townley, seeing our good success, went ashore with his men to kill some cows; for here were no inhabitants near to oppose us. The land is very woody, of a good fertile soil watered with many small rivers; yet it has but few inhabitants near the sea. Captain Townley killed 18 beefs, and after he came aboard our men, contrary to Captain Swan's inclination, gave Captain Townley part of the flour which we took ashore. Afterwards we gave the woman some clothes for her and her children, and put her and two of them ashore; but one of them, a very pretty boy about seven or eight years old, Captain Swan kept. The woman cried and begged hard to have him; but Captain Swan would not, but promised to make much of him and was as good as his word. He proved afterwards a very fine boy for wit, courage, and dexterity; I have often wondered at his expressions and actions.

The 21st day in the evening we sailed hence with the land-wind. The land-winds on this part of the coast are at north and the sea-winds at west-south-west. We had fair weather and coasted along to the westward. The land is high and full of ragged hills; and west from these ragged hills the land makes many pleasant and fruitful valleys among the mountains. The 25th day we were abreast of a very remarkable hill which, towering above the rest of his fellows, is divided in the top and makes two small parts. It is in latitude 18 degrees 8 minutes north.

A hill near Thelupan.

The Spaniards make mention of a town called Thelupan near this hill, which we would have visited if we could have found the way to it. The 26th day Captain Swan and Captain Townley with 200 men, of whom I was one, went in our canoes to seek for the city of Colima, a rich place by report, but how far within land I could never learn: for, as I said before, here is no trade by sea, and therefore we could never get guides to inform us or conduct us to any town but one or two on this coast: and there is never a town that lies open to the sea but Acapulco; and therefore our search was commonly fruitless, as now; for we rowed above 20 leagues along shore and found it a very bad coast to land. We saw no house nor sign of inhabitants, although we passed by a fine valley called the valley of Maguella; only at two places, the one at our first setting out on this expedition, and the other at the end of it, we saw a horseman set, as we supposed, as a sentinel to watch us. At both places we landed with difficulty, and at each place we followed the track of the horse on the sandy bay; but where they entered the woods we lost the track and, although we diligently searched for it, yet we could find it no more; so we were perfectly at a loss to find out the houses or town they came from.

The coast hereabouts.

The 28th day, being tired and hopeless to find any town, we went aboard our ships, that were now come abreast of the place where we were: for always when we leave our ships we either order a certain place of meeting, or else leave them a sign to know where we are by making one or more great smokes; yet we had all like to have been ruined by such a signal as this in a former voyage under Captain Sharp, when we made that unfortunate attempt upon Arica, which is mentioned in the

History of the Buccaneers. For upon the routing our men, and taking several of them, some of those so taken told the Spaniards that it was agreed between them and their companions on board to make two great smokes at a distance from each other as soon as the town should be taken, as a signal to the ship that it might safely enter the harbour. The Spaniards made these smokes presently: I was then among those who stayed on board; and whether the signal was not so exactly made or some other discouragement happened I remember not, but we forbore going in till we saw our scattered crew coming off in their canoes. Had we entered the port upon the false signal we must have been taken or sunk; for we must have passed close by the fort and could have had no wind to bring us out till the land-wind should rise in the night.

The volcano, town, valley, and bay of Colima.

But to our present voyage: after we came aboard we saw the volcano of Colima. This is a very high mountain in about 18 degrees 36 minutes north, standing five or six leagues from the sea in the midst of a pleasant valley. It appears with two sharp peaks, from each of which there do always issue flames of fire or smoke. The valley in which this volcano stands is called the valley of Colima from the town itself which stands there not far from the volcano. The town is said to be great and rich, the chief of all its neighbourhood: and the valley in which it is seated, by the relation which the Spaniards give of it, is the most pleasant and fruitful valley in all the kingdom of Mexico. This valley is about ten or twelve leagues wide by the sea, where it makes a small bay: but how far the vale runs into the country I know not. It is said to be full of cocoa-gardens, fields of corn, wheat, and plantain-walks. The neighbouring sea is bounded with a sandy shore; but there is no going ashore for the violence of the waves. The land within it is low all along and woody for about two leagues from the east side; at the end of the woods there is a deep river runs out into the sea, but it has such a great bar, or sandy shoal, that when we were here no boat or canoe could possibly enter, the sea running so high upon the bar: otherwise, I judge, we should have made some farther discovery into this pleasant valley. On the west side of the river the savannah-land begins and runs to the other side of the valley. We had but little wind when we came aboard, therefore we lay off this bay that afternoon and the night ensuing.

The 29th day our captains went away from our ships with 200 men, intending at the first convenient place to land and search about for a path: for the Spanish books make mention of two or three other towns hereabouts, especially one called Sallagua, to the west of this bay. Our canoes rowed along as near the shore as they could, but the sea went so high that they could not land. About 10 or 11 o'clock two horsemen came near the shore, and one of them took a bottle out of his pocket and drank to our men. While he was drinking, one of our men snatched up his gun and let drive at him and killed his horse: so his consort immediately set spurs to his horse and rode away, leaving the other to come after a-foot. But he being booted made but slow haste; therefore two of our men stripped themselves and swam ashore to take him. But he had a machete, or long knife, wherewith he kept them both from seizing him, they having nothing in their hands wherewith to defend themselves or offend him. The 30th day our men came all aboard again, for they could not find any place to land in.

Sallagua Port.

The first day of December we passed by the Port of Sallagua. This port is in latitude 18 degrees 52 minutes. It is only a pretty deep bay, divided in the middle with a rocky point, which makes, as it were, two harbours. Ships may ride securely in either but the west harbour is the best: there is good anchoring anywhere in 10 or 12 fathom, and a brook of fresh water runs into the sea. Here we saw a great new thatched house, and a great many Spaniards both horse and foot, with drums beating and colours flying in defiance of us, as we thought. We took no notice of them till the next morning, and then we landed about 200 men to try their courage; but they presently withdrew. The foot never stayed to exchange one shot, but the horsemen stayed till two or three were knocked down, and then they drew off, our men pursuing them. At last two of our men took two horses that had lost their riders and, mounting them, rode after the Spaniards full drive till they came among them, thinking to have taken a prisoner for intelligence, but had like to have been taken themselves: for four Spaniards surrounded them, after they had discharged their pistols, and unhorsed them; and if some of our best footmen had not come to their rescue they must have yielded or have been killed. They were both cut in two or three places but their wounds were not mortal. The four Spaniards got away before our men could hurt them and, mounting their horses, speeded after their consorts, who were marched away into the country. Our men, finding a broad road leading into the country, followed it about four leagues in a dry stony country, full of short wood; but finding no sign of inhabitants they returned again. In their way back they took two Mulattos who were not able to march as fast as their consorts; therefore they had skulked in the woods and by that means thought to have escaped our men.

Orrha.

These prisoners informed us that this great road did lead to a great city called Oarrha, from whence many of those horsemen before spoken of came: that this city was distant from hence as far as a horse will go in four days; and that there is no place of consequence nearer: that the country is very poor and thinly inhabited.

They said also that these men came to assist the Philippine ship that was every day expected here to put ashore passengers for Mexico. The Spanish pilot-books mention a town also called Sallagua hereabouts; but we could not find it, nor hear anything of it by our prisoners.

We now intended to cruise off Cape Corrientes to wait for the Philippine ship. So the 6th day of December we set sail, coasting to the westward towards Cape Corrientes. We had fair weather and but little wind; the sea-breezes at north-west and the land-wind at north.

Ragged hills.

The land is of an indifferent height, full of ragged points which at a distance appear like islands: the country is very woody, but the trees are not high, nor very big.

Here I was taken sick of a fever and ague that afterwards turned to a dropsy which I laboured under a long time after; and many of our men died of this distemper, though our surgeons used their greatest skill to preserve their lives. The dropsy is a general distemper on this coast, and the natives say that the best remedy they can find for it is the stone or cod of an alligator (of which they have four, one near each leg, within the flesh) pulverized and drunk in water: this recipe we also found mentioned in an almanac made at Mexico: I would have tried it but we found no alligators here though there are several.

There are many good harbours between Sallagua and Cape Corrientes but we passed by them all. As we drew near the Cape the land by the sea appeared of an indifferent height, full of white cliffs; but in the country the land is high and barren and full of sharp peaked hills, unpleasant to the sight.

Coronada, or the Crown Land.

To the west of this ragged land is a chain of mountains running parallel with the shore; they end on the west with a gentle descent; but on the east side they keep their height, ending with a high steep mountain which has three small sharp peaked tops, somewhat resembling a crown and therefore called by the Spaniards Coronada, the Crown Land.

Cape Corrientes.

The 11th day we were fair in sight of Cape Corrientes, it bore north by west and the Crown Land bore north. The cape is of an indifferent height with steep rocks to the sea. It is flat and even on the top, clothed with woods: the land in the country is high and doubled. This cape lies in 20 degrees 8 minutes north.

I find its longitude from Tenerife to be 230 degrees 56 minutes, but I keep my longitude westward, according to our course; and according to this reckoning I find it is from the Lizard in England 121 degrees 41 minutes, so that the difference of time is eight hours and almost six minutes.

Here we had resolved to cruise for the Philippine ship because she always makes this cape in her voyage homeward. We were (as I have said) four ships in company; Captain Swan and his tender; Captain Townley and his tender. It was so ordered that Captain Swan should lie eight or ten leagues off shore, and the rest about a league distant each from other, between him and the cape, that so we might not miss the Philippine ship; but we wanted provision and therefore we sent Captain Townley's bark with 50 or 60 men to the west of the cape to search about for some town or plantations where we might get provision of any sort. The rest of us in the meantime cruising in our stations. The 17th day the bark came to us again but had got nothing, for they could not get about the cape because the wind on this coast is commonly between the north-west and the south-west, which makes it very difficult getting to the westward; but they left four canoes with 46 men at the cape, who resolved to row to the westward. The 18th day we sailed to the keys of Chametly to fill our water.

Isles of Chametly. The city Purification.

The keys or islands of Chametly are about 16 or 18 leagues to the eastward of Cape Corrientes. They are small, low, and woody, environed with rocks, there are five of them lying in the form of a half moon, not a mile from the shore, and between them and the Main is very good riding, secure from any wind. The Spaniards do report that here live fishermen, to fish for the inhabitants of the city of Purification. This is said to be a large town, the best hereabouts; but is 14 leagues up in the country.

The 20th instant we entered within these islands, passing in on the south-east side, and anchored between the islands and the Main in five fathom clean sand. Here we found good fresh water and wood, and caught plenty of rock-fish with hook and line, a sort of fish I described at the isle of Juan Fernandez, but we saw no sign of inhabitants besides three or four old huts; therefore I do believe that the Spanish or Indian fishermen come hither only at Lent, or some other such season, but that they do not live here constantly. The 21st day Captain Townley went away with about 60 men to take an Indian village seven or eight leagues from hence to the westward more towards the cape, and the next day we went to cruise off the cape, where Captain Townley was to meet us. The 24th day, as we were cruising off the cape, the four canoes before mentioned, which Captain Townley's bark left at the cape, came off to us.

Valderas; or the Valley of Flags.

They, after the bark left them, passed to the west of the cape and rowed into the valley Valderas, or perhaps Val d'Iris; for it signifies the valley of Flags.

This valley lies in the bottom of a pretty deep bay that runs in between Cape Corrientes on the south-east and the point of Pontique on the north-west, which two places are about 10 leagues asunder. The valley is about three leagues wide; there is a level sandy bay against the sea and good smooth landing. In the midst of the bay is a fine river whereinto boats may enter; but it is brackish at the latter end of the dry season, which is in February, March, and part of April. I shall speak more of the seasons in my Chapter of Winds in the Appendix. This valley is bounded within land with a small green hill that makes a very gentle descent into the valley and affords a very pleasant prospect to seaward. It is enriched with fruitful savannahs, mixed with groves of trees fit for any uses, beside fruit-trees in abundance, as guavas, oranges and limes, which here grow wild in such plenty as if nature had designed it only for a garden. The savannahs are full of fat bulls and cows and some horses, but no house in sight.

They miss their design on this coast.

When our canoes came to this pleasant valley they landed 37 men and marched into the country seeking for some houses. They had not gone passed three mile before they were attacked by 150 Spaniards, horse and foot: there was a small thin wood close by them, into which our men retreated to secure themselves from the fury of the horse: yet the Spaniards rode in among them and attacked them very furiously till the Spanish captain and 17 more tumbled dead off their horses: then the rest retreated, being many of them wounded. We lost four men and had two desperately wounded. In this action the foot, who were armed with lances and swords and were the greatest number, never made any attack; the horsemen had each a brace of pistols and some short guns. If the foot had come in they had certainly destroyed all our men. When the skirmish was over our men placed the two wounded men on horses and came to their canoes. There they killed one of the horses and dressed it, being afraid to venture into the savannah to kill a bullock, of which there was store. When they had eaten and satisfied themselves they returned aboard. The 25th day, being Christmas, we cruised in pretty near the cape and sent in three canoes with the strikers to get fish, being desirous to have a Christmas dinner. In the afternoon they returned aboard with three great jew-fish which feasted us all; and the next day we sent ashore our canoes again and got three or four more.

Captain Townley, who went from us at Chametly, came aboard the 28th day and brought about 40 bushels of maize. He had landed to the eastward of Cape Corrientes and marched to an Indian village that is four or five leagues in the country. The Indians, seeing him coming, set two houses on fire that were full of maize and ran away; yet he and his men got in other houses as much as they could bring down on their backs, which he brought aboard.

1686.

We cruised off the cape till the first day of January 1686 and then made towards the valley Valderas to hunt for beef, and before night we anchored in the bottom of the bay in 60 fathom water a mile from the shore. Here we stayed hunting till the 7th day, and Captain Swan and Captain Townley went ashore every morning with about 240 men and marched to a small hill; where they remained with 50 or 60 men to watch the Spaniards, who appeared in great companies on other hills not far distant but did never attempt anything against our men. Here we killed and salted above two months' meat besides what we spent fresh; and might have killed as much more if we had been better stored with salt. Our hopes of meeting the Philippine ship were now over; for we did all conclude that while we were necessitated to hunt here for provisions she was passed by to the eastward, as indeed she was, as we did understand afterwards by prisoners. So this design failed through Captain Townley's eagerness after the Lima ship which he attempted in Acapulco Harbour, as I have related. For though we took a little flour hard by, yet the same guide which told us of that ship would have conducted us where we might have had store of beef and maize: but instead thereof we lost both our time and the opportunity of providing ourselves; and so we were forced to be victualling when we should have been cruising off Cape Corrientes in expectation of the Manila ship.

Hitherto we had coasted along here with two different designs; the one was to get the Manila ship, which would have enriched us beyond measure; and this Captain Townley was most for. Sir Thomas Cavendish formerly took the Manila ship off Cape San Lucas in California (where we also would have waited for her, had we been early enough stored with provisions, to have met her there) and threw much rich goods overboard. The other design, which Captain Swan and our crew were most for, was to search along the coast for rich towns and mines chiefly of gold and silver, which we were assured were in this country, and we hoped near the shore: not knowing (as we afterwards found) that it was in effect an inland country, its wealth remote from the South Sea coast and having little or no commerce with it, its trade being driven eastward with Europe by La Vera Cruz. Yet we had still some expectation of mines, and so resolved to steer on farther northward; but Captain Townley, who had no other design in coming on this coast but to meet this ship, resolved to return again towards the coast of Peru.

Captain Townley leaves them with the Darien Indians.

In all this voyage on the Mexican coast we had with us a captain and two or three of his men of our friendly Indians of the Isthmus of Darien; who, having conducted over some parties of our privateers, and expressing a desire to go along with us, were received and kindly entertained aboard our ships; and we were pleased in having, by this means, guides ready provided should we be for returning overland, as several of us thought to do, rather than sail round about. But at this time, we of Captain Swan's ship designing farther to the north-west and Captain Townley going back, we committed these our Indian friends to his care to carry them home. So here we parted; he to the eastward and we to the westward, intending to search as far to the westward as the Spaniards were settled.

It was the 7th day of January in the morning when we sailed from this pleasant valley. The wind was at north-east and the weather fair. At eleven o'clock the sea-wind came at north-west. Before night we passed by Point Pontique; this is the west point of the bay of the valley of Valderas and is distant from Cape Corrientes 10 leagues. This point is in latitude 20 degrees 50 minutes north; it is high, round, rocky, and barren. At a distance it appears like an island.

The point and isles of Pontique. Other isles of Chametly.

A league to the west of this point are two small barren islands, called the islands of Pontique. There are several high, sharp, white rocks that lie scattering about them: we passed between these rocky islands on the left and the Main on the right, for there is no danger. The sea-coast beyond this point runs northward for about 18 leagues, making many ragged points with small sandy bays between them. The land by the seaside is low and pretty woody; but in the country full of high, sharp, barren, rugged, unpleasant hills.

The 14th day we had sight of a small white rock, which appears very much like a ship under sail. This rock is in latitude 21 degrees 15 minutes. It is three leagues from the Main. There is a good channel between it and the Main where you will have 12 or 14 fathom water near the island; but running nearer the Main you will have gradual soundings till you come in with the shore. At night we anchored in six fathom water near a league from the Main in good oazy ground. We caught a great many cat-fish here and at several places on this coast, both before and after this.

From this island the land runs more northerly, making a fair sandy bay; but the sea falls in with such violence on the shore that there is no landing, but very good anchoring on all the coast, and gradual soundings. About a league off shore you will have six fathom, and four mile off shore you will have seven fathom water. We came to an anchor every evening; and in the mornings we sailed off with the land-wind, which we found at north-east, and the sea-breezes at north-west.

The 20th day we anchored about three miles on the east side of the islands Chametly, different from those of that name before mentioned; for these are six small islands in latitude 23 degrees 11 minutes, a little to the south of the Tropic of Cancer, and about 3 leagues from the Main, where a salt lake has its outlet into the sea. These isles are of an indifferent height: some of them have a few shrubby bushes; the rest are bare of any sort of wood. They are rocky round by the sea, only one or two of them have sandy bays on the north side. There is a sort of fruit growing on these islands called penguins; and it is all the fruit they have.

Of the river of Culiacan, and the trade of a town there with California.

Captain Swan went away from hence with 100 men in our canoes to the northward to seek for the river Culiacan, possibly the same with the river of Pastla, which some maps lay down in the province or region of Culiacan. This river lies in about 24 degrees north latitude. We were informed that there is a fair rich Spanish town seated on the east side of it, with savannahs about it, full of bulls and cows; and that the inhabitants of this town pass over in boats to the island California where they fish for pearl.

I have been told since by a Spaniard that said he had been at the island California, that there are great plenty of pearl-oysters there, and that the native Indians of California near the pearl-fishery are mortal enemies to the Spaniards. Our canoes were absent three or four days and said they had been above 30 leagues but found no river; that the land by the sea was low, and all sandy bay; but such a great sea that there was no landing. They met us in their return in the latitude 23 degrees 30 minutes coasting along shore after them towards Culiacan; so we returned again to the eastward. This was the farthest that I was to the north on this coast.

Six or seven leagues north-north-west from the isles of Chametly there is a small narrow entrance into a lake which runs about 12 leagues easterly, parallel with the shore, making many small low mangrove islands. The mouth of this lake is in latitude about 23 degrees 30 minutes. It is called by the Spaniards Rio de Sal: for it is a salt lake. There is water enough for boats and canoes to enter, and smooth landing after you are in. On the west side of it there is an house and an estancia, or farm of large cattle. Our men went into the lake and landed and, coming to the house, found seven or eight bushels of maize: but the cattle were driven away by the Spaniards, yet there our men took the owner of the estancia and brought him aboard. He said that the beefs were driven a great way in the country for fear we should kill them. While we lay here Captain Swan went into this lake again and landed 150 men on the north-east side and marched into the country: about a mile from the landing-place, as they were entering a dry salina, or salt-pond, they fired at two Indians that crossed the way before them; one of them, being wounded in the thigh, fell down and, being examined, he told our men that there was an Indian town four or five leagues off, and that the way which they were going would bring them thither. While they were in discourse with the Indian they were attacked by 100 Spanish horsemen who came with a design to scare them back but wanted both arms and hearts to do it.

Our men passed on from hence and in their way marched through a savannah of long dry grass. This the Spaniards set on fire, thinking to burn them, but that did not hinder our men from marching forward, though it did trouble them a little. They rambled for want of guides all this day and part of the next before they came to the town the Indian spoke of. There they found a company of Spaniards and Indians who made head against them, but were driven out of the town after a short dispute. Here our surgeon and one man more were wounded with arrows but none of the rest were hurt.

Massaclan.

When they came into the town they found two or three Indians wounded who told them that the name of the town was Massaclan; that there were a few Spaniards living in it, and the rest were Indians; that five leagues from this town there were two rich gold-mines where the Spaniards of Compostella, which is the chiefest town in these parts, kept many slaves and Indians at work for gold. Here our men lay that night, and the next morning packed up all the maize that they could find and brought it on their backs to the canoes and came aboard.

We lay here till the 2nd of February, and then Captain Swan went away with about 80 men to the river Rosario; where they landed and marched to an Indian town of the same name. They found it about nine mile from the sea; the way to it fair and even.

River and town of Rosario.

This was a fine little town of about 60 or 70 houses with a fair church; and it was chiefly inhabited with Indians, they took prisoners there, which told them that the river Rosario is rich in gold and that the mines are not above two leagues from the town. Captain Swan did not think it convenient to go to the mines but made haste aboard with the maize which he took there, to the quantity of about 80 or 90 bushels; and which to us, in the scarcity we were in of provisions, was at that time more valuable than all the gold in the world; and had he gone to the mines the Spaniards would probably have destroyed the corn before his return. The 3rd of February we went with our ships also towards the river Rosario and anchored the next day against the river's mouth, seven fathom, good oazy ground, a league from the shore. This river is in latitude 22 degrees 51 minutes north.

Caput Cavalli, and another hill.

When you are at an anchor against this river you will see a round hill, like a sugarloaf, a little way within land, right over the river, and bearing north-east by north. To the westward of that hill there is another pretty long hill, called by the Spaniards Caput Cavalli, or the horse's head.

The 7th day Captain Swan came aboard with the maize which he got. This was but a small quantity for so many men as we were, especially considering the place we were in, being strangers, and having no pilots to direct or guide us into any river; and we being without all sort of provision, but what we were forced to get in this manner from the shore.

The difficulty of intelligence on this coast.

And though our pilot-book directed us well enough to find the rivers, yet for want of guides to carry us to the settlements we were forced to search two or three days before we could find a place to land: for, as I have said before, besides the seas being too rough for landing in many places they have neither boat, bark, nor canoe that we could ever see or hear of: and therefore as there are no such landing-places in these rivers as there are in the North Seas so when we were landed we did not know which way to go to any town except we accidentally met with a path. Indeed the Spaniards and Indians whom we had aboard knew the names of several rivers and towns near them, and knew the towns when they saw them; but they knew not the way to go to them from the sea.

The river of Oletta. River of St. Jago. Maxentelba Rock, and Zelisco hill.

The 8th day Captain Swan sent about 40 men to seek for the river Oletta which is to the eastward of the river Rosario. The next day we followed after with the ships, having the wind at west-north-west and fair weather. In the afternoon our canoes came again to us for they could not find the river Oletta; therefore we designed next for the river St. Jago, to the eastward still. The 11th day in the evening we anchored against the mouth of the river in seven fathom water, good soft oazy ground, and about two mile from the shore. There was a high white rock without us called Maxentelba. This rock at a distance appears like a ship under sail; it bore from us west-north-west distant about three leagues. The hill Zelisco bore south-east which is a very high hill in the country, with a saddle or bending on the top. The river St. Jago is in latitude 22 degrees 15 minutes. It is one of the principal rivers on this coast; there is 10 foot water on the bar at low-water but how much it flows here I know not. The mouth of this river is near half a mile broad and very smooth entering. Within the mouth it is broader for there are three or four rivers more meet there and issue all out together, it is brackish a great way up; yet there is fresh water to be had by digging or making wells in the sandy bay, two or three foot deep, just at the mouth of the river.

The 11th day Captain Swan sent 70 men in four canoes into this river to seek a town; for although we had no intelligence of any yet the country appearing very promising we did not question but they would find inhabitants before they returned. They spent two days in rowing up and down the creeks and rivers; at last they came to a large field of maize which was almost ripe: they immediately fell to gathering as fast as they could and intended to lade the canoes; but, seeing an Indian that was set to watch the corn, they quitted that troublesome and tedious work, and seized him and brought him aboard, in hopes by his information to have some more easy and expedite way of a supply by finding corn ready cut and dried. He being examined said that there was a town called Santa Pecaque four leagues from the place where he was taken; and that if we designed to go thither he would undertake to be our guide. Captain Swan immediately ordered his men to make ready and the same evening went away with eight canoes and 140 men, taking the Indian for their guide.

He rowed about five leagues up the river and landed the next morning. The river at this place was not above pistol-shot wide, and the banks pretty high on each side and the land plain and even. He left 23 men to guard the canoes and marched with the rest to the town. He set out from the canoes at six o'clock in the morning and reached the town by 10. The way through which he passed was very plain, part of it woodland, part savannahs. The savannahs were full of horses, bulls, and cows. The Spaniards seeing him coming ran all away; so he entered the town without the least opposition.

Of Compostella.

Compostella is a rich town about 21 leagues from hence. It is the chiefest in all this part of the kingdom and is reported to have 70 white families; which is a great matter in these parts; for it may be that such a town has not less than 500 families of copper-coloured people besides the white. The silver mines are about five or six leagues from Santa Pecaque; where, as we were told, the inhabitants of Compostella had some hundreds of slaves at work. The silver here and all over the kingdom of Mexico is said to be finer and richer in proportion than that of Potosi or Peru, though the ore be not so abundant; and the carriers of this town of Santa Pecaque carry the ore to Compostella where it is refined. These carriers, or sutlers, also furnish the slaves at the mines with maize, whereof here was great plenty now in the town designed for that use: here was also sugar, salt, and salt-fish.

Captain Swan's only business at Santa Pecaque was to get provision; therefore he ordered his men to divide themselves into two parts and by turns carry down the provision to the canoes; one half remaining in the town to secure what they had taken while the other half were going and coming. In the afternoon they caught some horses, and the next morning, being the 17th day, 57 men and some horses went laden with maize to the canoes. They found them and the men left to guard them in good order; though the Spaniards had given them a small diversion and wounded one man: but our men of the canoes landed and drove them away. These that came loaded to the canoes left seven men more there, so that now they were 30 men to guard the canoes. At night the other returned; and the 18th day in the morning the half which stayed the day before at the town took their turn of going with every man his burden, and 24 horses laden. Before they returned Captain Swan and his other men at the town caught a prisoner who said that there were near a thousand men of all colours, Spaniards and Indians, Negroes and Mulattos, in arms, at a place called St. Jago, but three leagues off, the chief town on this river; that the Spaniards were armed with guns and pistols, and the copper-coloured with swords and lances. Captain Swan, fearing the ill consequence of separating his small company, was resolved the next day to march away with the whole party; and therefore he ordered his men to catch as many horses as they could, that they might carry the more provision with them.

Many of them cut off at Santa Pecaque.

Accordingly, the next day being the 19th day of February 1686, Captain Swan called out his men betimes to be gone; but they refused to go and said that they would not leave the town till all the provision was in the canoes: therefore he was forced to yield to them and suffered half the company to go as before: they had now 54 horses laden, which Captain Swan ordered to be tied one to another, and the men to go in two bodies, 25 before, and as many behind; but the men would go at their own rate, every man leading his horse. The Spaniards, observing their manner of marching, had laid an ambush about a mile from the town, which they managed with such success that, falling on our body of men who were guarding the corn to the canoes, they killed them every one. Captain Swan, hearing the report of their guns, ordered his men, who were then in the town with him, to march out to their assistance; but some opposed him, despising their enemies, till two of the Spaniards' horses that had lost their riders came galloping into the town in a great fright, both bridled and saddled, with each a pair of holsters by their sides, and one had a carbine newly discharged; which was an apparent token that our men had been engaged, and that by men better armed than they imagined they should meet with. Therefore Captain Swan immediately marched out of the town and his men all followed him; and when he came to the place where the engagement had been he saw all his men that went out in the morning lying dead. They were stripped and so cut and mangled that he scarce knew one man. Captain Swan had not more men then with him than those were who lay dead before him, yet the Spaniards never came to oppose him but kept at a great distance; for it is probable the Spaniards had not cut off so many men of ours, but with the loss of a great many of their own. So he marched down to the canoes and came aboard the ship with the maize that was already in the canoes. We had about 50 men killed, and among the rest my ingenious friend Mr. Ringrose was one, who wrote that part of the History of the Buccaneers which relates to Captain Sharp. He was at this time cape-merchant, or supercargo of Captain Swan's ship. He had no mind to this voyage; but was necessitated to engage in it or starve.

This loss discouraged us from attempting anything more hereabouts. Therefore Captain Swan proposed to go to Cape San Lucas on California to careen. He had two reasons for this: first, that he thought he could lie there secure from the Spaniards, and next, that if he could get a commerce with the Indians there he might make a discovery in the Lake of California, and by their assistance try for some of the plate of New Mexico.

Of California; whether an island or not: and of the north-west and north-east passage.

This Lake of California (for so the sea, channel or strait, between that and the continent, is called) is but little known to the Spaniards, by what I could ever learn; for their charts do not agree about it. Some of them do make California an island, but give no manner of account of the tides flowing in the lake, or what depth of water there is, or of the harbours, rivers, or creeks, that border on it: whereas on the west side of the island towards the Asiatic coast their pilot-book gives an account of the coast from Cape San Lucas to 40 degrees north. Some of their charts newly made do make California to join to the Main. I do believe that the Spaniards do not care to have this lake discovered for fear lest other European nations should get knowledge of it and by that means visit the mines of New Mexico. We heard that not long before our arrival here the Indians in the province of New Mexico made an insurrection and destroyed most of the Spaniards there, but that some of them, flying towards the Gulf or Lake of California, made canoes in that lake and got safe away; though the Indians of the lake of California seem to be at perfect enmity with the Spaniards. We had an old intelligent Spaniard now aboard who said that he spoke with a friar that made his escape among them.

New Mexico, by report of several English prisoners there and Spaniards I have met with, lies north-west from Old Mexico between 4 and 500 leagues, and the biggest part of the treasure which is found in this kingdom is in that province; but without doubt there are plenty of mines in other parts as well in this part of the kingdom where we now were as in other places; and probably on the Main bordering on the lake of California; although not yet discovered by the Spaniards, who have mines enough, and therefore, as yet, have no reason to discover more.

A *method proposed for discovery of the north-west and north-east passages.*

In my opinion here might be very advantageous discoveries made by any that would attempt it: for the Spaniards have more than they can well manage. I know yet they would lie like the dog in the manger; although not able to eat themselves yet they would endeavour to hinder others. But the voyage thither being so far I take that to be one reason that has hindered the discoveries of these parts: yet it is possible that a man may find a nearer way hither than we came; I mean by the north-west.

I know there have been divers attempts made about a north-west passage, and all unsuccessful: yet I am of opinion that such a passage may be found. All our countrymen that have gone to discover the north-west passage have endeavoured to pass to the westward, beginning their search along Davis's or Hudson's Bay. But if I was to go on this discovery I would go first into the South Seas, bend my course from thence along by California, and that way seek a passage back into the West Seas. For as others have spent the summer in first searching on this more known side nearer home, and so, before they got through, the time of the year obliged them to give over their search, and provide for a long course back again for fear of being left in the winter; on the contrary I would search first on the less known coast of the South Sea side, and then as the year passed away I should need no retreat, for I should come farther into my knowledge if I succeeded in my attempt, and should be without that dread and fear which the others must have in passing from the known to the unknown: who, for aught I know, gave over their search just as they were on the point of accomplishing their desires.

I would take the same method if I was to go to discover the north-east passage. I would winter about Japan, Korea, or the north-east part of China; and, taking the spring and summer before me, I would make my first trial on the coast of Tartary, wherein if I succeeded I should come into some known parts and have a great deal of time before me to reach Archangel or some other port. Captain Wood indeed says this north-east passage is not to be found for ice: but how often do we see that sometimes designs have been given over as impossible, and at another time, and by other ways, those very things have been accomplished; but enough of this.

Captain Swan proposes a voyage to the East Indies.

The 8th day we ran near the island and anchored in five fathom, and moored head and stern and unrigged both ship and bark in order to careen. Here Captain Swan proposed to go into the East Indies. Many were well pleased with the voyage; but some thought, such was their ignorance, that he would carry them out of the world; for about two-thirds of our men did not think there was any such way to be found; but at last he gained their consents.

At our first coming hither we did eat nothing but seal; but after the first two or three days our strikers brought aboard turtle every day; on which we fed all the time that we lay here, and saved our maize for our voyage. Here also we measured all our maize, and found we had about eighty bushels. This we divided into three parts; one for the bark and two for the ship; our men were divided also, a hundred men aboard the ship, and fifty aboard the bark, besides three or four slaves in each.

I had been a long time sick of a dropsy, a distemper whereof, as I said before, many of our men died; so here I was laid and covered all but my head in the hot sand: I endured it near half an hour, and then was taken out and laid to sweat in a tent. I did sweat exceedingly while I was in the sand, and I do believe it did me much good for I grew well soon after.

CHAPTER 10

Guam: Small Boats and Coconuts

The coconut-tree, fruit, etc.

The coconut-trees grow by the sea on the western side in great groves, three or four miles in length and a mile or two broad. This tree is in shape like the cabbage-tree, and at a distance they are not to be known each from other, only the coconut-tree is fuller of branches; but the cabbage-tree generally is much higher, though the coconut-trees in some places are very high.

The nut or fruit grows at the head of the tree among the branches and in clusters, 10 or 12 in a cluster. The branch to which they grow is about the bigness of a man's arm and as long, running small towards the end. It is of a yellow colour, full of knots, and very tough. The nut is generally bigger than a man's head. The outer rind is near two inches thick before you come to the shell; the shell itself is black, thick, and very hard. The kernel in some nuts is near an inch thick, sticking to the inside of the shell clear round, leaving a hollow in the middle of it which contains about a pint, more or less, according to the bigness of the nut, for some are much bigger than others.

This cavity is full of sweet, delicate, wholesome and refreshing water. While the nut is growing all the inside is full of this water, without any kernel at all; but as the nut grows towards its maturity the kernel begins to gather and settle round on the inside of the shell and is soft like cream; and as the nut ripens it increases in substance and becomes hard. The ripe kernel is sweet enough but very hard to digest, therefore seldom eaten, unless by strangers, who know not the effects of it; but while it is young and soft like pap some men will eat it, scraping it out with a spoon after they have drunk the water that was within it. I like the water best when the nut is almost ripe for it is then sweetest and briskest.

When these nuts are ripe and gathered the outside rind becomes of a brown rusty colour so that one would think that they were dead and dry; yet they will sprout out like onions after they have been hanging in the sun three or four months or thrown about in a house or ship, and if planted afterward in the earth they will grow up to a tree. Before they thus sprout out there is a small spongy round knob grows in the inside, which we call an apple. This at first is no bigger than the top of one's finger, but increases daily, sucking up the water till it is grown so big as to fill up the cavity of the coconut, and then it begins to sprout forth. By this time the nut that was hard begins to grow oily and soft, thereby giving passage to the sprout that springs from the apple, which nature has so contrived that it points to the hole in the shell (of which there are three, till it grows ripe, just where it's fastened by its stalk to the tree; but one of these holes remains open, even when it is ripe) through which it creeps and spreads forth its branches. You may let these teeming nuts sprout out a foot and a half or two foot high before you plant them, for they will grow a great while like an onion out of their own substance.

Their proas, a remarkable sort of boats: and of those used in the East Indies.

The natives are very ingenious beyond any people in making boats, or proas, as they are called in the East Indies, and therein they take great delight. These are built sharp at both ends; the bottom is of one piece, made like the bottom of a little canoe, very neatly dug, and left of a good substance. This bottom part is instead of a keel. It is about 26 or 28 foot long; the under-part of this keel is made round, but inclining to a wedge, and smooth; and the upper-part is almost flat, having a very gentle hollow, and is about a foot broad: from hence both sides of the boat are carried up to about five foot high with narrow plank, not above four or five inches broad, and each end of the boat turns up round, very prettily. But, what is very singular, one side of the boat is made perpendicular, like a wall, while the other side is rounding, made as other vessels are, with a pretty full belly. Just in the middle it is about four or five foot broad aloft, or more, according to the length of the boat. The mast stands exactly in the middle, with a long yard that peeps up and down like a mizzen-yard. One end of it reaches down to the end or head of the boat where it is placed in a notch that is made there purposely to receive it and keep it fast. The other end hangs over the stern: to this yard the sail is fastened. At the foot of the sail there is another small yard to keep the sail out square and to roll up the sail on when it blows hard; for it serves instead of a reef to take up the sail to what degree they please according to the strength of the wind. Along the belly-side of the boat, parallel with it, at about six or seven foot distance, lies another small boat, or canoe, being a log of very light wood, almost as long as the great boat but not so wide, being not above a foot and a half wide at the upper part, and very sharp like a wedge at each end. And there are two bamboos of about eight or 10 foot long and as big as one's leg placed over the great boat's side, one near each end of it and reaching about six or seven foot from the side of the boat: by the help of which, the little boat is made firm and contiguous to the other. These are generally called by the Dutch, and by the English from them, outlayers. The use of them is to keep the great boat upright from oversetting; because the wind here being in a manner constantly east (or if it were at west it would be the same thing) and the range of these islands, where their business lies to and fro, being mostly north and south, they turn the flat side of the boat against the wind, upon which they sail, and the belly-side, consequently with its little boat, is upon the lee: and the vessel having a head at each end so as to sail with either of them foremost (indifferently) they need not tack or go about, as all our vessels do, but each end of the boat serves either for head or stern as they please. When they ply to windward and are minded to go about he that steers bears away a little from the wind, by which means the stern comes to the wind; which is now become the head, only by shifting the end of the yard. This boat is steered with a broad paddle instead of a rudder. I have been the more particular in describing these boats because I do believe they sail the best of any boats in the world. I did here for my own satisfaction try the swiftness of one of them; sailing by our log we had 12 knots on our reel, and she run it all out before the half minute-glass was half out; which, if it had been no more, is after the rate of 12 mile an hour; but I do believe she would have run 24 mile an hour. It was very pleasant to see the little boat running along so swift by the other's side.

The native Indians are no less dextrous in managing than in building these boats. By report they will go from hence to another of the Ladrone Islands about 30 leagues off, and there do their business and return again in less than 12 hours. I was told that one of these boats was sent express to Manila, which is above 400 leagues, and performed the voyage in four days' time. There are of these proas or boats used in many places of the East Indies but with a belly and a little boat on each side. Only at Mindanao I saw one like these with the belly

A proa such as the one Dampier tried.

and a little boat only on one side and the other flat, but not so neatly built.

The state of Guam: and the provisions with which they were furnished there.

The Indians of Guam have neat little houses, very handsomely thatched with palmetto-thatch. They inhabit together in villages built by the sea on the west side, and have Spanish priests to instruct them in the Christian religion.

The Spaniards have a small fort on the west side near the south end, with six guns in it. There is a governor, and 20 or 30 Spanish soldiers. There are no more Spaniards on this island beside two or three priests. Not long before we arrived here the natives rose on the Spaniards to destroy them and did kill many: but the governor with his soldiers at length prevailed and drove them out of the fort: so when they found themselves disappointed of their intent they destroyed the plantations and stock and then went away to other islands: there were then three or 400 Indians on this island; but now there are not above 100; for all that were in this conspiracy went away. As for these who yet remain, if they were not actually concerned in that broil yet their hearts also are bent against the Spaniards: for they offered to carry us to the fort and assist us in the conquest of the island; but Captain Swan was not for molesting the Spaniards here.

Before we came to an anchor here one of the priests came aboard in the night with three Indians. They first hailed us to know from whence we came and what we were: to whom answer was made in Spanish that we were Spaniards and that we came from Acapulco. It being dark they could not see the make of our ship nor very well discern what we were: therefore we came aboard but, perceiving the mistake they were in in taking us for a Spanish ship they endeavoured to get from us again, but we held their boat fast and made them come in. Captain Swan received the priest with much civility and, conducting him into the great cabin, declared that the reason of our coming to this island was want of provision, and that he came not in any hostile manner but as a friend to purchase with his money what he wanted: and therefore desired the priest to write a letter to the governor to inform him what we were and on what account we came. For, having him now aboard, the captain was willing to detain him as an hostage till we had provision. The padre told Captain Swan that provision was now scarce on the island but he would engage that the governor would do his utmost to furnish us.

In the morning the Indians in whose boat or proa the friar came aboard were sent to the governor with two letters; one from the friar, and another very obliging one from Captain Swan, and a present of four yards of scarlet cloth and a piece of broad silver and gold lace. The governor lives near the south end of the island on the west side; which was about five leagues from the place where we were; therefore we did not expect an answer till the evening, not knowing then how nimble they were. Therefore when the Indian canoe was dispatched away to the governor we hoisted out two of our canoes, and sent one a-fishing and the other ashore for coconuts. Our fishing canoe got nothing; but the men that went ashore for coconuts came off laden.

About 11 o'clock that same morning the governor of the island sent a letter to Captain Swan, complimenting him for his present and promising to support us with as much provision as he could possibly spare; and as a token of his gratitude he sent a present of six hogs, of a small sort, most excellent meat, the best I think, that ever I ate: they are fed with coconuts and their flesh is as hard as brisket-beef. They were doubtless of that breed in America which came originally from Spain. He sent also 12 musk-melons, larger than ours in England, and as many watermelons, both sorts here being a very excellent fruit; and sent an order to the Indians that lived in a village not far from our ship to bake every day as much of the bread-fruit as we did desire, and to assist us in getting as many dry coconuts as we would have; which they accordingly did, and brought off the bread-fruit every day hot, as much as we could eat. After this the governor sent every day a canoe or two with hogs and fruit and desired for the same powder, shot, and arms; which were sent according to his request. We had a delicate large English dog which the governor did desire and had it given him very freely by the captain, though much against the grain of many of his men, who had a great value for that dog. Captain Swan endeavoured to get this governor's letter of recommendation to some merchants at Manila, for he had then a design to go to Fort St. George, and from thence intended to trade to Manila: but this his design was concealed from the company. While we lay here the Acapulco ship arrived in sight of the island but did not come in the sight of us; for the governor sent an Indian proa with advice of our being here. Therefore she stood off to the southward of the island and, coming foul of the same shoal that our bark had run over before, was in great danger of being lost there, for she struck off her rudder and with much ado got clear; but not till after three days' labour. For though the shoal be so near the island and the Indians go off and fish there every day yet the master of the Acapulco ship, who should (one would think) know these parts, was utterly ignorant of it. This their striking on the shoal we heard afterward when we were on the coast of Manila; but these Indians of Guam did speak of her being in sight of the island while we lay there, which put our men in a great heat to go out after her but Captain Swan persuaded them out of that humour, for he was now wholly averse to any hostile action.

The 30th day of May the governor sent his last present which was some hogs, a jar of pickled mangoes, a jar of excellent pickled fish, and a jar of fine rusk, or bread of fine wheat-flour, baked like biscuit but not so hard. He sent besides six or seven packs of rice, desiring to be excused from sending any more provision to us, saying he had no more on the island that he could spare. He sent word also that the west monsoon was at hand, that therefore it behoved us to be jogging from hence unless we were resolved to return back to America again. Captain Swan returned him thanks for his kindness and advice and took his leave; and the same day sent the friar ashore that was seized on at our first arrival, and gave him a large brass clock, an astrolabe, and a large telescope; for which present the friar sent us aboard six hogs and a roasting-pig, three or four bushels of potatoes, and 50 pound of Manila tobacco. Then we prepared to be gone, being pretty well furnished with provision to carry us to Mindanao, where we designed next to touch. We took aboard us as many coconuts as we could well stow, and we had a good stock of rice and about 50 hogs in salt.

CHAPTER 11

First Sight of Mindanao

They resolve to go to Mindanao.

While we lay at Guam we took up a resolution of going to Mindanao, one of the Philippine Islands, being told by the friar and others that it was exceedingly well stored with provisions; that the natives were Mohammedans, and that they had formerly a commerce with the Spaniards, but that now they were at wars with them. This island was therefore thought to be a convenient place for us to go; for besides that it was in our way to the East Indies, which we had resolved to visit; and that the westerly monsoon was at hand, which would oblige us to shelter somewhere in a short time, and that we could not expect good harbours in a better place than in so large an island as Mindanao: besides all this, I say, the inhabitants of Mindanao being then, as we were told (though falsely) at wars with the Spaniards, our men, who it should seem were very squeamish of plundering without licence, derived hopes from thence of getting a commission there from the prince of the island to plunder the Spanish ships about Manila, and so to make Mindanao their common rendezvous. And if Captain Swan was minded to go to an English port yet his men, who thought he intended to leave them, hoped to get vessels and pilots at Mindanao fit for their turn, to cruise on the coast of Manila. As for Captain Swan he was willing enough to go thither as best suiting his own design; and therefore this voyage was concluded on by general consent.

The island described.

Some of our books gave us an account that Mindanao City and Isle lies in 7 degrees 40 minutes. We guessed that the middle of the island might lie in this latitude but we were at a great loss where to find the city, whether on the east or west side. Indeed, had it been a small island lying open in the eastern wind we might probably have searched first on the west side; for commonly the islands within the tropics, or within the bounds of the trade-winds, have their harbours on the west side, as best sheltered; but the island Mindanao being guarded on the east side by St. John's Island we might as reasonably expect to find the harbour and city on this side as anywhere else: but, coming into the latitude in which we judged the city might be, found no canoes or people that might give us any umbrage of a city or place of trade near at hand, though we coasted within a league of the shore.

Its fertility.

The island Mindanao is the biggest of all the Philippine Islands except Luconia. It is about 60 leagues long and 40 or 50 broad. The south end is in about 5 degrees north and the north-west end reaches almost to 8 degrees north. It is a very mountainous island, full of hills and valleys. The mould in general is deep and black and extraordinary fat and fruitful. The sides of the hills are stony yet productive enough of very large tall trees. In the heart of the country there are some mountains that yield good gold. The valleys are well moistened with pleasant brooks and small rivers of delicate water; and have trees of divers sorts flourishing and green all the year. The trees in general are very large, and most of them are of kinds unknown to us.

The libby-trees, and the sago made of them.

There is one sort which deserves particular notice; called by the natives libby-trees. These grow wild in great groves of 5 or 6 miles long by the sides of the rivers. Of these trees sago is made, which the poor country people eat instead of bread 3 or 4 months in the year. This tree for its body and shape is much like the palmetto-tree or the cabbage-tree, but not so tall as the latter. The bark and wood is hard and thin like a shell, and full of white pith like the pith of an elder. This tree they cut down and split it in the middle and scrape out all the pith; which they beat lustily with a wooden pestle in a great mortar or trough, and then put it into a cloth or strainer held over a trough; and, pouring water in among the pith, they stir it about in the cloth: so the water carries all the substance of the pith through the cloth down into the trough, leaving nothing in the cloth but a light sort of husk which they throw away; but that which falls into the trough settles in a short time to the bottom like mud; and then they draw off the water, and take up the muddy substance, wherewith they make cakes; which being baked proves very good bread.

The Mindanao people live 3 or 4 months of the year on this food for their bread-kind. The native Indians of Ternate and Tidore and all the Spice Islands have plenty of these trees, and use them for food in the same manner; as I have been informed by Mr. Caril Rofy who is now commander of one of the king's ships. He was one of our company at this time; and, being left with Captain Swan at Mindanao, went afterwards to Ternate and lived there among the Dutch a year or two. The sago which is transported into other parts of the East Indies is dried in small pieces like little seeds or comfits and commonly eaten with milk of almonds by those that are troubled with the flux; for it is a great binder and very good in that distemper.

In some places of Mindanao there is plenty of rice; but in the hilly land they plant yams, potatoes, and pumpkins; all which thrive very well. The other fruits of this island are watermelons, musk-melons, plantains, bananas, guavas, nutmegs, cloves, betel-nuts, Durians, jacks, or jacas, coconuts, oranges, etc.

The banana.

The banana-tree is exactly like the plantain for shape and bigness, not easily distinguishable from it but by its fruit, which is a great deal smaller and not above half so long as a plantain, being also more mellow and soft, less luscious yet of a more delicate taste. They use this for the making drink oftener than plantains, and it is best when used for drink, or eaten as fruit; but it is not so good for bread, nor does it eat well at all when roasted or boiled; so it is only necessity that makes any use it this way. They grow generally where plantains do, being set intermixed with them purposely in their plantain-walks.

Centipedes or forty-legs, a venomous insect, and others.

Of the venomous kind of creatures here are scorpions, whose sting is in their tail; and centipedes, called by the English 40-legs, both which are also common in the West Indies, in Jamaica, and elsewhere. These centipedes are 4 or 5 inches long, as big as a goose-quill but flattish; of a dun or reddish colour on the back, but belly whitish, and full of legs on each side the belly. Their sting or bite is more raging than the scorpion. They lie in old houses and dry timber. There are several sorts of snakes, some very poisonous. There is another sort of creature like an iguana both in colour and shape but four times as big, whose tongue is like a small harpoon, having two beards like the beards of a fish-hook. They are said to be very venomous, but I know not their names. I have seen them in other places also, as at Pulo Condore, or the island Condore, and at Achin, and have been told that they are in the Bay of Bengal.

Mindanayan Ways

Of the inhabitants, and civil state of the isle of Mindanao.

This island is not subject to one prince, neither is the language one and the same; but the people are much alike in colour, strength, and stature. They are all or most of them of one religion, which is Mohammedanism, and their customs and manner of living are alike. The Mindanao people, more particularly so called, are the greatest nation in the island and, trading by sea with other nations, they are therefore the more civil. I shall say but little of the rest, being less known to me but, so much as has come to my knowledge, take as follows.

Of the Mindanayans, properly so called; their manners and habits.

The Mindanayans properly so-called are men of mean statures; small limbs, straight bodies, and little heads. Their faces are oval, their foreheads flat, with black small eyes, short low noses, pretty large mouths; their lips thin and red, their teeth black, yet very sound, their hair black and straight, the colour of their skin tawny but inclining to a brighter yellow than some other Indians, especially the women. They have a custom to wear their thumb-nails very long, especially that on their left thumb, for they do never cut it but scrape it often. They are endued with good natural wits, are ingenious, nimble, and active, when they are minded but generally very lazy and thievish, and will not work except forced by hunger. This laziness is natural to most Indians; but these people's laziness seems rather to proceed and so much from their natural inclinations, as from

The coast of Mindanao today.

the severity of their prince of whom they stand in awe: for he, dealing with them very arbitrarily, and taking from them what they get, this damps their industry, so they never strive to have anything but from hand to mouth. They are generally proud and walk very stately. They are civil enough to strangers and will easily be acquainted with them and entertain them with great freedom; but they are implacable to their enemies and very revengeful if they are injured, frequently poisoning secretly those that have affronted them.

They wear but few clothes; their heads are circled with a short turban, fringed or laced at both ends; it goes once about the head, and is tied in a knot, the laced ends hanging down. They wear frocks and breeches, but no stockings nor shoes.

The habits and manners of their women.

The women are fairer than the men; and their hair is black and long; which they tie in a knot that hangs back in their poles. They are more round-visaged than the men and generally well-featured; only their noses are very small and so low between their eyes that in some of the female children the rising that should be between the eyes is scarce discernible; neither is there any sensible rising in their foreheads. At a distance they appear very well; but being nigh these impediments are very obvious. They have very small limbs. They wear but two garments; a frock and a sort of petticoat; the petticoat is only a piece of cloth, sowed both ends together: but it is made two foot too big for their waists, so that they may wear either end uppermost: that part that comes up to their waist, because it is so much too big, they gather it in their hands and twist it till it fits close to their waists, tucking in the twisted part between their waist and the edge of the petticoat, which keeps it close. The frock fits loose about them and reaches down a little below the waist. The sleeves are a great deal longer than their arms and so small at the end that their hands will scarce go through. Being on, the sleeve fits in folds about the wrist, wherein they take great pride.

The better sort of people have their garments made of long cloth; but the ordinary sort wear cloth made of plantain-tree which they call saggen, by which name they call the plantain. They have neither stocking or shoe, and the women have very small feet.

The women are very desirous of the company of strangers, especially of white men; and doubtless would be very familiar if the custom of the country did not debar them from that freedom, which seems coveted by them. Yet from the highest to the lowest they are allowed liberty to converse with or treat strangers in the sight of their husbands.

A comical custom at Mindanao.

There is a kind of begging custom at Mindanao that I have not met elsewhere with in all my travels; and which I believe is owing to the little trade they have; which is thus: when strangers arrive here the Mindanao men will come aboard and invite them to their houses and inquire who has a comrade (which word I believe they have from the Spaniards) or a pagally, and who has not. A comrade is a familiar male friend; a pagally is an innocent platonic friend of the other sex. All strangers are in a manner obliged to accept of this acquaintance and familiarity, which must be first purchased with a small present and afterwards confirmed with some gift or other to continue the acquaintance: and as often as the stranger goes ashore he is welcome to his comrade or pagally's house, where he may be entertained for his money, to eat, drink, or sleep; and complimented as often as he comes ashore with tobacco and betel-nut, which is all the entertainment he must expect gratis. The richest men's wives are allowed the freedom to converse with her pagally in public, and may give or receive presents from him. Even the sultans and the generals wives, who are always cooped up, will yet look out of their cages when a stranger passes by and demand of him if he wants a pagally: and, to invite him to their friendship, will send a present of tobacco and betel-nut to him by their servants.

Their houses, their diet, and washings.

The sultan's house is much bigger than any of the rest. It stands on about 180 great posts or trees a great deal higher than the common building, with great broad stairs made to go up. In the first room he has about 20 iron guns, all Saker and Minion, placed on field-carriages. The general and other great men have some guns also in their houses. About 20 paces from the sultan's house there is a small low house built purposely for the reception of ambassadors or merchant strangers. This also stands on posts but the floor is not raised above three or four foot above the ground, and is neatly matted purposely for the sultan and his council to sit on; for they use no chairs but sit cross-legged like tailors on the floor.

The common food at Mindanao is rice or sago, and a small fish or two. The better sort eat buffalo or fowls ill dressed, and abundance of rice with it. They use no spoons to eat their rice but every man takes a handful out of the platter and, by wetting his hand in water, that it may not stick to his hand, squeezes it into a lump as hard as possibly he can make it, and then crams it into his mouth. They all strive to make these lumps as big as their mouth can receive them and seem to vie with each other and glory in taking in the biggest lump; so that sometimes they almost choke themselves. They always wash after meals or if they touch anything that is unclean; for which reason they spend abundance of water in their houses. This water, with the washing of their dishes and what other filth they make, they pour down near their fireplace: for their chambers are not boarded but floored with split bamboos like lath, so that the water presently falls underneath their dwelling rooms where it breeds maggots and makes a prodigious stink. Besides this filthiness the sick people case themselves and make water in their chambers, there being a small hole made purposely in the floor to let it drop through. But healthy sound people commonly ease themselves and make water in the river. For that reason you shall always see abundance of people of both sexes in the river from morning till night; some easing themselves, others washing their bodies or clothes. If they come into the river purposely to wash their clothes they strip and stand naked till they have done then put them on and march out again: both men and women take great delight in swimming and washing themselves, being bred to it from their infancy. I do believe it is very wholesome to wash mornings and evenings in these hot countries at least three or four days in the week: for I did use myself to it when I lived afterwards at Bencoolen, and found it very refreshing and comfortable. It is very good for those that have fluxes to wash and stand in the river mornings and evenings. I speak it experimentally for I was brought very low with that distemper at Achin; but by washing constantly mornings and evenings I found great benefit and was quickly cured by it.

Their fear of the Dutch, and seeming desire of the English.

They are now most afraid of the Dutch, being sensible how they have enslaved many of the neighbouring islands. For that reason they have a long time desired the English to settle among them and have offered them any convenient place to build a fort in, as the general himself told us; giving this reason, that they do not find the English so encroaching as the Dutch or Spanish. The Dutch are no less jealous of their admitting the English for they are sensible what detriment it would be to them if the English should settle here.

A sort of leprosy there, and other distempers.

The Mindanao people are much troubled with a sort of leprosy, the same as we observed at Guam. This distemper runs with a dry scurf all over their bodies and causes great itching in those that have it, making them frequently scratch and scrub themselves, which raises the outer skin in small whitish flakes like the scales of little fish when they are raised on end with a knife. This makes their skin extraordinary rough, and in some you shall see broad white spots in several parts of their body. I judge such have had it but were cured; for their skins were smooth and I did not perceive them to scrub themselves: yet I have learnt from their own mouths that these spots were from this distemper. Whether they use any means to cure themselves or whether it goes away of itself, I know not: but I did not perceive that they made any great matter of it, for they did never refrain any company for it; none of our people caught it of them, for we were afraid of it, and kept off. They are sometimes troubled with the smallpox but their ordinary distempers are fevers, agues, fluxes, with great pains and gripings in their guts. The country affords a great many drugs and medicinal herbs whose virtues are not unknown to some of them that pretend to cure the sick.

Their marriages.

The Mindanao men have many wives: but what ceremonies are used when they marry I know not. There is commonly a great feast made by the bridegroom to entertain his friends, and the most part of the night is spent in mirth.

The Sultan of Mindanao, his poverty, power, family, etc.

The sultan is absolute in his power over all his subjects. He is but a poor prince; for, as I mentioned before, they have but little trade and therefore cannot be rich. If the sultan understands that any man has money, if it be but 20 dollars, which is a great matter among them, he will send to borrow so much money, pretending urgent occasions for it; and they dare not deny him. Sometimes he will send to sell one thing or another that he has to dispose of to such whom he knows to have money, and they must buy it and give him his price; and if afterwards he has occasion for the same thing he must have it if he sends for it. He is but a little man, between 50 or 60 years old, and by relation very good-natured but overruled by those about him. He has a queen and keeps about 29 women, or wives, more, in whose company he spends most of his time. He has one daughter by his sultaness or queen, and a great many sons and daughters by the rest. These walk about the streets and would be always begging things of us; but it is reported that the young princess is kept in a room and never stirs out, and that she did never see any man but her father and Raja Laut her uncle, being then about fourteen years old.

When the sultan visits his friends he is carried in a small couch on four men's shoulders, with eight or ten armed men to guard him; but he never goes far this way for the country is very woody and they have but little paths, which renders it the less commodious.

The proas or boats here.

When he takes his pleasure by water he carries some of his wives along with him. The proas that are built for this purpose are large enough to entertain 50 or 60 persons or more. The hull is neatly built, with a round head and stern, and over the hull there is a small slight house built with bamboos; the sides are made up with split bamboos about four foot high, with little windows in them of the same to open and shut at their pleasure. The roof is almost flat, neatly thatched with palmetto-leaves. This house is divided into two or three small partitions or chambers, one particularly for himself. This is neatly matted underneath and round the sides; and there is a carpet and pillows for him to sleep on. The second room is for his women, much like the former. The third is for the servants, who tend them with tobacco and betel-nut; for they are always chewing or smoking. The fore and after-parts of the vessel are for the mariners to sit and row. Besides this they have outlayers, such as those I described at Guam; only the boats and outlayers here are larger. These boats are more round, like a half moon almost; and the bamboos or outlayers that reach from the boat are also crooked. Besides, the boat is not flat on one side here, as at Guam; but has a belly and outlayers on each side: and whereas at Guam there is a little boat fastened to the outlayers that lies in the water; the beams or bamboos here are fastened traverse-wise to the outlayers on each side, and touch not the water like boats, but 1, 3 or 4 foot above the water, and serve for the barge-men to sit and row and paddle on; the inside of the vessel, except only just afore and abaft, being taken up with the apartments for the passengers. There run across the outlayers two tier of beams for the paddlers to sit on, on each side the vessel. The lower tier of these beams is not above a foot from the water: so that, upon any the least reeling of the vessel, the beams are dipped in the water and the men that sit are wet up to their waist, their feet seldom escaping the water. And thus, as all our vessels are rowed from within, these are paddled from without.

Raja Laut the general, brother to the sultan, and his family.

The sultan has a brother called Raja Laut, a brave man. He is the second man in the kingdom. All strangers that come hither to trade must make their address to him, for all sea-affairs belong to him. He licenses strangers to import or export any commodity, and it is by his permission that the natives themselves are suffered to trade: nay, the very fishermen must take a permit from him: so that there is no man can come into the river or go out but by his leave. He is two or three years younger than the sultan, and a little man like him. He has eight women, by some of whom he has issue. He has only one son, about twelve or fourteen years old, who was circumcised while we were there. His eldest son died a little before we came hither, for whom he was still in great heaviness. If he had lived a little longer he should have married the young princess; but whether this second son must have her I know not, for I did never hear any discourse about it. Raja Laut is a very sharp man; he speaks and writes Spanish, which he learned in his youth. He has by often conversing with strangers got a great sight into the customs of other nations, and by Spanish books has some knowledge of Europe. He is general of the Mindanayans, and is accounted an expert soldier, and a very stout man; and the women in their dances sing many songs in his praise.

Raja Laut's devotion.

Raja Laut never goes to the mosque but prays at certain hours, eight or ten times in a day, wherever he is, he is very punctual to his canonical hours, and if he be aboard will go ashore on purpose to pray. For no business nor company hinders him from this duty. Whether he is at home or abroad, in a house or in the field, he leaves all his company and goes about 100 yards off, and there kneels down to his devotion. He first kisses the ground then prays aloud, and divers time in his prayers he kisses the ground and does the same when he leaves off. His servants and his wives and children talk and sing, or play how they please all the time, but himself is very serious. The meaner sort of people have little devotion: I did never see any of them at their prayers or go into a mosque.

A clock or drum in their mosques.

In the sultan's mosque there is a great drum with but one head called a gong; which is instead of o'clock. This gong is beaten at 12 o'clock, at 3, 6, and 9; a man being appointed for that service. He has a stick as big as a man's arm, with a great knob at the end, bigger than a man's fist, made with cotton bound fast with small cords: with this he strikes the gong as hard as he can, about twenty strokes; beginning to strike leisurely the first five or six strokes; then he strikes faster, and at last strikes as fast as he can; and then he strikes again slower and slower so many more strokes: thus he rises and falls three times, and then leaves off till three hours after. This is done night and day.

Of their circumcision, and the solemnity then used.

They circumcise the males at 11 or 12 years of age, or older; and many are circumcised at once. This ceremony is performed with a great deal of solemnity. There had been no circumcision for some years before our being here; and then there was one for Raja Laut's son. They choose to have a general circumcision when the sultan or general or some other great person has a son fit to be circumcised; for with him a great many more are circumcised. There is notice given about eight or ten days before for all men to appear in arms. And great preparation is made against the solemn day. In the morning before the boys are circumcised presents are sent to the father of the child that keeps the feast; which, as I said before, is either the sultan or some great person: and about 10 or 11 o'clock the Mohammedan priest does his office. He takes hold of the foreskin with two sticks and with a pair of scissors snips it off.

Of their other religious observations and superstitions.

After this most of the men, both in city and country being in arms before the house, begin to act as if they were engaged with an enemy, having such arms as I described. Only one acts at a time, the rest make a great ring of 2 or 300 yards round about him. He that is to exercise comes into the ring with a great shriek or two and a horrid look; then he fetches two or three large stately strides and falls to work. He holds his broadsword in one hand, and his lance in the other, and traverses his ground, leaping from one side of the ring to the other; and, in a menacing posture and look, bids defiance to the enemy whom his fancy frames to him; for there is nothing but air to oppose him. Then he stamps and shakes his head and, grinning with his teeth, makes many rueful faces. Then he throws his lance and nimbly snatches out his cresset, with which he hacks and hews the air like a madman, often shrieking. At last, being almost tired with motion, he flies to the middle of the ring, where he seems to have his enemy at his mercy, and with two or three blows cuts on the ground as if he was cutting off his enemy's head. By this time he is all of a sweat, and withdraws triumphantly out of the ring, and presently another enters with the like shrieks and gestures. Thus they continue combating their imaginary enemy all the rest of the day; towards the conclusion of which the richest men act, and at last the general, and then the sultan concludes this ceremony: he and the general, with some other great men, are in armour, but the rest have none. After this the sultan returns home, accompanied with abundance of people, who wait on him there till they are dismissed. But at the time when we were there there was an after-game to be played; for, the general's son being then circumcised, the sultan intended to give him a second visit in the night, so they all waited to attend him thither. The general also provided to meet him in the best manner, and therefore desired Captain Swan with his men to attend him. Accordingly Captain Swan ordered us to get our guns and wait at the general's house till further orders. So about 40 of us waited till eight o'clock in the evening when the general with Captain Swan and about 1000 men went to meet the sultan, with abundance of torches that made it as light as day. The manner of the march was thus: first of all there was a pageant, and upon it two dancing women gorgeously apparelled, with coronets on their heads, full of glittering spangles, and pendants of the same hanging down over their breast and shoulders. These are women bred up purposely for dancing: their feet and legs are but little employed except sometimes to turn round very gently; but their hands, arms, head, and body are in continual motion, especially their arms, which they turn and twist so strangely that you would think them to be made without bones. Besides the two dancing women there were two old women in the pageant holding each a lighted torch in their hands, close by the two dancing women, by which light the glittering spangles appeared very gloriously. This pageant was carried by six lusty men: then came six or seven torches lighting the general and Captain Swan who marched side by side next, and we that attended Captain Swan followed close after, marching in order six and six abreast, with each man his gun on his shoulder, and torches on each side. After us came twelve of the general's men with old Spanish matchlocks, marching four in a row. After them about forty lances, and behind them as many with great swords, marching all in order. After them came abundance only with cressets by their sides, who marched up close without any order. When we came near the sultan's house the sultan and his men met us, and we wheeled off to let them pass. The sultan had three pageants went before him: in the first pageant were four of his sons, who were about ten or eleven years old. They had gotten abundance of small stones which they roguishly threw about on the people's heads. In the next were four young maidens, nieces to the sultan, being his sister's daughters; and in the third, there was three of the sultan's children, not above six years old. The sultan himself followed next, being carried in his couch, which was not like your Indians' palanquins but open and very little and ordinary. A multitude of people came after without any order: but as soon as he was passed by the general and Captain Swan and all our men closed in just behind the sultan, and so all marched together to the general's house. We came thither between 10 and 11 o'clock, where the biggest part of the company were immediately dismissed; but the sultan and his children and his nieces and some other persons of quality entered the general's house. They were met at the head of the stairs by the general's women, who with a great deal of respect conducted them into the house. Captain Swan and we that were with him followed after. It was not long before the general caused his dancing women to enter the room and divert the company with that pastime. I had forgot to tell you that they have none but vocal music here, by what I could learn, except only a row of a kind of bells without clappers, 16 in number, and their weight increasing gradually from about three to ten pound weight. These are set in a row on a table in the general's house, where for seven or eight days together before the circumcision day they were struck each with a little stick, for the biggest part of the day making a great noise, and they ceased that morning. So these dancing women sung themselves and danced to their own music. After this the general's women and the sultan's sons and his nieces danced. Two of the sultan's nieces were about 18 or 19 years old, the other two were three or four years younger. These young ladies were very richly dressed with loose garments of silk, and small coronets on their heads. They were much fairer than any women I did ever see there, and very well featured; and their noses though but small yet higher than the other women's, and very well proportioned. When the ladies had very well diverted themselves and the company with dancing the general caused us to fire some sky-rockets that were made by his and Captain Swan's order, purposely for this night's solemnity; and after that the sultan and his retinue went away with a few attendants and we all broke up, and thus ended this day's solemnity: but the boys being sore with their amputation went straddling for a fortnight after.

Their abhorrence of swines' flesh, etc.

A main part of their religion consists in washing often to keep themselves from being defiled; or after they are defiled to cleanse themselves again. They also take great care to keep themselves from being polluted by tasting or touching anything that is accounted unclean; therefore swine's flesh is very abominable to them; nay, anyone that has either tasted of swine's flesh or touched those creatures is not permitted to come into their houses in many days after, and there is nothing will scare them more than a swine. Yet there are wild hogs in the islands, and those so plentiful that they will come in troops out of the woods in the night into the very city, and come under their houses to rummage up and down the filth that they find there. The natives therefore would even desire us to lie in wait for the hogs to destroy them, which we did frequently, by shooting them and carrying them presently on board, but were prohibited their houses afterwards.

And now I am on this subject I cannot omit a story concerning the general. He once desired to have a pair of shoes made after the English fashion, though he did very seldom wear any: so one of our men made him a pair, which the general liked very well. Afterwards somebody told him that the thread wherewith the shoes were sowed were pointed with hogs' bristles. This put him into a great passion; so he sent the shoes to the man that made them, and sent him withal more leather to make another pair with threads pointed with some other hair, which was immediately done, and then he was well pleased.

CHAPTER 13

Mindanao to Mutiny

*Their coasting along the isle of Mindanao,
from a bay on the east side to another at the
south-east end.*

Having in the last chapter given some account of the natural,
civil, and religious state of Mindanao, I shall now go on with
the prosecution of our affairs during our stay here.

It was in a bay on the north-east side of the island that we
came to an anchor, as has been said. We lay in this bay but
one night and part of the next day. Yet there we got speech
with some of the natives, who by signs made us to understand
that the City Mindanao was on the west side of the island. We
endeavoured to persuade one of them to go with us to be our
pilot but he would not: therefore in the afternoon we loosed
from hence, steering again to the south-east, having the wind
at south-west. When we came to the south-east end of the
island Mindanao we saw two small islands about three leagues
distant from it. We might have passed between them and the
main island, as we learnt since; but not knowing them, nor
what dangers we might encounter there, we chose rather to
sail to the eastward of them. But meeting very strong westerly
winds we got nothing forward in many days. In this time we
first saw the islands Meangis, which are about sixteen leagues
distant from the Mindanao, bearing south-east. I shall have
occasion to speak more of them hereafter.

The 18th day of July we arrived before the river of Mindanao,
the mouth of which lies in latitude 6 degrees 22 minutes north
and is laid in 231 degrees 12 minutes longitude west, from the
Lizard in England. We anchored right against the river in 15
fathom water, clear hard sand, about two miles from the shore
and three or four miles from a small island that lay without

us to the southward. We fired seven or nine guns, I remember not well which, and were answered again with three from the shore; for which we gave one again.

The sultan's brother and son come aboard them, and invite them to settle there.

Immediately after our coming to an anchor Raja Laut and one of the sultan's sons came off in a canoe, being rowed with ten oars, and demanded in Spanish what we were? and from whence we came? Mr. Smith (he who was taken prisoner at Leon in Mexico) answered in the same language that we were English, and that we had been a great while out of England. They told us that we were welcome and asked us a great many questions about England; especially concerning our East India merchants; and whether we were sent by them to settle a factory here? Mr. Smith told them that we came hither only to buy provision. They seemed a little discontented when they understood that we were not come to settle among them: for they had heard of our arrival on the east side of the island a great while before, and entertained hopes that we were sent purposely out of England hither to settle a trade with them; which it should seem they are very desirous of. For Captain Goodlud had been here not long before to treat with them about it; and when he went away told them (as they said) that in a short time they might expect an ambassador from England to make a full bargain with them.

Of the feasibleness and probable advantage of such a settlement from the neighbouring Gold and Spice Islands.

Indeed upon mature thoughts I should think we could not have done better than to have complied with the desire they seemed to have of our settling here; and to have taken up our quarters among them. For as thereby we might better have consulted our own profit and satisfaction than by the other loose roving way of life; so it might probably have proved of public benefit to our nation and been a means of introducing an English settlement and trade, not only here, but through several of the Spice Islands which lie in its neighbourhood.

For the islands Meangis, which I mentioned in the beginning of this chapter, lie within twenty leagues of Mindanao. These are three small islands that abound with gold and cloves, if I may credit my author Prince Jeoly, who was born on one of them and was at that time a slave in the city of Mindanao. He might have been purchased by us of his master for a small matter, as he was afterwards by Mr. Moody (who came hither to trade and laded a ship with clove-bark) and by transporting him home to his own country we might have gotten a trade there. But of Prince Jeoly I shall speak more hereafter. These islands are as yet probably unknown to the Dutch who, as I said before, endeavour to engross all the spice into their own hands.

There was another opportunity offered us here of settling on another Spice Island that was very well inhabited: for the inhabitants fearing the Dutch and understanding that the English were settling at Mindanao, their sultan sent his nephew to Mindanao while we were there to invite us thither: Captain Swan conferred with him about it divers times, and I do believe he had some inclination to accept the offer; and I am sure most of the men were for it: but this never came to a head for want of a true understanding between Captain Swan and his men, as may be declared hereafter.

Beside the benefit which might accrue from this trade with Meangis and other the Spice Islands the Philippine Islands themselves, by a little care and industry, might have afforded us a very beneficial trade, and all these trades might have been managed from Mindanao by settling there first. For that island lies very convenient for trading either to the Spice Islands or to the rest of the Philippine Islands: since, as its soil is much of the same nature with either of them, so it lies as it were in the centre of the gold and spice-trade in these parts, the islands north of Mindanao abounding most in gold, and those south of Meangis in spice.

As to the capacity we were then in, of settling ourselves at Mindanao, although we were not sent out of any such design of settling, yet we were as well provided, or better, considering all circumstances, than if we had. For there was scarce any useful trade but some or other of us understood it. We had sawyers, carpenters, joiners, brick-makers, bricklayers, shoemakers, tailors, etc. We only wanted a good smith for great work; which we might have had at Mindanao. We were very well provided with iron, lead, and all sorts of tools, as saws, axes, hammers, etc. We had powder and shot enough, and very good small arms. If we had designed to build a fort we could have spared 8 or 10 guns out of our ship and men enough to have managed it, and any affair of trade beside. We had also a great advantage above raw men that are sent out of England into these places, who proceed usually too cautiously, coldly, and formally to compass any considerable design, which experience better teaches than any rules whatsoever; besides the danger of their lives in so great and sudden a change of air: whereas we were all inured to hot climates, hardened by many fatigues, and in general, daring men, and such as would not be easily baffled. To add one thing more, our men were almost tired and began to desire a quietus est; and therefore they would gladly have seated themselves anywhere. We had a good ship too, and enough of us (beside what might have been spared to manage our new settlement) to bring the news with the effects to the owners in England: for Captain Swan had already five thousand pound in gold, which he and his merchants received for goods sold mostly to Captain Harris and his men: which if he had laid but part of it out in spice, as probably he might have done, would have satisfied the merchants to their hearts' content. So much by way of digression.

To proceed therefore with our first reception at Mindanao, Raja Laut and his nephew sat still in their canoe, and would not come aboard us; because, as they said, they had no orders for it from the sultan. After about half an hour's discourse they took their leaves; first inviting Captain Swan ashore and promising to assist him in getting provision; which they said at present was scarce, but in three or four month's time the rice would be gathered in and then he might have as much as he pleased: and that in the meantime he might secure his ship in some convenient place for fear of the westerly winds which they said would be very violent at the latter end of this month and all the next, as we found them.

Captain Swan's present to the sultan: his reception of it, and audience given to Captain Swan, with Raja Laut, the sultan's brother's entertainment of him.

Captain Swan, considering that the season of the year would oblige us to spend some time at this island, thought it convenient to make what interest he could with the sultan; who might afterwards either obstruct or advance his designs. He therefore immediately provided a present to send ashore to the sultan, namely, three yards of scarlet cloth, three yards of broad gold lace, a Turkish scimitar and a pair of pistols: and to Raja Laut he sent three yards of scarlet cloth and three yards of silver lace. This present was carried by Mr. Henry More in the evening. He was first conducted to Raja Laut's house; where he remained till report thereof was made to the sultan, who immediately gave order for all things to be made ready to receive him.

About nine o'clock at night a messenger came from the sultan to bring the present away. Then Mr. More was conducted all the way with torches and armed men till he came to the house where the sultan was. The sultan with eight or ten men of his council were seated on carpets, waiting his coming. The present that Mr. More brought was laid down before them, and was very kindly accepted by the sultan, who caused Mr. More to sit down by them and asked a great many questions of him. The discourse was in Spanish by an interpreter. This conference lasted about an hour and then he was dismissed and returned again to Raja Laut's house. There was a supper provided for him, and the boat's crew; after which he returned aboard.

The next day the sultan sent for Captain Swan: he immediately went ashore with a flag flying in the boat's head and two trumpets sounding all the way. When he came ashore he was met at his landing by two principal officers, guarded along with soldiers and abundance of people gazing to see him. The sultan waited for him in his chamber of audience, where Captain Swan was treated with tobacco and betel, which was all his entertainment.

The contents of two English letters shown them by the Sultan of Mindanao.

The sultan sent for two English letters for Captain Swan to read, purposely to let him know that our East India merchants did design to settle here, and that they had already sent a ship hither. One of these letters was sent to the sultan from England by the East India merchants. The chiefest things contained in it, as I remember, for I saw it afterwards in the secretary's hand, who was very proud to show it to us, was to desire some privileges in order to the building of a fort there. This letter was written in a very fair hand; and between each line there was a gold line drawn. The other letter was left by Captain Goodlud, directed to any English-men who should happen to come thither. This related wholly to trade, giving an account at what rate he had agreed with them for goods of the island, and how European goods should be sold to them with an account of their weights and measures, and their difference from ours.

Of the commodities and the punishments there.

The rate agreed on for Mindanao gold was 14 Spanish dollars (which is a current coin all over India) the English ounce, and 18 dollars the Mindanao ounce. But for beeswax and clove-bark I do not remember the rates, neither do I well remember the rates of Europe commodities; but I think the rate of iron was not above 4 dollars a hundred. Captain Goodlud's letter concludes thus. "Trust none of them, for they are all thieves, but tace is Latin for a candle." We understood afterwards that Captain Goodlud was robbed of some goods by one of the general's men, and that he that robbed him was fled into the mountains and could not be found while Captain Goodlud was here. But, the fellow returning back to the city some time after our arrival here, Raja Laut brought him bound to Captain Swan and told him what he had done, desiring him to punish him for it as he pleased; but Captain Swan excused himself and said it did not belong to him, therefore he would have nothing to do with it. However the General Raja Laut would not pardon him, but punished him according to their own custom, which I did never see but at this time.

He was stripped stark naked in the morning at sun-rising, and bound to a post, so that he could not stir hand nor foot but as he was moved; and was placed with his face eastward against the sun. In the afternoon they turned his face towards the west that the sun might still be in his face; and thus he stood all day, parched in the sun (which shines here excessively hot) and tormented with the mosquitoes or gnats: after this the general would have killed him if Captain Swan had consented to it. I did never see any put to death; but I believe they are barbarous enough in it. The general told us himself that he put two men to death in a town where some of us were with him; but I heard not the manner of it. Their common way of punishing is to strip them in this manner and place them in the sun; but sometimes they lay them flat on their backs on the sand, which is very hot; where they remain a whole day in the scorching sun with the mosquitoes biting them all the time.

This action of the general in offering Captain Swan the punishment of the thief caused Captain Swan afterwards to make him the same offer of his men when any had offended the Mindanao men: but the general left such offenders to be punished by Captain Swan as he thought convenient. So that for the least offence Captain Swan punished his men, and that in the sight of the Mindanayans; and I think sometimes only for revenge; as he did once punish his chief mate Mr. Teat, he that came captain of the bark to Mindanao. Indeed at that time Captain Swan had his men as much under command as if he had been in a king's ship: and had he known how to use his authority he might have led them to any settlement, and have brought them to assist him in any design he had pleased.

The general's caution how to demean themselves; at his persuasion they lay up their ships in the river.

Captain Swan being dismissed from the sultan, with abundance of civility, after about two hours' discourse with him, went

thence to Raja Laut's house. Raja Laut had then some difference
with the sultan, and therefore he was not present at the sultan's
reception of our captain but waited his return and treated
him and all his men with boiled rice and fowls. He then told
Captain Swan again, and urged it to him, that it would be best
to get his ship into the river as soon as he could because of the
usual tempestuous weather at this time of the year; and that he
should want no assistance to further him in anything. He told
him also that, as we must of necessity stay here some time, so
our men would often come ashore; and he therefore desired
him to warn his men to be careful to give no affront to the
natives; who, he said, were very revengeful. That their customs
being different from ours, he feared that Captain Swan's men
might some time or other offend them, though ignorantly; that
therefore he gave him this friendly warning to prevent it: that
his house should always be open to receive him or any of
his men, and that he, knowing our customs, would never be
offended at anything. After a great deal of such discourse he
dismissed the Captain and his company, who took their leave
and came aboard.

Captain Swan, having seen the two letters, did not doubt but
that the English did design to settle a factory here: therefore
he did not much scruple the honesty of these people, but
immediately ordered us to get the ship into the river. The river
upon which the city of Mindanao stands is but small and has
not above 10 or 11 foot water on the bar at a spring-tide:
therefore we lightened our ship and, the spring coming on, we
with much ado got her into the river, being assisted by 50 or
60 Mindanayan fishermen who lived at the mouth of the river;
Raja Laut himself being aboard our ship to direct them. We
carried her about a quarter of a mile up, within the mouth of
the river, and there moored her head and stern in a hole where
we always rode afloat.

The Mindanayans' caresses.

After this the citizens of Mindanao came frequently aboard
to invite our men to their houses, and to offer us pagallies. It
was a long time since any of us had received such friendship,

and therefore we were the more easily drawn to accept of their kindnesses; and in a very short time most of our men got a comrade or two, and as many pagallies; especially such of us as had good clothes and store of gold, as many had who were of the number of those that accompanied Captain Harris over the Isthmus of Darien, the rest of us being poor enough. Nay, the very poorest and meanest of us could hardly pass the streets but we were even hauled by force into their houses to be treated by them: although their treats were but mean, namely, tobacco, or betel-nut, or a little sweet spiced water; yet their seeming sincerity, simplicity, and the manner of bestowing these gifts made them very acceptable. When we came to their houses they would always be praising the English, as declaring that the English and Mindanayans were all one. This they expressed by putting their two forefingers close together and saying that the English and Mindanayans were "samo, samo," that is, all one. Then they would draw their forefingers half a foot asunder and say the Dutch and they were "bugeto," which signifies so, that they were at such distance in point of friendship: and for the Spaniards they would make a greater representation of distance than for the Dutch: fearing these, but having felt and smarted from the Spaniards who had once almost brought them under.

Captain Swan did seldom go into any house at first but into Raja Laut's. There he dined commonly every day; and as many of his men as were ashore and had no money to entertain themselves resorted thither about 12 o'clock, where they had rice enough boiled and well dressed, and some scraps of fowls, or bits of buffalo, dressed very nastily. Captain Swan was served a little better, and his two trumpeters sounded all the time that he was at dinner. After dinner Raja Laut would sit and discourse with him most part of the afternoon. It was now the Ramdam time, therefore the general excused himself that he could not entertain our captain with dances and other pastimes, as he intended to do when this solemn time was past; besides, it was the very height of the wet season, and therefore not so proper for pastimes.

How their women dance.

When the Ramdam time was over, and the dry time set in a little, the general, to oblige Captain Swan, entertained him every night with dances. The dancing women that are purposely bred up to it and make it their trade I have already described. But beside them all the women in general are much addicted to dancing. They dance 40 or 50 at once; and that standing all round in a ring, joined hand in hand and singing and keeping time. But they never budge out of their places nor make any motion till the chorus is sung; then all at once they throw out one leg and bawl out aloud; and sometimes they only clap their hands when the chorus is sung. Captain Swan, to retaliate the general's favours, sent for his violins and some that could dance English dances; wherewith the general was very well pleased. They commonly spent the biggest part of the night in these sort of pastimes.

A story of one John Thacker.

Among the rest of our men that did use to dance thus before the general there was one John Thacker who was a seaman bred, and could neither write nor read but had formerly learnt to dance in the music houses about Wapping: this man came into the South Seas with Captain Harris and, getting with him a good quantity of gold, and being a pretty good husband of his share, had still some left besides what he laid out in a very good suit of clothes. The general supposed by his garb and his dancing that he had been of noble extraction; and to be satisfied of his quality asked of one of our men if he did not guess aright of him? The man of whom the general asked this question told him he was much in the right; and that most of our ship's company were of the like extraction; especially all those that had fine clothes; and that they came aboard only to see the world, having money enough to bear their expenses wherever they came; but that for the rest, those that had but mean clothes, they were only common seamen. After this the general showed a great deal of respect to all that had good clothes, but especially to John Thacker, till Captain Swan came to know the business, and marred all; undeceiving the general and drubbing the nobleman: for he was so much incensed against John Thacker that he could never endure him afterwards; though the poor fellow knew nothing of the matter.

Their bark eaten up, and their ship endangered by the worm.

About the middle of November we began to work on our ship's bottom, which we found very much eaten with the worm: for this is a horrid place for worms. We did not know this till after we had been in the river a month, and then we found our canoes' bottoms eaten like honeycombs; our bark, which was a single bottom, was eaten through; so that she could not swim. But our ship was sheathed, and the worm came no further than the hair between the sheathing plank and the main plank.

Raja Laut, the general's deceitfulness.

We did not mistrust the general's knavery till now: for when he came down to our ship, and found us ripping off the sheathing plank, and saw the firm bottom underneath, he shook his head, and seemed to be discontented; saying he did never see a ship with two bottoms before. We were told that in this place where we now lay a Dutch ship was eaten up in 2 months' time, and the general had all her guns; and it is probable he did expect to have had ours: which I do believe was the main reason that made him so forward in assisting us to get our ship into the river, for when we came out again we had no assistance from him.

Of Captain Swan.

Having thus ripped off all our worm-eaten plank and clapped on new, by the beginning of December 1686, our ship's bottom was sheathed and tallowed, and the 10th day we went over the bar and took aboard the iron and lead that we could not sell, and began to fill our water and fetch aboard rice for our voyage: but Captain Swan remained ashore still and was not yet determined when to sail or whither. But I am well assured that he did never intend to cruise about Manila, as his crew designed; for I did once ask him, and he told me that what he had already done of that kind he was forced to; but now being at liberty he would never more engage in any such design: for, said he, there is no prince on Earth is able to wipe off the stain of such actions. What other designs he had I know not, for he was commonly very cross; yet he did never propose doing anything else, but only ordered the provision to be got aboard in order to sail; and I am confident if he had made a motion to go to any English factory most of his men would have consented to it, though probably some would have still opposed it. However his authority might soon have over-swayed those that were refractory; for it was very strange to see the awe that these men were in of him, for he punished the most stubborn and daring of his men. Yet when we had brought the ship out into the road they were not altogether so submissive as while it lay in the river, though even then it was that he punished Captain Teat.

Hunting wild kine.

I was at that time a-hunting with the general for beef, which he had a long time promised us. But now I saw that there was no credit to be given to his word; for I was a week out with him and saw but four cows which were so wild that we did not get one. There were five or six more of our company with me; these who were young men and had Delilahs there, which made them fond of the place, all agreed with the general to tell Captain Swan that there were beeves enough, only they were wild. But I told him the truth, and advised him not to be too credulous of the general's promises. He seemed to be very angry, and stormed behind the general's back, but in his presence was very mute, being a man of small courage.

It was about the 20th day of December when we returned from hunting, and the general designed to go again to another place to hunt for beef; but he stayed till after Christmas Day because some of us designed to go with him; and Captain Swan had desired all his men to be aboard that day that we might keep it solemnly together: and accordingly he sent aboard a buffalo the day before that we might have a good dinner. So the 25th day about 10 o'clock Captain Swan came aboard and all his men who were ashore: for you must understand that near a third of our men lived constantly ashore with their comrades and pagallies, and some with women-servants whom they hired of their masters for concubines.

The prodigality of some of the English.

Some of our men also had houses which they hired or bought, for houses are very cheap, for 5 or 6 dollars. For many of them, having more money than they knew what to do with, eased themselves here of the trouble of telling it, spending it very lavishly, their prodigality making the people impose upon them, to the making the rest of us pay the dearer for what we bought, and to endangering the like impositions upon such Englishmen as may come here hereafter. For the Mindanayans knew how to get our squires gold from them (for we had no silver) and when our men wanted silver they would change now and then an ounce of gold and could get for it no more than ten or eleven dollars for a Mindanao ounce, which they would not part with again under eighteen dollars. Yet this and the great prices the Mindanayans set on their goods were not the only way to lessen their stocks; for their pagallies and comrades would often be begging somewhat of them, and our men were generous enough and would bestow half an ounce of gold at a time, in a ring for their pagallies, or in a silver wrist-band, or hoop to come about their arms, in hopes to get a night's lodging with them.

When we are all aboard on Christmas Day, Captain Swan and his two merchants; I did expect that Captain Swan would have made some proposals or have told us his designs; but he only dined and went ashore again without speaking anything of his mind.

Captain Swan treats with a young Indian of a Spice Island.

Yet even then I do think that he was driving on a design of going to one of the Spice Islands to load with Spice; for the young man before mentioned, who I said was sent by his uncle, the sultan of a Spice Island near Ternate, to invite the English to their island, came aboard at this time, and after some private discourse with Captain Swan they both went ashore together. This young man did not care that the Mindanayans should be privy to what he said. I have heard Captain Swan say that he offered to load his ship with spice provided he would build a small fort and leave some men to secure the island from the Dutch; but I am since informed that the Dutch have now got possession of the island.

A *hunting-voyage with the general.*

The next day after Christmas, the general went away again, and 5 or 6 Englishmen with him, of whom I was one, under pretence of going a-hunting; and we all went together by water in his proa, together with his women and servants, to the hunting-place. The general always carried his wives and children, his servants, his money and goods with him: so we all embarked in the morning and arrived there before night. I have already described the fashion of their proas and the rooms made in them. We were entertained in the general's room or cabin. Our voyage was not so far but that we reached our fort before night.

His *punishing a servant of his.*

At this time one of the general's servants had offended, and was punished in this manner: he was bound fast flat on his belly on a bamboo belonging to the prow, which was so near the water that by the vessel's motion it frequently delved under water, and the man along with it; and sometimes when hoisted up he had scarce time to blow before he would be carried under water again.

When we had rowed about two leagues we entered a pretty large deep river and rowed up a league further, the water salt all the way. There was a pretty large village, the houses built after the country fashion. We landed at this place, where there was a house made ready immediately for us. The general and his women lay at one end of the house and we at the other end, and in the evening all the women in the village danced before the general.

Of his wives and women.

While we stayed here the general with his men went out every morning betimes and did not return till four or five o'clock in the afternoon, and he would often compliment us by telling us what good trust and confidence he had in us, saying that he left his women and goods under our protection and that he thought them as secure with us six (for we had all our arms with us) as if he had left 109 of his own men to guard them. Yet for all this great confidence he always left one of his principal men for fear some of us should be too familiar with his women.

They did never stir out of their own room when the general was at home, but as soon as he was gone out they would presently come into our room and sit with us all day, and ask a thousand questions of us concerning our Englishwomen and our customs. You may imagine that before this time some of us had attained so much of their language as to understand them and give them answers to their demands. I remember that one day they asked how many wives the King of England had? We told them but one, and that our English laws did not allow of any more. They said it was a strange custom that a man should be confined to one woman; some of them said it was a very bad law, but others again said it was a good law; so there was a great dispute among them about it. But one of the general's women said positively that our law was better than theirs, and made them all silent by the reason which she gave for it. This was the War Queen, as we called her, for she did always accompany the general whenever he was called out to engage his enemies, but the rest did not. By this familiarity among the women, and by often discoursing them, we came to be acquainted with their customs and privileges. The general lies with his wives by turns; but she by whom he had the first son has a double portion of his company: for when it comes to her turn she has him two nights, whereas the rest have him but one. She with whom he is to lie at night seems to have a particular respect shown her by the rest all the precedent day; and for a mark of distinction wears a striped silk handkerchief about her neck, by which we knew who was queen that day.

We lay here about 5 or 6 days but did never in all that time see the least sign of any beef, which was the business we came about, neither were we suffered to go out with the general to see the wild kine, but we wanted for nothing else: however this did not please us, and we often importuned him to let us go out among the cattle. At last he told us that he had provided a jar of rice-drink to be merry with us, and after that we should go with him.

The general's foul dealing and exactions.

Captain Swan was much vexed at the general's actions for he promised to supply us with as much beef as we should want, but now either could not or would not make good his promise. Besides, he failed to perform his promise in a bargain of rice that we were to have for the iron which we sold him, but he put us off still from time to time and would not come to any account. Neither were these all his tricks; for a little before his son was circumcised (of which I spoke in the foregoing chapter) he pretended a great strait for money to defray the charges of that day; and therefore desired Captain Swan to lend him about twenty ounces of gold; for he knew that Captain Swan had a considerable quantity of gold in his possession, which the general thought was his own, but indeed he had none but what belonged to the merchants. However he lent it the general; but when he came to an account with Captain Swan he told him that it was usual at such solemn times to make presents, and that he received it as a gift. He also demanded payment for the victuals that our captain and his men did eat at his house.

Captain Swan's uneasiness and indiscreet management.

These things startled Captain Swan, yet how to help himself he knew not. But all this, with other inward troubles, lay hard on our captain's spirits and put him very much out of humour; for his own company were pressing him every day to be gone, because now was the height of the easterly monsoon, the only wind to carry us farther into the Indies.

About this time some of our men, who were weary and tired with wandering, ran away into the country and absconded, they being assisted, as was generally believed by Raja Laut. There were others also who, fearing we should not go to an English port, bought a canoe and designed to go in her to Borneo: for not long before the Mindanao vessel came from thence and brought a letter directed to the chief of the English factory at Mindanao. This letter the general would have Captain Swan have opened, but he thought it might come from some of the East India merchants whose affairs he would not intermeddle with, and therefore did not open it. I since met with Captain Bowry at Achin and, telling him this story, he said that he sent that letter, supposing that the English were settled there at Mindanao; and by this letter we also thought that there was an English factory at Borneo: so here was a mistake on both sides. But this canoe, wherewith some of them thought to go to Borneo, Captain Swan took from them, and threatened the undertakers very hardly. However this did not so far discourage them, for they secretly bought another; but their designs taking air they were again frustrated by Captain Swan.

The whole crew were at this time under a general disaffection and full of very different projects; and all for want of action. The main division was between those that had money and those that had none. There was a great difference in the humours of these; for they that had money lived ashore and did not care for leaving Mindanao; whilst those that were poor lived aboard and urged Captain Swan to go to sea. These began to be unruly as well as dissatisfied, and sent ashore the merchants' iron to sell for rack and honey to make punch, wherewith they grew drunk and quarrelsome: which disorderly actions deterred me from going aboard; for I did ever abhor drunkenness, which now our men that were aboard abandoned themselves wholly to.

Yet these disorders might have been crushed if Captain Swan had used his authority to suppress them: but he with his merchants living always ashore there was no command; and therefore every man did what he pleased and encouraged each other in his villainies. Now Mr. Harthop, who was one of Captain Swan's merchants, did very much importune him to settle his resolutions and declare his mind to his men; which at last he consented to do. Therefore he gave warning to all his men to come aboard the 13th day of January 1687.

We did all earnestly expect to hear what Captain Swan would propose and therefore were very willing to go aboard. But, unluckily for him, two days before this meeting was to be Captain Swan sent aboard his gunner to fetch something ashore out of his cabin. The gunner, rummaging to find what he was sent for, among other things took out the captain's journal from America to the island Guam, and laid down by him. This journal was taken up by one John Read, a Bristol man whom I have mentioned in my 4th chapter. He was a pretty ingenious young man, and of a very civil carriage and behaviour. He was also accounted a good artist, and kept a journal, and was now prompted by his curiosity to peep into Captain Swan's journal to see how it agreed with his own, a thing very usual among the seamen that keep journals, when they have an opportunity, and especially young men who have no great experience. At the first opening of the book he lit on a place in which Captain Swan had inveighed bitterly against most of his men, especially against another John Reed a Jamaica man. This was such stuff as he did not seek after: but, hitting so pat on this subject, his curiosity led him to pry further; and therefore, while the gunner was busy, he conveyed the book away to look over it at his leisure. The gunner, having dispatched his business, locked up the cabin-door, not missing the book, and went ashore. Then John Reed showed it to his namesake and to the rest that were aboard, who were by this time the biggest part of them ripe for mischief; only wanting some fair pretence to set themselves to work about it.

His men mutiny.

Therefore looking on what was written in this journal to be matter sufficient for them to accomplish their ends Captain Teat who, as I said before, had been abused by Captain Swan, laid hold on this opportunity to be revenged for his injuries and aggravated the matter to the height; persuading the men to turn out Captain Swan from being commander in hopes to have commanded the ship himself. As for the seamen they were easily persuaded to anything; for they were quite tired with this long and tedious voyage, and most of them despaired of ever getting home and therefore did not care what they did or whither they went. It was only want of being busied in some action that made them so uneasy; therefore they consented to what Teat proposed, and immediately all that were aboard bound themselves by oath to turn Captain Swan out and to conceal this design from those that were ashore until the ship was under sail; which would have been presently if the surgeon or his mate had been aboard; but they were both ashore, and they thought it no prudence to go to sea without a surgeon: therefore the next morning they sent ashore one John Cookworthy to hasten off either the surgeon or his mate by pretending that one of the men in the night broke his leg by falling into the hold. The surgeon told him that he intended to come aboard the next day with the captain and would not come before; but sent his mate, Herman Coppinger.

Of a snake twisting about one of their necks.

This man some time before this was sleeping at his pagallies and a snake twisted himself about his neck; but afterwards went away without hurting him. In this country it is usual to have the snakes come into the houses and into the ships too; for we had several came aboard our ship when we lay in the river. But to proceed, Herman Coppinger provided to go aboard; and the next day, being the time appointed for Captain Swan and all his men to meet aboard, I went aboard with him, neither of us distrusted what was designing by those aboard till we came thither. Then we found it was only a trick to get the surgeon off; for now, having obtained their desires, the canoe was sent ashore again immediately to desire as many as they could meet to come aboard; but not to tell the reason lest Captain Swan should come to hear of it.

The 13th day in the morning they weighed and fired a gun: Captain Swan immediately sent aboard Mr. Nelly, who was now his chief mate, to see what the matter was: to him they told all their grievances and showed him the journal. He persuaded them to stay till the next day for an answer from Captain Swan and the merchants. So they came to an anchor again and the next morning Mr. Harthop came aboard: he persuaded them to be reconciled again, or at least to stay and get more rice: but they were deaf to it and weighed again while he was aboard. Yet at Mr. Harthop's persuasion they promised to stay till two o'clock in the afternoon for Captain Swan and the rest of the men, if they would come aboard; but they suffered no man to go ashore except one William Williams that had a wooden leg and another that was a sawyer.

The main part of the crew go away with the ship, leaving Captain Swan and some of his men: several others poisoned there.

If Captain Swan had yet come aboard he might have dashed all their designs; but he neither came himself, as a captain of any prudence and courage would have done, nor sent till the time was expired. So we left Captain Swan and about 36 men ashore in the city, and six or eight that ran away; and about 16 we had buried there, the most of which died by poison. The natives are very expert at poisoning and do it upon small occasions: nor did our men want for giving offence through their general rogueries, and sometimes by dallying too familiarly with their women, even before their faces. Some of their poisons are slow and lingering; for we had some now aboard who were poisoned there but died not till some months after.

CHAPTER 14

Pulo Condore

They depart from the river of Mindanao.

The 14th day of January 1687 at three of the clock in the afternoon we sailed from the river of Mindanao, designing to cruise before Manila.

Of the time lost or gained in sailing round the world: with a caution to seamen, about the allowance they are to take for the difference of the sun's declination.

It was during our stay at Mindanao that we were first made sensible of the change of time in the course of our voyage. For, having travelled so far westward, keeping the same course with the sun, we must consequently have gained something insensibly in the length of the particular days, but have lost in the tale the bulk, or number of the days or hours. According to the different longitudes of England and Mindanao this isle, being west from the Lizard, by common computation, about 210 degrees, the difference of time at our arrival at Mindanao ought to be about 14 hours: and so much we should have anticipated our reckoning, having gained it by bearing the sun company. Now the natural day in every particular place must be consonant to itself: but this going about with or against the sun's course will of necessity make a difference in the calculation of the civil day between any two places. Accordingly at Mindanao and all other places in the East Indies we found them reckoning a day before us, both natives and Europeans; for the Europeans, coming eastward by the Cape of Good Hope in a course contrary to the sun and us, wherever we met they were a full day before us in their accounts. So among the Indian Mohammedans here their Friday, the day of their sultan's going to their mosques, was Thursday with us; though it were Friday also with those who came eastward from Europe. Yet at the Ladrone Islands we found the Spaniards of Guam keeping the same computation with ourselves; the reason of which I take to be that they settled that colony by a course westward from Spain; the Spaniards going first to America and thence to the Ladrones and Philippines. But how the reckoning was at Manila and the rest of the Spanish colonies in the Philippine Islands I know not; whether they keep it as they brought it or corrected it by the accounts of the natives and of the Portuguese, Dutch, and English, coming the contrary way from Europe.

One great reason why seamen ought to keep the difference of time as exact as they can is that they may be the more exact in their latitudes. For our tables of the sun's declination, being calculated for the meridians of the places in which they were made, differ about 12 minutes from those parts of the world that lie on their opposite meridians in the months of March and September; and in proportion to the sun's declination at other times of the year also. And should they run farther as we did the difference would still increase upon them, and be an occasion of great errors. Yet even able seamen in these voyages are hardly made sensible of this, though so necessary to be observed, for want of duly attending to the reason of it, as it happened among those of our crew; who after we had passed 180 degrees began to decrease the difference of declination, whereas they ought still to have increased it, for it all the way increased upon us.

Isle of Mindoro.

The 18th day of February we anchored at the north-west end of the island Mindoro, in 10 fathom water, about three quarters of a mile from the shore. Mindoro is a large island; the middle of it lying in latitude 13, about 40 leagues long, stretching north-west and south-east. It is high and mountainous and not very woody. At this place where we anchored the land was neither very high nor low. There was a small brook of water, and the land by the sea was very woody, and the trees high and tall, but a league or two farther in the woods are very thin and small. Here we saw great tracks of hog and beef, and we saw some of each and hunted them; but they were wild and we could kill none.

While we were here there was a canoe with four Indians came from Manila. They were very shy of us a while but at last, hearing us speak Spanish, they came to us and told us that they were going to a friar that lived at an Indian village towards the south-east end of the island. They told us also that the harbour of Manila is seldom or never without 20 or 30 sail of vessels, most Chinese, some Portuguese, and some few the Spaniards have of their own. They said that when they had done their business with the friar they would return to Manila, and hope to be back again at this place in four days' time. We told them that we came for a trade with the Spaniards at Manila, and should be glad if they would carry a letter to some merchant there, which they promised to do. But this was only a pretence of ours to get out of them what intelligence we could as to their shipping, strength, and the like, under colour of seeking a trade; for our business was to pillage. Now if we had really designed to have traded there this was as fair an opportunity as men could have desired: for these men could have brought us to the friar that they were going to, and a small present to him would have engaged him to do any kindness for us in the way of trade: for the Spanish governors do not allow of it and we must trade by stealth.

The 21st day we went from hence with the wind at east-north-east a small gale. The 23rd day in the morning we were fair by the south-east end of the island Luconia, the place that had been so long desired by us.

They go off Pulo Condore to lie there.

The time of the year being now too far spent to do anything here it was concluded to sail from hence to Pulo Condore, a little parcel of islands on the coast of Cambodia, and there careen if we could find any convenient place for it, designing to return hither again by the latter end of May and wait for the Acapulco ship that comes about that time. By our charts (which we were guided by, being strangers to these parts) this seemed to us then to be a place out of the way where we might lie snug for a while, and wait the time of returning for our prey. For we avoided as much as we could the going to lie by at any great place of commerce lest we should become too much exposed, and perhaps be assaulted by a force greater than our own.

So, we sailed from Luconia the 26th day of February, with the wind east-north-east and fair weather, and a brisk gale. We were in latitude 14 degrees north when we began to steer away for Pulo Condore, and we steered south by west.

Pulo Condore.

It was the 13th day of March before we came in sight of Pulo Condore, or the island Condore, as Pulo signifies. The 14th day about noon we anchored on the north side of the island against a sandy bay two mile from the shore, in ten fathom clean hard sand, with both ship and prize. Pulo Condore is the principal of a heap of islands and the only inhabited one of them. They lie in latitude 8 degrees 40 minutes north, and about twenty leagues south and by east from the mouth of the river of Cambodia. These islands lie so near together that at a distance they appear to be but one island.

Two of these islands are pretty large and of a good height, they may be seen fourteen or fifteen leagues at sea; the rest are but little spots. The biggest of the two (which is the inhabited one) is about four or five leagues long and lies east and west. It is not above three mile broad at the broadest place, in most places not above a mile wide. The other large island is about three mile long and half a mile wide. This island stretches north and south. It is so conveniently placed at the west end of the biggest island that between both there is formed a very commodious harbour. The entrance of this harbour is on the north side where the two islands are near a mile asunder. There are three or four small keys and a good deep channel between them and the biggest island. Towards the south end of the harbour the two islands do in a manner close up, leaving only a small passage for boats and canoes. There are no more islands on the north side but five or six on the south side of the great island. See the Table.

The mould of these islands for the biggest part is blackish and pretty deep, only the hills are somewhat stony. The eastern part of the biggest island is sandy yet all clothed with trees of divers sorts. The trees do not grow so thick as I have seen them in some places, but they are generally large and tall and fit for any use.

The tar-tree.

There is one sort of tree much larger than any other on this island and which I have not seen anywhere else. It is about three or four foot diameter in the body, from whence is drawn a sort of clammy juice, which being boiled a little becomes perfect tar; and if you boil it much it will become hard as pitch. It may be put to either use; we used it both ways, and found it to be very serviceable. The way that they get this juice is by cutting a great gap horizontally in the body of the tree half through, and about a foot from the ground; and then cutting the upper part of the body aslope inwardly downward, till in the middle of the tree it meets with the traverse cutting or plain. In this plain horizontal semicircular stump they make a hollow like a basin, that may contain a quart or two. Into this hole the juice which drains from the wounded upper part of the tree falls; from whence you must empty it every day. It will run thus for some months and then dry away, and the tree will recover again.

Their animals.

The animals of these islands are some hogs, lizards and iguanas; and some of those creatures which are like but much bigger than the iguanas.

Here are many sorts of birds, as parrots, parakeets, doves and pigeons. Here are also a sort of wild cocks and hens: they are much like our tame fowl of that kind; but a great deal less, for they are about the bigness of a crow. The cocks do crow like ours but much more small and shrill; and by their crowing we do first find them out in the woods where we shoot them. Their flesh is very white and sweet.

There are a great many limpets and mussels, and plenty of green turtle.

Of the migration of the turtle from place to place.

And upon this mention of turtle again I think it not amiss to add some reasons to strengthen the opinion that I have given concerning these creatures removing from place to place. I have said in Chapter 5 that they leave their common feeding-places and go to places a great way from thence to lay, as particularly to the island Ascension. Now I have discoursed with some since that subject was printed who are of opinion that when the laying-time is over they never go from thence, but lie somewhere in the sea about the island, which I think is very improbable: for there can be no food for them there, as I could soon make appear; as particularly from hence, that the sea about the isle of Ascension is so deep as to admit of no anchoring but at one place, where there is no sign of grass: and we never bring up with our sounding-lead any grass or weeds out of very deep seas, but sand or the like only. But if this be granted, that there is food for them, yet I have a great deal of reason to believe that the turtle go from hence; for after the laying-time you shall never see them, and wherever turtle are you will see them rise and hold their head above water to breathe once in seven or eight minutes, or at longest in ten or twelve. And if any man does but consider how fish take their certain seasons of the year to go from one sea to another this should not seem strange; even fowls also having their seasons to remove from one place to another.

These islands are pretty well watered with small brooks of fresh water that run flush into the sea for ten months in the year. The latter end of March they begin to dry away, and in April you shall have none in the brooks but what is lodged in deep holes; but you may dig wells in some places. In May

when the rain comes the land is again replenished with water
and the brooks run out into the sea.

Of the Malayan tongue.

The inhabitants of this island are by nation Cochin-chinese,
as they told us, for one of them spoke good Malayan: which
language we learnt a smattering of, and some of us so as to
speak it pretty well, while we lay at Mindanao; and this is the
common tongue of trade and commerce (though it be not in
several of them the native language) in most of the East India
Islands, being the Lingua Franca, as it were, of these parts. I
believe it is the vulgar tongue at Malacca, Sumatra, Java, and
Borneo; but at Celebes, the Philippine Islands, and the Spice
Islands it seems borrowed for the carrying on of trade.

The inhabitants of Pulo Condore are but a small people
in stature, well enough shaped, and of a darker colour than
the Mindanayans. They are pretty long-visaged; their hair is
black and straight, their eyes are but small and black, their
noses of a mean bigness, and pretty high, their lips thin, their
teeth white, and little mouths. They are very civil people but
extraordinary poor. Their chiefest employment is to draw the
juice of those trees that I have described to make tar. They
preserve it in wooden troughs; and when they have their cargo
they transport it to Cochin-china, their mother country. Some
others of them employ themselves to catch turtle, and boil up
their fat to oil, which they also transport home. These people
have great large nets with wide meshes to catch the turtle. The
Jamaica turtlers have such; and I did never see the like nets but
at Jamaica and here.

The idolatry here, at Tonquin, and among the Chinese seamen, and of a procession at Fort St. George.

These people are idolaters: but their manner of worship I know
not. There are a few scattering houses and plantations on the
great island, and a small village on the south side of it where

there is a little idol-temple, and an image of an elephant, about five foot high and in bigness proportionable, placed on one side of the temple; and a horse not so big, placed on the other side of it; both standing with their heads towards the south. The temple itself was low and ordinary, built of wood and thatched like one of their houses; which are but very meanly.

The images of the horse and the elephant were the most general idols that I observed in the temples of Tonquin when I travelled there. There were other images also, of beasts, birds and fish. I do not remember I saw any human shape there; nor any such monstrous representations as I have seen among the Chinese. Wherever the Chinese seamen or merchants come (and they are very numerous all over these seas) they have always hideous idols on board their junks or ships, with altars, and lamps burning before them. These idols they bring ashore with them: and beside those they have in common every man has one in his own house. Upon some particular solemn days I have seen their bonzies, or priests, bring whole armfuls of painted papers and burn them with a great deal of ceremony, being very careful to let no piece escape them. The same day they killed a goat which had been purposely fatting a month before; this they offer or present before their idol, and then dress it and feast themselves with it. I have seen them do this in Tonquin, where I have at the same time been invited to their feasts; and at Bencoolen in the isle of Sumatra they sent a shoulder of the sacrificed goat to the English, who ate of it, and asked me to do so too; but I refused.

When I was at Madras, or Fort St. George, I took notice of a great ceremony used for several nights successively by the idolaters inhabiting the suburbs: both men and women (these very well clad) in a great multitude went in solemn procession with lighted torches, carrying their idols about with them. I knew not the meaning of it. I observed some went purposely carrying oil to sprinkle into the lamps to make them burn the brighter. They began their round about 11 o'clock at night and, having paced it gravely about the streets till two or three o'clock in the morning, their idols were carried with much ceremony into the temple by the chief of the procession, and some of the women I saw enter the temple, particularly. Their idols were different from those of Tonquin, Cambodia, etc., being in human shape.

They refit their ship.

I have said already that we arrived at these islands the 14th day of March 1687. The next day we searched about for a place to careen in; and the 16th day we entered the harbour and immediately provided to careen. Some men were set to fell great trees to saw into planks; others went to unrigging the ship; some made a house to put our goods in and for the sail-maker to work in. The country people resorted to us and brought us of the fruits of the island, with hogs, and sometimes turtle; for which they received rice in exchange, which we had a shipload of, taken at Manila. We bought of them also a good quantity of their pitchy liquor, which we boiled, and used about our ship's bottom. We mixed it first with lime which we made here, and it made an excellent coat and stuck on very well.

We stayed in this harbour from the 16th day of March till the 16th of April; in which time we made a new suit of sails of the cloth that was taken in the prize. We cut a spare main-top-mast and sawed plank to sheath the ship's bottom; for she was not sheathed all over at Mindanao, and that old plank that was left on then we now ripped off and clapped on new.

Two of them die of poison they took at Mindanao.

While we lay here two of our men died, who were poisoned at Mindanao, they told us of it when they found themselves poisoned and had lingered ever since. They were opened by our doctor, according to their own request before they died, and their livers were black, light and dry, like pieces of cork.

They take in water, and a pilot for the Bay of Siam.

Our business being finished here we left the Spanish prize taken at Manila, and most of the rice, taking out enough for ourselves, and on the 17th day we went from hence to the place where we first anchored, on the north side of the great island, purposely to water; for there was a great stream when we first came to the island, and we thought it was so now. But we found it dried up, only it stood in holes, two or three hogsheads or a tun in a hole: therefore we did immediately cut bamboos and made spouts through which we conveyed the water down to the seaside by taking it up in bowls, and pouring it into these spouts or troughs. We conveyed some of it thus near half a mile. While we were filling our water Captain Read engaged an old man, one of the inhabitants of this island, the same who I said could speak the Malayan language, to be his pilot to the Bay of Siam; for he had often been telling us that he was well acquainted there, and that he knew some islands there where there were fishermen lived who he thought could supply us with salt-fish to eat at sea; for we had nothing but rice to eat. The easterly monsoon was not yet done; therefore it was concluded to spend some time there and then take the advantage of the beginning of the western monsoon to return to Manila again.

The 21st day of April 1687 we sailed from Pulo Condore, directing our course west by south for the Bay of Siam. We had fair weather and a fine moderate gale of wind at east-north-east.

Pulo Ubi; and Point of Cambodia.

The 23rd day we arrived at Pulo Ubi, or the island Ubi. This island is about 40 leagues to the westward of Pulo Condore; it lies just at the entrance of the Bay of Siam, at the south-west point of land that makes the bay; namely, the Point of Cambodia. This island is about seven or eight leagues round, and it is higher land than any of Pulo Condore isles. Against the south-east part of it there is a small key, about a cable's length from the main island. This Pulo Ubi is very woody and it has good water on the north side, where you may anchor; but the best anchoring is on the east side against a small bay; then you will have the little island to the southward of you.

Two Cambodian vessels.

At Pulo Ubi we found two small barks laden with rice. They belonged to Cambodia, from whence they came not above two or three days before, and they touched here to fill water. Rice is the general food of all these countries, therefore it is transported by sea from one country to another, as corn in these parts of the world. For in some countries they produce more than enough for themselves and send what they can spare to those places where there is but little.

The 24th day we went into the Bay of Siam: this is a large deep bay, of which, and of this kingdom, I shall at present speak but little, because I design a more particular account of all this coast, to wit, of Tonquin, Cochin-china, Siam, Champa, Cambodia, and Malacca, making all the most easterly part of the continent of Asia, lying south of China: but to do it in the course of this voyage would too much swell this volume; and I shall choose therefore to give a separate relation of what I know or have learnt of them, together with the neighbouring parts of Sumatra, Java, etc., where I have spent some time.

The tight vessels and seamen of the kingdom of Champa.

We had yet fair weather and very little wind; so that, being often becalmed, we were till the 13th day of May before we got to Pulo Ubi again. There we found two small vessels at an anchor on the east side: they were laden with rice and lacquer, which is used in japanning of cabinets. One of these came from Champa, bound to the town of Malacca, which belongs to the Dutch who took it from the Portuguese; and this shows that they have a trade with Champa. This was a very pretty neat vessel, her bottom very clean and curiously coated, she had about forty men all armed with cortans, or broadswords, lances, and some guns, that went with a swivel upon their gunwale. They were of the idolaters, natives of Champa, and some of the briskest, most sociable, without fearfulness or shyness, and the most neat and dextrous about their shipping, of any such I have met with in all my travels. The other vessel came from the river of Cambodia and was bound towards the Straits of Malacca. Both of them stopped here, for the westerly-winds now began to blow, which were against them, being somewhat bleated.

Storms.

We anchored also on the east side, intending to fill water. While we lay here we had very violent wind at south-west and a strong current setting right to windward. The fiercer the wind blew, the more strong the current set against it. This storm lasted till the 20th day, and then it began to abate.

The 21st day of May we went back from hence towards Pulo Condore.

A Chinese junk from Palimbam in Sumatra. They come again to Pulo Condore.

In our way we overtook a great junk that came from Palimbam, a town on the island Sumatra: she was full laden with pepper which they bought there and was bound to Siam: but, it blowing so hard, she was afraid to venture into that bay, and therefore came to Pulo Condore with us, where we both anchored May the 24th. This vessel was of the Chinese make, full of little rooms or partitions, like our well-boats. I shall describe them in the next chapter. The men of this junk told us that the English were settled on the island Sumatra, at a place called Sillabar; and the first knowledge we had that the English had any settlement on Sumatra was from these.

A bloody fray with a Malayan vessel.

When we came to an anchor we saw a small bark at an anchor near the shore; therefore Captain Read sent a canoe aboard her to know from whence they came; and, supposing that it was a Malayan vessel, he ordered the men not to go aboard for they are accounted desperate fellows and their vessels are commonly full of men who all wear cressets, or little daggers, by their sides. The canoe's crew, not minding the captain's orders, went aboard, all but one man that stayed in the canoe. The Malayans, who were about 20 of them, seeing our men all armed, thought that they came to take their vessel; therefore at once, on a signal given, they drew out their cressets and stabbed five or six of our men before they knew what the matter was. The rest of our men leapt overboard, some into the canoe and some into the sea, and so got away. Among the rest one Daniel Wallis leapt into the sea who could never swim before nor since; yet now he swam very well a good while before he was taken up. When the canoes came aboard Captain Read manned two canoes and went to be revenged on the Malayans; but they seeing him coming did cut a hole in the vessel's bottom and went ashore in their boat. Captain Read followed them but they ran into the woods and hid themselves. Here we stayed ten or eleven days for it blew very hard all the time.

The surgeon's and the author's desires of leaving their crew.

While we stayed here Herman Coppinger our surgeon went ashore, intending to live here; but Captain Read sent some men to fetch him again. I had the same thoughts, and would have gone ashore too but waited for a more convenient place. For neither he nor I, when we were last on board at Mindanao, had any knowledge of the plot that was laid to leave Captain Swan and run away with the ship; and, being sufficiently weary of this mad crew, we were willing to give them the slip at any place from whence we might hope to get a passage to an English factory. There was nothing else of moment happened while we stayed here.

CHAPTER 15

China to the Red Sea

The inhabitants; and of the Tartars forcing the Chinese to cut off their hair.

The natives of this island are Chinese. They are subject to the crown of China, and consequently at this time to the tartars. The Chinese in general are tall, straight-bodied, raw-boned men. They are long-visaged, and their foreheads are high; but they have little eyes. Their noses are pretty large with a rising in the middle. Their mouths are of a mean size, pretty thin lips. They are of an ashy complexion; their hair is black, and their beards thin and long, for they pluck the hair out by the roots, suffering only some few very long straggling hairs to grow about their chin, in which they take great pride, often combing them and sometimes tying them up in a knot, and they have such hairs too growing down from each side of their upper lip like whiskers. The ancient Chinese were very proud of the hair of their heads, letting it grow very long and stroking it back with their hands curiously, and then winding the plaits all together round a bodkin thrust through it at the hinder part of the head; and both men and women did thus. But when the Tartars conquered them they broke them of this custom they were so fond of by main force; insomuch that they resented this imposition worse than their subjection and rebelled upon it but, being still worsted, were forced to acquiesce; and to this day they follow the fashion of their masters the tartars, and shave all their heads, only reserving one lock, which some tie up, others let it hang down a great or small length as they please. The Chinese in other countries still keep their old custom, but if any of the Chinese is found wearing long hair in China he forfeits his head; and many of them have abandoned their country to preserve their liberty of wearing their hair, as I have been told by themselves.

The Chinese have no hats, caps, or turbans; but when they walk abroad they carry a small umbrella in their hands wherewith they fence their head from the sun or the rain by holding it over their heads. If they walk but a little way they carry only a large fan made of paper, or silk, of the same fashion as those our ladies have, and many of them are brought over hither; one of these every man carried in his hand if he do but cross the street, screening his head with it if he has not an umbrella with him.

Their habits, and the little feet of their women, china-ware, china-roots, tea, etc.

The common apparel of the men is a loose frock and breeches. They seldom wear stockings but they have shoes, or a sort of slippers rather. The men's shoes are made diversely. The women have very small feet and consequently but little shoes; for from their infancy their feet are kept swathed up with bands as hard as they can possibly endure them; and from the time they can go till they have done growing they bind them up every night. This they do purposely to hinder them from growing, esteeming little feet to be a great beauty. But by this unreasonable custom they do in a manner lose the use of their feet, and instead of going they only stumble about their houses, and presently squat down on their breeches again, being as it were confined to sitting all days of their lives. They seldom stir abroad and one would be apt to think that, as some have conjectured, their keeping up their fondness for this fashion were a stratagem of the men to keep them from gadding and gossiping about and confine them at home. They are kept constantly to their work, being fine needlewomen, and making many curious embroideries, and they make their own shoes; but if any stranger be desirous to bring away any for novelty's sake he must be a great favourite to get a pair of shoes of them, though he give twice their value. The poorer sort of women trudge about streets and to the market without shoes or stockings; and these cannot afford to have little feet, being to get their living with them.

The Chinese both men and women are very ingenious; as may appear by the many curious things that are brought from thence, especially the porcelain or China earthenware. The Spaniards of Manila that we took on the coast of Luconia told me that this commodity is made of conch-shells, the inside of which looks like mother-of-pearl. But the Portuguese lately mentioned, who had lived in China and spoke that and the neighbouring languages very well, said that it was made of a fine sort of clay that was dug in the province of Canton. I have often made enquiry about it but could never be well satisfied in it: but while I was on the coast of Canton I forgot to enquire about it. They make very fine lacquer-ware also, and good silks; and they are curious at painting and carving.

China affords drugs in great abundance, especially China-root; but this is not peculiar to that country alone; for there is much of this root growing at Jamaica, particularly at 16-mile walk, and in the Bay of Honduras it is very plentiful. There is a great store of sugar made in this country; and tea in abundance is brought from thence; being much used there, and in Tonquin and Cochin-china as common drinking; women sitting in the streets and selling dishes of tea hot and ready made; they call it chau and even the poorest people sip it. But the tea at Tonquin of Cochin-china seems not so good, or of so pleasant a bitter, or of so fine a colour, or such virtue as this in China; for I have drunk of it in these countries; unless the fault be in the way of making it, for I made none there myself; and by the high red colour it looks as if they made a decoction of it or kept it stale. Yet at Japan I was told there is a great deal of pure tea, very good.

The Chinese are very great gamesters and they will never be tired with it, playing night and day till they have lost all their estates; then it is usual with them to hang themselves. This was frequently done by the Chinese factors at Manila, as I was told by Spaniards that lived there. The Spaniards themselves are much addicted to gaming and are very expert at it; but the Chinese are too subtle for them, being in general a very cunning people.

Of the China-junks, and their rigging.

While we lay at this place we saw several small China junks
sailing in the lagoon between the islands and the main, one
came and anchored by us. I and some more of our men went
aboard to view her: she was built with a square flat head as
well as stern, only the head or fore part was not so broad
as the stern. On her deck she had little thatched houses like
hovels, covered with palmetto-leaves and raised about three
foot high, for the seamen to creep into. She had a pretty large
cabin wherein there was an altar and a lamp burning. I did but
just look in and saw not the idol. The hold was divided into
many small partitions, all of them made so tight that if a leak
should spring up in any one of them it could go no farther,
and so could do but little damage but only to the goods in
the bottom of that room where the leak springs up. Each of
these rooms belong to one or two merchants, or more; and
every man freights his goods in his own room; and probably
lodges there if he be on board himself. These junks have only
two masts, a main-mast and a fore-mast. The fore-mast has
a square yard and a square sail, but the main-mast has a sail
narrow aloft like a sloop's sail, and in fair weather they use
a topsail which is to haul down on the deck in foul weather,
yard and all; for they did not go up to furl it. The main-mast
in their biggest junks seem to me as big as any third-rate man-
of-war's mast in England, and yet not pieced as ours but made
of one grown tree; and in an all my travels I never saw any
single-tree-masts so big in the body, and so long and yet so well
tapered, as I have seen in the Chinese junks.

Some of our men went over to a pretty large town on the
continent of China where we might have furnished ourselves
with provision, which was a thing we were always in want of
and was our chief business here; but we were afraid to lie in
this place any longer for we had some signs of an approaching
storm; this being the time of the year in which storms are
expected on this coast; and here was no safe riding. It was
now the time of the year for the south-west monsoon but the
wind had been whiffing about from one part of the compass
to another for two or three days, and sometimes it would be

A Chinese junk.

quite calm. This caused us to put to sea, that we might have sea-room at least; for such flattering weather is commonly the forerunner of a tempest.

They leave St. John's and the coast of China. A most outrageous storm.

Accordingly we weighed anchor and set out; yet we had very little wind all the next night. But the day ensuing, which was the 4th day of July, about four o'clock in the afternoon, the wind came to the north-east and freshened upon us, and the sky looked very black in that quarter, and the black clouds began to rise apace and moved towards us; having hung all the morning in the horizon. This made us take in our topsails and, the wind still increasing, about nine o'clock we reefed our mainsail and foresail; at ten we furled our foresail, keeping under a mainsail and mizzen. At eleven o'clock we furled our mainsail and ballasted our mizzen; at which time it began to rain, and by twelve o'clock at night it blew exceeding hard and the rain poured down as through a sieve. It thundered and lightened prodigiously, and the sea seemed all of a fire about us; for every sea that broke sparkled like lightning. The violent wind raised the sea presently to a great height, and it ran very short and began to break in on our deck. One sea struck away the rails of our head, and our sheet-anchor, which was stowed with one flook or bending of the iron over the ship's gunwale, and lashed very well down to the side, was violently washed off, and had like to have struck a hole in our bow as it lay beating against it. Then we were forced to put right before the wind to stow our anchor again; which we did with much ado; but afterwards we durst not adventure to bring our ship to the wind again for fear of foundering, for the turning the ship either to or fro from the wind is dangerous in such violent storms. The fierceness of the weather continued till four o'clock that morning; in which time we did cut away two canoes that were towing astern.

Corpus Sant, a light, or meteor appearing in storms.

After four o'clock the thunder and the rain abated and then we saw a corpus sant at our main-top-mast head, on the very top of the truck of the spindle. This sight rejoiced our men exceedingly; for the height of the storm is commonly over when the corpus sant is seen aloft; but when they are seen lying on the deck it is generally accounted a bad sign.

A corpus sant is a certain small glittering light; when it appears as this did on the very top of the main-mast or at a yard-arm it is like a star; but when it appears on the deck it resembles a great glow-worm. The Spaniards have another name for it (though I take even this to be a Spanish or Portuguese name, and a corruption only of corpus sanctum) and I have been told that when they see them they presently go to prayers and bless themselves for the happy sight. I have heard some ignorant seamen discoursing how they have seen them creep, or, as they say, travel about in the scuppers, telling many dismal stories that happened at such times: but I did never see anyone stir out of the place where it was first fixed, except upon deck, where every sea washes it about: neither did I ever see any but when we have had hard rain as well as wind; and therefore do believe it is some jelly: but enough of this.

We continued scudding right before wind and sea from two till seven o'clock in the morning, and then the wind being much abated we set our mizzen again, and brought our ship to the wind, and lay under a mizzen till eleven. Then it fell flat calm, and it continued so for about two hours: but the sky looked very black and rueful, especially in the south-west, and the sea tossed us about like an eggshell for want of wind. About one o'clock in the afternoon the wind sprung up at south-west out of the quarter from whence we did expect it: therefore we presently brailed up our mizzen and wore our ship: but we had no sooner put our ship before the wind but it blew a storm again and rained very hard, though not so violently as the night before: but the wind was altogether as boisterous and so continued till ten or eleven o'clock at night. All which time we scudded and run before the wind very swift, though only with our bare poles, that is, without any sail abroad. Afterwards the wind died away by degrees, and before day we had but little wind and fine clear weather.

I was never in such a violent storm in all my life; so said all the company. This was near the change of the moon: it was two or three days before the change. The 6th day in the morning, having fine handsome weather, we got up our yards again and began to dry ourselves and our clothes for we were all well sopped. This storm had deadened the hearts of our men so much that, instead of going to buy more provision at the same place from whence we came before the storm, or of seeking any more for the island Prata, they thought of going somewhere to shelter before the full moon, for fear of another storm at that time: for commonly, if there is any very bad weather in the month, it is about two or three days before or after the full or change of the moon.

The Piscadores, or Fishers Islands near Formosa.

These thoughts, I say, put our men on thinking where to go, and, the charts or sea-plats being first consulted, it was concluded to go to certain islands lying in latitude 23 degrees north called Piscadores. For there was not a man aboard that was anything acquainted on these coasts; and therefore all our dependence was on the charts, which only pointed out to us where such and such places or islands were without giving us any account what harbour, roads or bays there were, or the produce, strength, or trade of them; these we were forced to seek after ourselves.

The Piscadores are a great many inhabited islands lying near the island Formosa, between it and China, in or near the latitude of 23 degrees north latitude, almost as high as the Tropic of Cancer. These Piscadore islands are moderately high and appear much like our Dorsetshire and Wiltshire Downs in England. They produce thick short grass and a few trees. They are pretty well watered and they feed abundance of goats and some great cattle. There are abundance of mounts and old fortifications on them: but of no use now, whatever they have been.

We now directed our course for some islands we had chosen to go to that lie between Formosa and Luconia. They are laid down in our plots without any name, only with a figure of 5, denoting the number of them. It was supposed by us that these islands had no inhabitants, because they had not any name by our hydrographers. Therefore we thought to lie there secure, and be pretty near the island Luconia, which we did still intend to visit.

The inhabitants and their clothing.

Monmouth and Grafton Islands are very thick inhabited; and Bashee Island has one town on it. The natives of these islands are short squat people; they are generally round-visaged, with low foreheads and thick eyebrows; their eyes of a hazel colour and small, yet bigger than the Chinese; short low noses and their lips and mouths middle proportioned; their teeth are white; their hair is black, and thick, and lank, which they wear but short; it will just cover their ears, and so it is cut round very even. Their skins are of a very dark copper colour.

They wear no hat, cap, nor turban, nor anything to keep off the sun. The men for the biggest part have only a small clout to cover their nakedness; some of them have jackets made of plantain leaves which were as rough as any bear's skin: I never saw such rugged things. The women have a short petticoat made of cotton which comes a little below their knees. It is a thick sort of stubborn cloth which they make themselves of their cotton.

Of the ship's first intercourse with these people, and bartering with them.

To proceed therefore with our affairs: I have said before that we anchored here the 6th day of August. While we were furling our sails there came near 100 boats of the natives aboard, with three or four men in each; so that our deck was full of men. We were at first afraid of them, and therefore got up 20 or 30 small arms on our poop and kept three or four men as sentinels, with guns in their hands, ready to fire on them if they had offered to molest us. But they were pretty quiet, only they picked up such old iron that they found on our deck, and they also took out our pump bolts and linchpins out of the carriages of our guns before we perceived them. At last one of our men perceived one of them very busy getting out one of our linchpins; and took hold of the fellow who immediately bawled out, and all the rest presently leapt overboard, some into their boats, others into the sea; and they all made away for the shore. But when we perceived their fright we made much of him that was in hold, who stood trembling all the while; and at last we gave him a small piece of iron, with which he immediately leapt overboard and swam to his consorts who hovered about our ship to see the issue. Then we beckoned to them to come aboard again, being very loth to lose a commerce with them. Some of the boats came aboard again, and they were always very honest and civil afterward.

We presently after this sent a canoe ashore to see their manner of living and what provision they had: the canoe's crew were made very welcome with bashee-drink and saw abundance of hogs, some of which they bought and returned aboard. After this the natives brought aboard both hogs and goats to us in their own boats; and every day we should have fifteen or twenty hogs and goats in boats aboard by our side. These we bought for a small matter; we could buy a good fat goat for an old iron hoop, and a hog of seventy or eighty pounds weight for two or three pound of iron. Their drink also they brought off in jars, which we bought for old nails, spikes and leaden bullets. Beside the fore-mentioned commodities they brought aboard great quantities of yams and potatoes; which we purchased for nails, spikes or bullets. It was one man's work to be all day cutting out bars of iron into small pieces with a cold chisel: and these were for the great purchases of hogs and goats, which they would not sell for nails, as their drink and roots. We never let them know what store we have, that they may value it the more. Every morning as soon as it was light they would thus come aboard with their commodities which we bought as we had occasion. We did commonly furnish ourselves with as many goats and roots as served us all the day; and their hogs we bought in large quantities as we thought convenient; for we salted them. Their hogs were very sweet; but I never saw so many measled ones.

Their course among the islands; their stay there, and provision to depart.

We filled all our water at a curious brook close by us in Grafton's Isle where we first anchored. We stayed there about three or four days before we went to other islands. We sailed to the southward, passing on the east side of Grafton Island, and then passed through between that and Monmouth Island; but we found no anchoring till we came to the north end of Monmouth Island, and there we stopped during one tide. The tide runs very strong here and sometimes makes a short chopping sea. Its course among these islands is south by east and north by west. The flood sets to the north, and ebb to the south, and it rises and falls eight foot.

When we went from hence we coasted about two leagues to the southward on the west side of Monmouth Island; and, finding no anchor-ground we stood over to the Bashee Island and came to an anchor on the north-east part of it, against a small sandy bay, in seven fathom clean hard sand and about a quarter of a mile from the shore. Here is a pretty wide channel between these two islands and anchoring all over it. The depth of water is twelve, fourteen, and sixteen fathom.

We presently built a tent ashore to mend our sails in, and stayed all the rest of our time here, namely, from the 13th day of August till the 26th day of September. In which time we mended our sails and scrubbed our ship's bottom very well; and every day some of us went to their towns and were kindly entertained by them. Their boats also came aboard with their merchandise to sell, and lay aboard all day; and if we did not take it off their hands one day they would bring the same again the next.

We had yet the winds at south-west and south-south-west mostly fair weather. In October we did expect the winds to shift to the north-east and therefore we provided to sail (as soon as the eastern monsoon was settled) to cruise off of Manila. Accordingly we provided a stock of provision. We salted seventy or eighty good fat hogs and bought yams and potatoes good store to eat at sea.

They are driven off by a violent storm, and return.

About the 24th day of September the winds shifted about to the east, and from thence to the north-east fine fair weather. The 25th it came at north and began to grow fresh, and the sky began to be clouded, and the wind freshened on us.

At twelve o'clock at night it blew a very fierce storm. We were then riding with our best bower ahead; and though our yards and top-mast were down yet we drove. This obliged us to let go our sheet-anchor, veering out a good scope of cable, which stopped us till ten or eleven o'clock the next day. Then the wind came on so fierce that she drove again, with both anchors ahead. The wind was now at north by west and we kept driving till three or four o'clock in the afternoon: and it was well for us that there were no islands, rocks, or sands in our way, for if there had we must have been driven upon them. We used our utmost endeavours to stop here, being loth to go to sea because we had six of our men ashore who could not get off now. At last we were driven out into deep water, and then it was in vain to wait any longer: therefore we hove in our sheet-cable, and got up our sheet-anchor, and cut away our best bower (for to have heaved her up then would have gone near to have foundered us) and so put to sea. We had very violent weather the night ensuing, with very hard rain, and we were forced to scud with our bare poles till three o'clock in the morning. Then the wind slackened and we brought our ship to under a mizzen, and lay with our head to the westward. The 27th day the wind abated much, but it rained very hard all day and the night ensuing. The 28th day the wind came about to the north-east and it cleared up and blew a hard gale, but it stood not there, for it shifted about to the eastward, thence to the south-east, then to the south, and at last settled at south-west, and then we had a moderate gale and fair weather.

It was the 29th day when the wind came to the south-west. Then we made all the sail we could for the island again. The 30th day we had the wind at west and saw the islands but could not get in before night. Therefore we stood off to the southward till two o'clock in the morning; then we tacked and stood in all the morning, and about twelve o'clock the 1st day of October we anchored again at the place from whence we were driven.

The natives' kindness to six of them left behind.

Then our six men were brought aboard by the natives, to whom we gave three whole bars of iron for their kindness and civility, which was an extraordinary present to them. Mr. Robert Hall was one of the men that was left ashore. I shall speak more of him hereafter. He and the rest of them told me that, after the ship was out of sight, the natives began to be more kind to them than they had been before, and persuaded them to cut their hair short, as theirs was, offering to each of them if they would do it a young woman to wife, and a small hatchet and other iron utensils fit for a planter, in dowry; and withal showed them a piece of land for them to manage. They were courted thus by several of the town where they then were: but they took up their headquarters at the house of him with whom they first went ashore. When the ship appeared in sight again then they importuned them for some iron, which is the chief thing that they covet, even above their earrings. We might have bought all their earrings, or other gold they had, with our iron bars, had we been assured of its goodness; and yet when it was touched and compared with other gold we could not discern any difference, though it looked so pale in the lump; but the seeing them polish it so often was a new discouragement.

The crew discouraged by those storms, quit their design of cruising off Manila for the Acapulco ship; and it is resolved to fetch a compass to Cape Comorin, and so for the Red Sea.

This last storm put our men quite out of heart: for although it was not altogether so fierce as that which we were in on the coast of China, which was still fresh in memory, yet it wrought more powerfully and frightened them from their design of cruising before Manila, fearing another storm there. Now every man wished himself at home, as they had done a hundred times before: but Captain Read and Captain Teat the master persuaded them to go towards Cape Comorin, and then they would tell them more of their minds, intending doubtless to cruise in the Red Sea; and they easily prevailed with the crew.

The eastern monsoon was now at hand, and the best way had been to go through the Straits of Malacca: but Captain Teat said it was dangerous by reason of many islands and shoals there with which none of us were acquainted. Therefore he thought it best to go round on the east side of the Philippine Islands and so, keeping south toward the Spice Islands, to pass out into the East Indian Ocean about the island Timor.

This seemed to be a very tedious way about, and as dangerous altogether for shoals; but not for meeting with English or Dutch ships, which was their greatest fear. I was well enough satisfied, knowing that the farther we went the more knowledge and experience I should get, which was the main thing that I regarded; and should also have the more variety of places to attempt an escape from them, being fully resolved to take the first opportunity of giving them the slip.

CHAPTER 16

Terra Australis Incognita

*They stop at the two isles near Mindanao;
where they refit their ship, and make a pump
after the Spanish fashion.*

The 14th day of October we came close by a small low woody island that lies east from the south-east end of Mindanao, distant from it about 20 leagues. I do not find it set down in any sea-chart.

The 15th day we had the wind at north-east and we steered west for the island Mindanao, and arrived at the south-east end again on the 16th day. There we went in and anchored between two small islands which lie in about 5 degrees 10 minutes north latitude. I mentioned them when we first came on this coast. Here we found a fine small cove on the north-west end of the easternmost island, fit to careen in or haul ashore; so we went in there and presently unrigged our ship and provided to haul our ship ashore to clean her bottom. These islands are about three or four leagues from the island Mindanao; they are about four or five leagues in circumference and of a pretty good height. The mould is black and deep and there are two small brooks of fresh water.

They are both plentifully stored with great high trees; therefore our carpenters were sent ashore to cut down some of them for our use; for here they made a new boltsprit, which we did set here also, our old one being very faulty. They made a new fore-yard too, and a fore-top-mast: and our pumps being faulty and not serviceable they did cut a tree to make a pump. They first squared it, then sawed it in the middle, and then hollowed each side exactly. The two hollow sides were made big enough to contain a pump box in the midst of them both when they were joined together;

and it required their utmost skill to close them exactly to the making a tight cylinder for the pump-box; being unaccustomed to such work. We learnt this way of pump-making from the Spaniards, who make their pumps that they use in their ships in the South Seas after this manner; and I am confident that there are no better hand-pumps in the world than they have.

By the young prince of the Spice Island they have news of Captain Swan, and his men, left at Mindanao.

While we lay here the young prince that I mentioned in the 13th chapter came aboard. He understanding that we were bound farther to the southward desired us to transport him and his men to his own island. He showed it to us in our chart and told us the name of it; which we put down in our chart, for it was not named there; but I quite forgot to put it into my journal.

This man told us that not above six days before this he saw Captain Swan and several of his men that we left there, and named the names of some of them, who he said were all well, and that now they were at the city of Mindanao; but that they had all of them been out with Raja Laut, fighting under him in his wars against his enemies the Alfoores; and that most of them fought with undaunted courage; for which they were highly honoured and esteemed, as well by the sultan as by the general Raja Laut; that now Captain Swan intended to go with his men to Fort St. George and that, in order thereto, he had proffered forty ounces of gold for a ship; but the owner and he were not yet agreed; and that he feared that the sultan would not let him go away till the wars were ended.

All this the prince told us in the Malayan tongue, which many of us had learnt; and when he went away he promised to return to us again in three days' time, and so long Captain Read promised to stay for him (for we had now almost finished our business) and he seemed very glad of the opportunity of going with us.

The author proposes to the crew to return to him; but in vain.

After this I endeavoured to persuade our men to return with the ship to the river of Mindanao and offer their service again to Captain Swan. I took an opportunity when they were filling of water, there being then half the ship's company ashore; and I found all these very willing to do it. I desired them to say nothing till I had tried the minds of the other half, which I intended to do the next day, it being their turn to fill water then; but one of these men, who seemed most forward to invite back Captain Swan, told Captain Read and Captain Teat of the project, and they presently dissuaded the men from any such designs. Yet fearing the worst they made all possible haste to be gone.

The story of his murder at Mindanao.

I have since been informed that Captain Swan and his men stayed there a great while afterward; and that many of the men got passages from thence in Dutch sloops to Ternate, particularly Mr. Rofy and Mr. Nelly. There they remained a great while and at last got to Batavia (where the Dutch took their journals from them) and so to Europe; and that some of Captain Swan's men died at Mindanao; of which number Mr. Harthrop and Mr. Smith, Captain Swan's merchants, were two. At last Captain Swan and his surgeon, going in a small canoe aboard of a Dutch ship then in the road, in order to get passage to Europe, were overset by the natives at the mouth of the river; who waited their coming purposely to do it, but unsuspected by them; where they both were killed in the water. This was done by the general's order, as some think, to get his gold, which he did immediately seize on. Others say it was because the general's house was burnt a little before, and Captain Swan was suspected to be the author of it; and others say that it was Captain Swan's threats occasioned his own ruin; for he would often say passionately that he had been abused by the general, and that he would have satisfaction for it; saying also that now he was well acquainted with their rivers, and knew how to come in at any time; that he also knew their manner of fighting and the weakness of their country; and therefore he would go away and get a band of men to assist him, and returning thither again he would spoil and take all that they had and their country too. When the general had been informed of these discourses he would say: "What, is Captain Swan made of iron and able to resist a whole kingdom? Or does he think that we are afraid of him that he speaks thus?" Yet did he never touch him till now the Mindanayans killed him. It is very probable there might be somewhat of truth in all this; for the captain was passionate, and the general greedy of gold. But, whatever was the occasion, so he was killed, as several have assured me, and his gold seized on, and all his things; and his journal also, from England as far as Cape Corrientes on the coast of Mexico. This journal was afterwards sent away from thence by Mr. Moody (who was there both a little before and a little after the murder) and he sent it to England by Mr. Goddard, chief mate of the Defence.

A spout: a description of them, with a story of one.

The 30th day we had a fresh land-wind and steered away south, passing between the two shoals which we saw the day before. These shoals lie in latitude 3 degrees south and about ten leagues from the island Celebes. Being past them the wind died away and we lay becalmed till the afternoon: then we had a hard tornado out of the south-west, and towards the evening we saw two or three spouts, the first I had seen since I came into the East Indies; in the West Indies I had often met with them. A spout is a small ragged piece or part of a cloud hanging down about a yard, seemingly from the blackest part thereof. Commonly it hangs down sloping from thence, or sometimes appearing with a small bending, or elbow in the middle. I never saw any hang perpendicularly down. It is small at the lower end, seeming no bigger than one's arm, but still fuller towards the cloud from whence it proceeds.

When the surface of the sea begins to work you shall see the water, for about 100 paces in circumference, foam and move gently round till the whirling motion increases: and then it flies upward in a pillar, about 100 paces in compass at the bottom, but lessening gradually upwards to the smallness of the spout itself, there where it reaches the lower end of the spout, through which the rising seawater seems to be conveyed into the clouds. This visibly appears by the clouds increasing in bulk and blackness. Then you shall presently see the cloud drive along, although before it seemed to be without any motion: the spout also keeping the same course with the cloud, and still sucking up the water as it goes along, and they make a wind as they go. Thus it continues for the space of half an hour, more or less, until the sucking is spent, and then, breaking off, all the water which was below the spout, or pendulous piece of cloud, falls down again into the sea, making a great noise with its fall and clashing motion in the sea.

It is very dangerous for a ship to be under a spout when it breaks, therefore we always endeavour to shun it by keeping at a distance, if possibly we can. But, for want of wind to carry us away, we are often in great fear and danger, for it is usually calm when spouts are at work; except only just where they are. Therefore men at sea, when they see a spout coming and know not how to avoid it, do sometimes fire shot out of their great guns into it, to give it air or vent, that so it may break; but I did never hear that it proved to be of any benefit.

And now being on this subject I think it not amiss to give you an account of an accident that happened to a ship once on the coast of Guinea, some time in or about the year 1674. One Captain Records of London, bound for the coast of Guinea, in a ship of 300 tuns and 16 guns called the Blessing: when he came into the latitude 7 or 8 degrees north he saw several spouts, one of which came directly towards the ship, and he, having no wind to get out of the way of the spout, made ready to receive it by furling his sails. It came on very swift and broke a little before it reached the ship; making a great noise and raising the sea round it, as if a great house or some such thing had been cast into the sea. The fury of the wind still lasted and took the ship on the starboard bow with such violence that it snapped off the boltsprit and foremast both at once, and blew which ship all along, ready to overset it, but the ship did presently right again, and the wind whirling round took the ship a second time with the like fury as before, but on the contrary side, and was again like to overset her the other way. The mizzen-mast felt the fury of this second blast and was snapped short off, as the foremast and boltsprit had been before. The mainmast and main-top-mast received no damage, for the fury of the wind (which was presently over) did not reach them. Three men were in the fore-top when the foremast broke and one on the boltsprit, and fell with them into the sea, but all of them were saved. I had this relation from Mr. John Canby, who was then quartermaster and steward of her; one Abraham Wise was chief mate, and Leonard Jefferies second mate.

We are usually very much afraid of them: yet this was the only damage that ever I heard done by them. They seem terrible enough, the rather because they come upon you while you lie becalmed, like a log in the sea, and cannot get out of their way: but though I have seen and been beset by them often, yet the fright was always the greatest of the harm.

Engraving showing a ship in peril from multiple waterspouts.

New Holland; laid down too much northward.

Being now clear of all the islands we stood off south, intending to touch at New Holland, a part of Terra Australis Incognita, to see what that country would afford us. Indeed as the winds were we could not now keep our intended course (which was first westerly and then northerly) without going to New Holland unless we had gone back again among the islands: but this was not a good time of the year to be among any islands to the south of the Equator, unless in a good harbour.

The 4th day of January 1688 we fell in with the land of New Holland in the latitude of 16 degrees 50 minutes, having, as I said before, made our course due south from the shoal that we passed by the 31st day of December. We ran in close by it and, finding no convenient anchoring because it lies open to the north-west, we ran along shore to the eastward, steering north-east by east for so the land lies. We steered thus about 12 leagues; and then came to a point of land from whence the land trends east and southerly for 10 or 12 leagues; but how afterwards I know not. About 3 leagues to the eastward of this point there is a pretty deep bay with abundance of islands in it, and a very good place to anchor in or to haul ashore. About a league to the eastward of that point we anchored January the 5th 1688, two mile from the shore in 29 fathom, good hard sand and clean ground.

Its soil, and dragon-trees.

New Holland is a very large tract of land. It is not yet determined whether it is an island or a main continent; but I am certain that it joins neither to Asia, Africa, nor America. This part of it that we saw is all low even land, with sandy banks against the sea, only the points are rocky, and so are some of the islands in this bay.

The land is of a dry sandy soil, destitute of water except you make wells; yet producing divers sorts of trees; but the woods are not thick, nor the trees very big. Most of the trees that we saw are dragon-trees as we supposed; and these too are the largest trees of any there. They are about the bigness of our large apple-trees, and about the same height; and the rind is blackish and somewhat rough. The leaves are of a dark colour; the gum distils out of the knots or cracks that are in the bodies of the trees. We compared it with some gum-dragon or dragon's blood that was aboard, and it was of the same colour and taste. The other sort of trees were not known by any of us. There was pretty long grass growing under the trees; but it was very thin. We saw no trees that bore fruit or berries.

We saw no sort of animal nor any track of beast but once; and that seemed to be the tread of a beast as big as a great mastiff-dog. Here are a few small land-birds but none bigger than a blackbird; and but few sea-fowls. Neither is the sea very plentifully stored with fish unless you reckon the manatee and turtle as such. Of these creatures there is plenty but they are extraordinary shy; though the inhabitants cannot trouble them much having neither boats nor iron.

The poor winking inhabitants: their feathers, habit, food, arms, etc.

The inhabitants of this country are the miserablest people in the world. The Hodmadods of Monomatapa, though a nasty people, yet for wealth are gentlemen to these; who have no houses, and skin garments, sheep, poultry, and fruits of the earth, ostrich eggs, etc., as the Hodmadods have: and, setting aside their human shape, they differ but little from brutes. They are tall, straight-bodied, and thin, with small long limbs. They have great heads, round foreheads, and great brows. Their eyelids are always half closed to keep the flies out of their eyes; they being so troublesome here that no fanning will keep them from coming to one's face; and without the assistance of both hands to keep them off they will creep into one's nostrils and mouth too if the lips are not shut very close; so that, from their infancy being thus annoyed with these insects, they do never open their eyes as other people: and therefore they cannot see far, unless they hold up their heads as if they were looking at somewhat over them.

They have great bottle-noses, pretty full lips, and wide mouths. The two fore-teeth of their upper jaw are wanting in all of them, men and women, old and young; whether they draw them out I know not: neither have they any beards. They are long-visaged, and of a very unpleasing aspect, having no one graceful feature in their faces. Their hair is black, short, and curled like that of the Negroes; and not long and lank like the common Indians. The colour of their skins, both of their faces and the rest of their body, is coal-black like that of the Negroes of Guinea.

They have no sort of clothes but a piece of the rind of a tree, tied like a girdle about their waists, and a handful of long grass, or three or four small green boughs full of leaves thrust under their girdle to cover their nakedness.

They have no houses but lie in the open air without any covering; the earth being their bed, and the heaven their canopy. Whether they cohabit one man to one woman or promiscuously I know not; but they do live in companies, 20 or 30 men, women, and children together. Their only food is a small sort of fish which they get by making weirs of stone across little coves or branches of the sea; every tide bringing in the small fish and there leaving them for a prey to these people who constantly attend there to search for them at low water. This small-fry I take to be the top of their fishery: they have no instruments to catch great fish should they come; and such seldom stay to be left behind at low water: nor could we catch any fish with our hooks and lines all the while we lay there. In other places at low-water they seek for cockles, mussels, and periwinkles: of these shellfish there are fewer still; so that their chiefest dependence is upon what the sea leaves in their weirs; which, be it much or little, they gather up, and march to the places of their abode. There the old people that are not able to stir abroad by reason of their age and the tender infants wait their return; and what providence has bestowed on them they presently broil on the coals and eat it in common. Sometimes they get as many fish as makes them a plentiful banquet; and at other times they scarce get everyone a taste: but be it little or much that they get, everyone has his part, as well the young and tender, the old and feeble, who are not able to go abroad, as the strong and lusty. When they have eaten they lie down till the next low-water, and then all that are able march out, be it night or day, rain or shine, it is all one; they must attend the weirs or else they must fast: for the earth affords them no food at all. There is neither herb, root, pulse, nor any sort of grain for them to eat that we saw; nor any sort of bird or beast that they can catch, having no instruments wherewithal to do so.

I did not perceive that they did worship anything. These poor creatures have a sort of weapon to defend their weir or fight with their enemies if they have any that will interfere with their poor fishery. They did at first endeavour with their weapons to frighten us, who lying ashore deterred them from one of their fishing-places. Some of them had wooden swords, others had a sort of lances. The sword is a piece of wood shaped somewhat like a cutlass. The lance is a long straight pole sharp at one end, and hardened afterwards by heat. I saw no iron nor any other sort of metal; therefore it is probable they use stone-hatchets, as some Indians in America do, described in Chapter 4.

The inhabitants on the islands.

These people speak somewhat through the throat; but we could not understand one word that they said. We anchored, as I said before, January the 5th and, seeing men walking on the shore, we presently sent a canoe to get some acquaintance with them: for we were in hopes to get some provision among them. But the inhabitants, seeing our boat coming, ran away and hid themselves. We searched afterwards three days in hopes to find their houses; but found none: yet we saw many places where they had made fires. At last, being out of hopes to find their habitations, we searched no farther; but left a great many toys ashore in such places where we thought that they would come. In all our search we found no water but old wells on the sandy bays.

Their habitations, unfitness for labour, etc.

At last we went over to the islands and there we found a great many of the natives: I do believe there were 40 on one

island, men, women, and children. The men at our first coming
ashore threatened us with their lances and swords; but they
were frightened by firing one gun which we fired purposely to
scare them. The island was so small that they could not hide
themselves: but they were much disordered at our landing,
especially the women and children: for we went directly to
their camp. The lustiest of the women, snatching up their
infants, ran away howling, and the little children ran after
squeaking and bawling; but the men stood still. Some of the
women and such people as could not go from us lay still by
a fire, making a doleful noise as if we had been coming to
devour them: but when they saw we did not intend to harm
them they were pretty quiet, and the rest that fled from us at
our first coming returned again. This their place of dwelling
was only a fire with a few boughs before it, set up on that side
the winds was of.

After we had been here a little while the men began to be
familiar and we clothed some of them, designing to have had
some service of them for it: for we found some wells of water
here, and intended to carry 2 or 3 barrels of it aboard. But it
being somewhat troublesome to carry to the canoes we thought
to have made these men to have carried it for us, and therefore
we gave them some old clothes; to one an old pair of breeches,
to another a ragged shirt, to the third a jacket that was scarce
worth owning; which yet would have been very acceptable at
some places where we had been, and so we thought they might
have been with these people. We put them on them, thinking
that this finery would have brought them to work heartily for
us; and, our water being filled in small long barrels, about six
gallons in each, which were made purposely to carry water
in, we brought these our new servants to the wells, and put a
barrel on each of their shoulders for them to carry to the canoe.
But all the signs we could make were to no purpose for they
stood like statues without motion but grinned like so many
monkeys staring one upon another: for these poor creatures
seem not accustomed to carry burdens; and I believe that one
of our ship-boys of 10 years old would carry as much as one
of them. So we were forced to carry our water ourselves, and
they very fairly put the clothes off again and laid them down,
as if clothes were only to work in. I did not perceive that they

had any great liking to them at first, neither did they seem to admire anything that we had.

At another time, our canoe being among these islands seeking for game, espied a drove of these men swimming from one island to another; for they have no boats, canoes, or bark-logs. They took up four of them and brought them aboard; two of them were middle-aged, the other two were young men about 18 or 20 years old. To these we gave boiled rice and with it turtle and manatee boiled. They did greedily devour what we gave them but took no notice of the ship, or anything in it, and when they were set on land again they ran away as fast as they could. At our first coming, before we were acquainted with them or they with us, a company of them who lived on the main came just against our ship, and, standing on a pretty high bank, threatened us with their swords and lances by shaking them at us: at last the captain ordered the drum to be beaten, which was done of a sudden with much vigour, purposely to scare the poor creatures. They hearing the noise ran away as fast as they could drive; and when they ran away in haste they would cry "Gurry, gurry," speaking deep in the throat. Those inhabitants also that live on the main would always run away from us; yet we took several of them. For, as I have already observed, they had such bad eyes that they could not see us till we came close to them. We did always give them victuals and let them go again, but the islanders, after our first time of being among them, did not stir for us.

CHAPTER 17

A Parting of Ways

Nicobar Island, and the rest called by that name.

We now directed our course towards the Nicobar Islands, intending there to clean the ship's bottom in order to make her sail well.

The 14th day in the evening we had sight of one of the Nicobar Islands. The southernmost of them lies about 40 leagues north-north-west from the north-west end of the island Sumatra. This most southerly of them is Nicobar itself, but all the cluster of islands lying south of the Andaman Islands are called by our seamen the Nicobar Islands.

The author projects and gets leave to stay ashore here, and with him two Englishmen more, the Portuguese, and four Malayans of Achin.

I thought now was my time to make my escape by getting leave if possible to stay here: for it seemed not very feasible to do it by stealth; and I had no reason to despair of getting leave: this being a place where my stay could probably do our crew no harm should I design it. Indeed one reason that put me on the thoughts of staying at this particular place, besides the present opportunity of leaving Captain Read, which I did always intend to do as soon as I could, was that I had here also a prospect of advancing a profitable trade for ambergris with these people, and of gaining a considerable fortune to myself: for in a short time I might have learned their language and, by accustoming myself to row with them in the proas or canoes, especially by conforming myself to their customs and manners of living, I should have seen how they got their ambergris, and have known what quantities they get, and the time of the year when most is found. And then afterwards I thought it would be easy for me to have transported myself from thence, either in some ship that passed this way, whether English, Dutch, or Portuguese; or else to have gotten one of the young men of the island to have gone with me in one of their canoes to Achin; and there to have furnished myself with such commodities as I found most coveted by them; and therewith at my return to have bought their ambergris.

I had till this time made no open show of going ashore here: but now, the water being filled and the ship in a readiness to sail, I desired Captain Read to set me ashore on this island. He, supposing that I could not go ashore in a place less frequented by ships than this, gave me leave: which probably he would have refused to have done if he thought I should have gotten from hence in any short time; for fear of my giving an account of him to the English or Dutch. I soon got up my chest and bedding and immediately got some to row me ashore; for fear lest his mind should change again.

Their first rencounters with the natives.

The canoe that brought me ashore landed me on a small sandy bay where there were two houses but no person in them. For the inhabitants were removed to some other house, probably for fear of us because the ship was close by: and yet both men and women came aboard the ship without any sign of fear. When our ship's canoe was going aboard again they met the owner of the houses coming ashore in his boat. He made a great many signs to them to fetch me off again: but they would not understand him. Then he came to me and offered his boat to carry me off; but I refused it. Then he made signs for me to go up into the house and, according as I did understand him by his signs and a few Malayan words that he used, he intimated that somewhat would come out of the woods in the night when I was a sleep and kill me, meaning probably some wild beast. Then I carried my chest and clothes up into the house.

I had not been ashore an hour before Captain Teat and one John Damarel, with three or four armed men more, came to fetch me aboard again. They need not have sent an armed posse for me; for had they but sent the cabin-boy ashore for me I would not have denied going aboard. For though I could have hid myself in the woods yet then they would have abused or have killed some of the natives, purposely to incense them against me. I told them therefore that I was ready to go with them and went aboard with all my things.

When I came aboard I found the ship in an uproar; for there were three men more who, taking courage by my example, desired leave also to accompany me. One of them was the surgeon Mr. Coppinger, the other was Mr. Robert Hall, and one named Ambrose; I have forgot his surname. These men had always harboured the same designs as I had. The two last were not much opposed; but Captain Read and his crew would not part with the surgeon. At last the surgeon leapt into the canoe and, taking up my gun, swore he would go ashore, and that if any man did oppose it he would shoot him: but John Oliver, who was then quartermaster, leapt into the canoe, taking hold of him took away the gun and, with the help of two or three more, they dragged him again into the ship.

Then Mr. Hall and Ambrose and I were again sent ashore; and one of the men that rowed us ashore stole an axe and gave it to us, knowing it was a good commodity with the Indians. It was now dark, therefore we lighted a candle and I, being the oldest stander in our new country, conducted them into one of the houses, where we did presently hang up our hammocks. We had scarce done this before the canoe came ashore again and brought the four Malayan men belonging to Achin (which we took in the proa we took off of Sumatra) and the Portuguese that came to our ship out of the Siam junk at Pulo Condore: the crew having no occasion for these, being leaving the Malayan parts, where the Portuguese spark served as an interpreter; and not fearing now that the Achinese could be serviceable to us in bringing us over to their country, forty leagues off; nor imagining that we durst make such an attempt, as indeed it was a bold one. Now we were men enough to defend ourselves against the natives of this island if they should prove our enemies: though if none of these men had come ashore to me

I should not have feared any danger: nay perhaps less because I should have been cautious of giving any offence to the natives. And I am of the opinion that there are no people in the world so barbarous as to kill a single person that falls accidentally into their hands or comes to live among them; except they have before been injured by some outrage or violence committed against them. Yet even then, or afterwards if a man could but preserve his life from their first rage, and come to treat with them (which is the hardest thing because their way is usually to abscond and, rushing suddenly upon their enemy, to kill him at unawares) one might by some slight insinuate one's self into their favours again; especially by showing some toy or knack that they did never see before: which any European that has seen the world might soon contrive to amuse them withal: as might be done generally, even with a lit fire struck with a flint and steel.

Of the common traditions concerning cannibals, or man-eaters.

As for the common opinion of anthropophagi, or man-eaters, I did never meet any such people: all nations or families in the world, that I have seen or heard of, having some sort of food to live on either fruit, grain, pulse, or roots, which grow naturally, or else planted by them; if not fish and land animals besides (yea even the people of New Holland had fish amidst all their penury) and would scarce kill a man purposely to eat him. I know not what barbarous customs may formerly have been in the world; and to sacrifice their enemies to their gods is a thing has been much talked of with relation to the savages of America. I am a stranger to that also if it be or have been customary in any nation there; and yet, if they sacrifice their enemies it is not necessary they should eat them too. After all I will not be peremptory in the negative, but I speak as to the compass of my own knowledge and know some of these cannibal stories to be false, and many of them have been disproved since I first went to the West Indies. At that time how barbarous were the poor Florida Indians accounted which now we find to be civil enough? What strange stories have we heard of the Indians whose islands were called the Isles of Cannibals? Yet we find that they do trade very civilly with the French and Spaniards; and have done so with us. I do own that they have formerly endeavoured to destroy our plantations at Barbados, and have since hindered us from settling in the island Santa Loca by destroying two or three colonies successively of those that were settled there; and even the island Tobago has been often annoyed and ravaged by them when settled by the Dutch, and still lies waste (though a delicate fruitful island) as being too near the Caribbees on the continent, who visit it every year. But this was to preserve their own right by endeavouring to keep out any that would settle themselves on those islands where they had planted themselves; yet even these people would not hurt a single person, as I have been told by some that have been prisoners among them. I could instance also in the Indians of Boca Toro and Boca Drago, and many other places where they do live, as the Spaniards call it, wild and savage: yet there they have been familiar with privateers, but by abuses have withdrawn their friendship again. As for these Nicobar people I found them affable enough, and therefore I did not fear them; but I did not much care whether I had gotten any more company or no.

But however I was very well satisfied, and the rather because we were now men enough to row ourselves over to the island Sumatra; and accordingly we presently consulted how to purchase a canoe of the natives.

It was a fine clear moonlight night in which we were left ashore. Therefore we walked on the sandy bay to watch when the ship would weigh and be gone, not thinking ourselves secure in our new-gotten liberty till then. About eleven or twelve o'clock we saw her under sail and then we returned to our chamber and so to sleep. This was the 6th of May.

Their entertainment ashore.

The next morning be times our landlord with four or five of his friends came to see his new guests, and was somewhat surprised to see so many of us for he knew of no more but myself. Yet he seemed to be very well pleased and entertained us with a large calabash of toddy, which he brought with him.

They buy a canoe, to transport them over to Achin; but overset her at first going out.

Before he went away again (for wheresoever we came they left their houses to us, but whether out of fear or superstition I know not) we bought a canoe of him for an axe, and we did presently put our chests and clothes in it, designing to go to the south end of the island and lie there till the monsoon shifted, which we expected every day.

When our things were stowed away we with the Achinese entered with joy into our new frigate and launched off from the shore. We were no sooner off but our canoe overset, bottom upwards. We preserved our lives well enough by swimming and dragged also our chests and clothes ashore; but all our things were wet. I had nothing of value but my journal and some draughts of land of my own taking which I much prized, and which I had hitherto carefully preserved. Mr. Hall had also such another cargo of books and draughts which were now like to perish. But we presently opened our chests and took out our books which, with much ado, we did afterwards dry; but some of our draughts that lay loose in our chests were spoiled.

We lay here afterwards three days, making great fires to dry our books. The Achinese in the meantime fixed our canoe with outlayers on each side; and they also cut a good mast for her and made a substantial sail with mats.

Having recruited and improved her, they set out again for the east side of the island.

The canoe being now very well fixed, and our books and clothes dry, we launched out a second time and rowed towards the east side of the island, leaving many islands to the north of us. The Indians of the island accompanied us with eight or ten canoes against our desire; for we thought that these men would make provision dearer at that side of the island we were going to by giving an account what rates we gave for it at the place from whence we came, which was owing to the ship's being there; for the ship's crew were not so thrifty in bargaining (as they seldom are) as single persons or a few men might be apt to be, who would keep to one bargain. Therefore to hinder them from going with us Mr. Hall scared one canoe's crew by firing a shot over them. They all leapt overboard and cried out but, seeing us row away, they got into their canoe again and came after us.

They have a war with the islanders; but peace being reestablished, they lay in stores, and make preparations for their voyage.

The firing of that gun made all the inhabitants of the island to be our enemies. For presently after this we put ashore at a bay where were four houses and a great many canoes: but they all went away and came near us no more for several days. We had then a great loaf of melory which was our constant food; and if we had a mind to coconuts or toddy our Malayans of Achin would climb the trees and fetch as many nuts as we would have, and a good pot of toddy every morning. Thus we lived till our melory was almost spent; being still in hopes that the natives would come to us and sell it as they had formerly done. But they came not to us; nay they opposed us wherever we came and, often shaking their lances at us, made all the show of hatred that they could invent.

At last when we saw that they stood in opposition to us we resolved to use force to get some of their food if we could not get it other ways. With this resolution we went into our canoe to a small bay on the north part of the island because it was smooth water there and good landing; but on the other side, the wind being yet on the quarter, we could not land without jeopardy of oversetting our canoe and wetting our arms, and then we must have lain at the mercy of our enemies who stood 2 or 300 men in every bay where they saw us coming to keep us off.

When we set out we rowed directly to the north end and presently were followed by seven or eight of their canoes. They keeping at a distance rowed away faster than we did and got to the bay before us; and there, with about 20 more canoes full of men, they all landed and stood to hinder us from landing. But we rowed in within a hundred yards of them. Then we lay still and I took my gun and presented at them; at which they all fell down flat on the ground. But I turned myself about and, to show that we did not intend to harm them, I fired my gun off towards the sea; so that they might see the shot graze on the water. As soon as my gun was loaded again we rowed gently in; at which some of them withdrew. The rest standing up did still cut and hew the air, making signs of their hatred; till I once more frightened them with my gun and discharged it as before. Then more of them sneaked away, leaving only five or six men on the bay. Then we rowed in again and Mr. Hall, taking his sword in his hand, leapt ashore; and I stood ready with my gun to fire at the Indians if they had injured him: but they did not stir till he came to them and saluted them.

He shook them by the hand, and by such signs of friendship as he made the peace was concluded, ratified, and confirmed by all that were present: and others that were gone were again called back, and they all very joyfully accepted of a peace. This became universal over all the island to the great joy of the inhabitants. There was no ringing of bells nor bonfires made, for that it is not the custom here; but gladness appeared in their countenances, for now they could go out and fish again without fear of being taken. This peace was not more welcome to them than to us; for now the inhabitants brought their melory again to us; which we bought for old rags and small strips of cloth about as broad as the palm of one's hand. I did not see above five or six hens, for they have but few on the island. At some places we saw some small hogs which we could have bought of them reasonably; but we could not offend our Achinese friends who were Mohammedans.

We stayed here two or three days and then rowed toward the south end of the island, keeping on the east side, and we were kindly received by the natives wherever we came. When we arrived at the south end of the island we fitted ourselves with melory and water. We bought three or four loaves of melory and about twelve large coconut-shells that had all the kernel taken out, yet were preserved whole, except only a small hole at one end; and all these held for us about three gallons and a half of water. We bought also two or three bamboos that held about four or five gallons more: this was our sea-store.

We now designed to go for Achin, a town on the north-west end of the island Sumatra, distant from hence about 40 leagues, bearing south-south-west. We only waited for the western monsoon, which we had expected a great while, and now it seemed to be at hand; for the clouds began to hang their heads to the eastward, and at last moved gently that way; and though the wind was still at east, yet this was an infallible sign that the western monsoon was nigh.

CHAPTER 18

The Long Journey Home

*The author, with some others, put to sea in an
open boat, designing for Achin.*

It was the 15th day of May 1688 about four o'clock in the
afternoon when we left Nicobar Island, directing our course
towards Achin, being eight men of us in company, namely,
three English, four Malayans, who were born at Achin, and
the mongrel Portuguese.

Their accommodations for their voyage.

Our vessel, the Nicobar canoe, was not one of the biggest nor
of the least size: she was much about the burden of one of our
London wherries below bridge, and built sharp at both ends
like the fore part of a wherry. She was deeper than a wherry,
but not so broad, and was so thin and light that when empty
four men could launch her or haul her ashore on a sandy bay.
We had a good substantial mast and a mat sail, and good
outlayers lashed very fast and firm on each side the vessel,
being made of strong poles. So that while these continued firm
the vessel could not overset which she should easily have done
without them, and with them too had they not been made very
strong; and we were therefore much beholden to our Achinese
companions for this contrivance. These men were none of them
so sensible of the danger as Mr. Hall and myself, for they all
confided so much in us that they did not so much as scruple
anything that we did approve of. Neither was Mr. Hall so well
provided as I was, for before we left the ship I had purposely
consulted our chart of the East Indies (for we had but one in
the ship) and out of that I had written in my pocket-book an

account of the bearing and distance of all the Malacca coast and that of Sumatra, Pegu, and Siam, and also brought away with me a pocket-compass for my direction in any enterprise that I should undertake. The weather at our setting out was very fair, clear and hot. The wind was still at south-east, a very small breeze just fanning the air, and the clouds were moving gently from west to east, which gave us hopes that the winds were either at west already abroad at sea, or would be so in a very short time. We took this opportunity of fair weather, being in hopes to accomplish our voyage to Achin before the western monsoon was set in strong, knowing that we should have very blustering weather after this fair weather, especially at the first coming of the western monsoon.

We rowed therefore away to the southward, supposing that when we were clear from the island we should have a true wind, as we call it; for the land hauls the wind; and we often find the wind at sea different from what it is near the shore. We rowed with four oars taking our turns: Mr. Hall and I steered also by turns, for none of the rest were capable of it. We rowed the first afternoon and the night ensuing about twelve leagues by my judgment. Our course was south-south-east; but the 16th day in the morning, when the sun was an hour high, we saw the island from whence we came bearing north-west by north. Therefore I found we had gone a point more to the east than I intended for which reason we steered south by east.

In the afternoon at 4 o'clock we had a gentle breeze at west-south-west which continued so till nine, all which time we laid down our oars and steered away south-south-east. I was then at the helm and I found by the rippling of the sea that there was a strong current against us. It made a great noise that might be heard near half a mile. At 9 o'clock it fell calm, and so continued till ten. Then the wind sprang up again and blew a fresh breeze all night.

The 17th day in the morning we looked out for the island Sumatra, supposing that we were now within 20 leagues of it; for we had rowed and sailed by our reckoning 24 leagues from Nicobar Island; and the distance from Nicobar to Achin is about 40 leagues. But we looked in vain for the island Sumatra; for, turning ourselves about, we saw to our grief Nicobar Island lying west-north-west and not above eight leagues distant. By this it was visible that we had met a very strong current against us in the night. But the wind freshened on us and we made the best use of it while the weather continued fair. At noon we had an observation of the sun, my latitude was 6 degrees 55 minutes and Mr. Hall's was 7 degrees north.

Change of weather; a halo about the sun, and a violent storm.

The 18th day the wind freshened on us again and the sky began to be clouded. It was indifferent clear till noon and we thought to have had an observation; but we were hindered by the clouds that covered the face of the sun when it came on the meridian. This often happens that we are disappointed of making observations by the sun's being clouded at noon though it shines clear both before and after, especially in places near the sun; and this obscuring of the sun at noon is commonly sudden and unexpected, and for about half an hour or more.

We had then also a very ill presage by a great circle about the sun (five or six times the diameter of it) which seldom appears but storms of wind or much rain ensue. Such circles about the moon are more frequent but of less import. We do commonly take great notice of these that are about the sun, observing if there be any breach in the circle, and in what quarter the breach is; for from thence we commonly find the greatest stress of the wind will come. I must confess that I was a little anxious at the sight of this circle and wished heartily that we were near some land. Yet I showed no sign of it to discourage any consorts, but made a virtue of necessity and put a good countenance on the matter.

Their great danger and distress. Cudda, a town and harbour on the coast of Malacca.

I told Mr. Hall that if the wind became too strong and violent, as I feared it would, it being even then very strong, we must of necessity steer away before the wind and sea till better weather presented; and that as the winds were now we should, instead of about twenty leagues to Achin, be driven sixty or seventy leagues to the coast of Cudda or Queda, a kingdom and town and harbour of trade on the coast of Malacca. The winds therefore bearing very hard we rolled up the foot of our sail on a pole fastened to it, and settled our yard within three foot of the canoe sides so that we had now but a small sail; yet it was still too big considering the wind; for the wind being on our broadside pressed her down very much, though supported by her outlayers; insomuch that the poles of the outlayers going from the sides of their vessel bent as if they would break; and should they have broken our overturning and perishing had been inevitable. Besides the sea increasing would soon have filled the vessel this way. Yet thus we made a shift to bear up with the side of the vessel against the wind for a while: but the wind still increasing about one o'clock in the afternoon we put away right before wind and sea, continuing to run thus all the afternoon and part of the night ensuing. The wind continued increasing all the afternoon, and the sea still swelled higher and often broke, but did us no damage; for the ends of the vessel being very narrow he that steered received and broke the sea on his back, and so kept it from coming in so much as to endanger the vessel: though much water would come in which we were forced to keep heaving out continually. And by this time we saw it was well that we had altered our course, every wave would else have filled and sunk us, taking the side of the vessel: and though our outlayers were well lashed down to the canoe's bottom with rattans, yet they must probably have yielded to such a sea as this; when even before they were plunged under water and bent like twigs.

The evening of this 18th day was very dismal. The sky looked very black, being covered with dark clouds, the wind blew hard and the seas ran high. The sea was already roaring in a white foam about us; a dark night coming on and no land in sight to shelter us, and our little ark in danger to be swallowed by every wave; and, what was worst of all, none of us thought ourselves prepared for another world. The reader may better guess than I can express the confusion that we were all in. I had been in many imminent dangers before now, some of which I have already related, but the worst of them all was but a play-game in comparison with this. I must confess that I was in great conflicts of mind at this time. Other dangers came not upon me with such a leisurely and dreadful solemnity. A sudden skirmish or engagement or so was nothing when one's blood was up and pushed forwards with eager expectations. But here I had a lingering view of approaching death and little or no hopes of escaping it; and I must confess that my courage, which I had hitherto kept up, failed me here; and I made very sad reflections on my former life, and looked back with horror and detestation on actions which before I disliked but now I trembled at the remembrance of. I had long before this repented me of that roving course of life but never with such concern as now. I did also call to mind the many miraculous acts of God's providence towards me in the whole course of my life, of which kind I believe few men have met with the like. For all these I returned thanks in a peculiar manner, and this once more desired God's assistance, and composed my mind as well as I could in the hopes of it, and as the event showed I was not disappointed of my hopes. Submitting ourselves therefore to God's good providence and taking all the care we could to preserve our lives, Mr. Hall and I took turns to steer and the rest took turns to heave out the water, and thus we provided to spend the most doleful night I ever was in. About ten o'clock it began to thunder, lightning, and rain; but the rain was very welcome to us, having drunk up all the water we brought from the island.

The wind at first blew harder than before, but within half an hour it abated and became more moderate; and the sea also assuaged of its fury; and then by a lighted match, of which we kept a piece burning on purpose, we looked on our compass to see how we steered, and found our course to be still east. We had no occasion to look on the compass before, for we steered right before the wind, which if it shifted we had been obliged to have altered our course accordingly. But now it being abated we found our vessel lively enough with that small sail which was then aboard to haul to our former course south-south-east, which accordingly we did, being now in hopes again to get to the island Sumatra. But about two o'clock in the morning of the 19th day we had another gust of wind with much thunder, lightning, and rain, which lasted till day, and obliged us to put before the wind again, steering thus for several hours. It was very dark and the hard rain soaked us so thoroughly that we had not one dry thread about us. The rain chilled us extremely; for any fresh water is much colder than that of the sea. For even in the coldest climates the sea is warm, and in the hottest climates the rain is cold and unwholesome for man's body. In this wet starveling plight we spent the tedious night. Never did poor mariners on a lee shore more earnestly long for the dawning light than we did now. At length the day appeared; but with such dark black clouds near the horizon that the first glimpse of the dawn appeared 30 or 40 degrees high; which was dreadful enough; for it is a common saying among seamen, and true as I have experienced, that a high dawn will have high winds, and a low dawn small winds. PULO WAY. We continued our course still east before wind and sea till about eight o'clock in the morning of this 19th day; and then one of our Malayan friends cried out "Pulo Way." Mr. Hall and Ambrose and I thought the fellow had said "pull away," an expression usual among English seamen when they are rowing. And we wondered what he meant by it till we saw him point to his consorts; and then we looking that way saw land appearing like an island, and all our Malayans said it was an island at the north-west end of Sumatra called Way; for Pulo Way is the island Way. We, who were dropping with wet, cold and hungry, were all overjoyed at the sight of the land and presently marked its bearing. It bore south and the wind was still at west, a strong gale; but the sea did not run so high as in the night. Therefore we trimmed our small sail no bigger than an apron and steered with it. Now our outlayers did us a great kindness again, for although we had but a small sail yet the wind was strong and pressed down our vessel's side very much: but being supported by the outlayers we could brook it well enough, which otherwise we could not have done.

Golden mountain on the Isle of Sumatra.

About noon we saw more land beneath the supposed Pulo Way; and, steering towards it, before night we saw all the coast of Sumatra, and found the errors of our Achinese; for the high land that we first saw, which then appeared like an island, was not Pulo Way but a great high mountain on the island Sumatra called by the English the Golden Mountain. Our wind continued till about seven o'clock at night; then it abated and at ten o'clock it died away: and then we stuck to our oars again, though all of us quite tired with our former fatigues and hardships.

River and town of Passange Jonca on Sumatra, near Diamond Point; where they go ashore very sick, and are kindly entertained by the Oromkay, and inhabitants.

The next morning, being the 20th day, we saw all the low land plain, and judged ourselves not above eight leagues off. About eight o'clock in the morning we had the wind again at west, a fresh gale and, steering in still for a shore, at five o'clock in the afternoon we ran to the mouth of a river on the island Sumatra called Passange Jonca. It is 34 leagues to the eastward of Achin and six leagues to the west of Diamond Point, which makes with three angles of a rhombus and is low land.

Our Malayans were very well acquainted here and carried us to a small fishing village within a mile of the river's mouth, called also by the name of the river Passange Jonca. The hardships of this voyage, with the scorching heat of the sun at our first setting out, and the cold rain, and our continuing wet for the last two days, cast us all into fevers, so that now we were not able to help each other, nor so much as to get our canoe up to the village; but our Malayans got some of the townsmen to bring her up.

The news of our arrival being noised abroad, one of the Oramkis, or noblemen, of the island came in the night to see us. We were then lying in a small hut at the end of the town and, it being late, this lord only viewed us and, having spoken with our Malayans, went away again; but he returned to us again the next day and provided a large house for us to live in till we should be recovered of our sickness, ordering the townspeople to let us want for nothing. The Achinese Malayans that came with us told them all the circumstances of our voyage; how they were taken by our ship, and where and how we that came with them were prisoners aboard the ship and had been set ashore together at Nicobar as they were. It was for this reason probably that the gentlemen of Sumatra were thus extraordinary kind to us, to provide everything that we had need of; nay they would force us to accept of presents from them that we knew not what to do with; as young buffaloes, goats, etc., for these we would turn loose at night after the gentlemen that gave them to us were gone, for we were prompted by our Achinese consorts to accept of them for fear of disobliging by our refusal. But the coconuts, plantains, fowls, eggs, fish, and rice we kept for our use. The Malayans that accompanied us from Nicobar separated themselves from us now, living at one end of the house by themselves, for they were Mohammedans, as all those of the kingdom of Achin are and, though during our passage by sea together we made them be contented to drink their water out of the same coconut-shell with us; yet being now no longer under that necessity they again took up their accustomed nicety and reservedness. They all lay sick, and as their sickness increased one of them threatened us that, if any of them died, the rest would kill us for having brought them this voyage; yet I question whether they would have attempted, or the country people have suffered it. We made a shift to dress our own food, for none of these people, though they were very kind in giving us anything that we wanted, would yet come near us to assist us in dressing our victuals: nay they would not touch anything that we used. We had all fevers and therefore took turns to dress victuals according as we had strength to do it, or stomachs to eat it. I found my fever to increase and my head so distempered that I could scarce stand, therefore I whetted and sharpened my penknife in order to let myself blood; but I could not for my knife was too blunt.

We stayed here ten or twelve days in hopes to recover our health but, finding no amendment, we desired to go to Achin. But we were delayed by the natives who had a desire to have kept Mr. Hall and myself to sail in their vessels to Malacca, Cudda, or to other places whither they trade. But, finding us more desirous to be with our countrymen in our factory at Achin, they provided a large proa to carry us thither, we not being able to manage our own canoe. Besides, before this three of our Malayan comrades were gone very sick into the country, and only one of them and the Portuguese remained with us, accompanying us to Achin and they both as sick as we.

They go thence to Achin.

It was the beginning of June 1686 [sic] when we left Passange Jonca. We had four men to row, one to steer, and a gentleman of the country that went purposely to give an information to the government of our arrival. We were but three days and nights in our passage, having sea-breezes by day and land-winds by night and very fair weather.

The author is examined before the shabander; and takes physick of a Malayan doctor. His long illness.

When we arrived at Achin I was carried before the shebander, the chief magistrate in the city. One Mr. Dennis Driscal, an Irishman and a resident there in the factory which our East India Company had there then, was interpreter. I being weak was suffered to stand in the shebander's presence: for it is their custom to make men sit on the floor as they do, cross-legged like tailors: but I had not strength then to pluck up my heels in that manner. The shebander asked of me several questions, especially how we durst adventure to come in a canoe from the Nicobar Islands to Sumatra. I told him that I had been accustomed to hardships and hazards therefore I did with much freedom undertake it. He enquired also concerning our ship, whence she came, etc. I told him from the South Seas; that she had ranged about the Philippine islands, etc., and was now gone towards Arabia and the Red Sea. The Malayans also and Portuguese were afterwards examined and confirmed what I declared, and in less than half an hour I was dismissed with Mr. Driscal, who then lived in the English East India Company's factory. He provided a room for us to lie in and some victuals. Three days after our arrival here our Portuguese died of a fever. What became of our Malayans I know not: Ambrose lived not long after, Mr. Hall also was so weak that I did not think he would recover. I was the best; but still very sick of a fever and little likely to live. Therefore Mr. Driscal and some other Englishmen persuaded me to take some purging physic of a Malayan doctor. I took their advice, being willing to get ease: but after three doses, each a large calabash of nasty stuff, finding no amendment, I thought to desist from more physic; but was persuaded to take one dose more; which I did, and it wrought so violently that I thought it would have ended my days. I struggled till I had been about twenty or thirty times at stool: but, it working so quick with me with little intermission, and my strength being almost spent, I even threw myself down once for all, and had above sixty stools in all before it left off working. I thought my Malayan doctor, whom they so much commended, would have killed me outright. I continued extraordinary weak for some days after his drenching me thus: but my fever left me for above a week: after which it returned upon me again for a twelvemonth and a flux with it. However when I was a little recovered from the effects of my drench I made a shift to go abroad: and, having been kindly invited to Captain Bowrey's house there, my first visit was to him; who had a ship in the road but lived ashore. This gentleman was extraordinary kind to us all, particularly to me, and importuned me to go his boatswain to Persia; whither he was bound, with a design to sell his ship there, as I was told, though not by himself. From thence he intended to pass with the caravan to Aleppo and so home for England. His business required him to stay some time longer at Achin; I judge to sell some commodities that he had not yet disposed of. Yet he chose rather to leave the disposal of them to some merchant there and make a short trip to the Nicobar Islands in the meantime, and on his return to take in his effects, and so proceed towards Persia. This was a sudden resolution of Captain Bowrey's, presently after the arrival of a small frigate from Siam with an ambassador from the king of Siam to the queen of Achin. The ambassador was a Frenchman by nation. The vessel that he came in was but small yet very well manned, and fitted for a fight. Therefore it was generally supposed here that Captain Bowrey was afraid to lie in Achin Road because the Siamers were now at wars with the English, and he was not able to defend his ship if he should be attacked by them.

He sets out towards Nicobar again, but returns suddenly to Achin road.

But whatever made him think of going to the Nicobar Islands he provided to sail; and took me, Mr. Hall, and Ambrose with him, though all of us so sick and weak that we could do him no service. It was some time about the beginning of June when we sailed out of Achin road: but we met with the winds at north-west with turbulent weather which forced us back again in two days' time. Yet he gave us each 12 mess apiece, a gold coin, each of which is about the value of 15 pence English. So he gave over that design: and, some English ships coming into Achin Road, he was not afraid of the Siamers who lay there.

After this he again invited me to his house at Achin, and treated me always with wine and good cheer, and still importuned me to go with him to Persia: but I being very weak, and fearing the westerly winds would create a great deal of trouble, did not give him a positive answer; especially because I thought I might get a better voyage in the English ships newly arrived, or some others now expected here. It was this Captain Bowrey who sent the letter from Borneo directed to the chief of the English factory at Mindanao, of which mention is made in Chapter 13.

He makes several voyages thence, to Tonquin, to Malacca, to Fort St. George, and to Bencoolen, an English factory on Sumatra.

A short time after this Captain Welden arrived here from Fort St. George in a ship called the Curtana bound to Tonquin. This being a more agreeable voyage than to Persia at this time of the year; besides that the ship was better accommodated, especially with a surgeon, and I being still sick; I therefore chose rather to serve Captain Welden than Captain Bowrey. But to go on with a particular account of that expedition were to carry my reader back again: whom, having brought thus far towards England in my circumnavigation of the globe, I shall not weary him with new rambles, nor so much swell this volume, as I must describe the tour I made in those remote parts of the East Indies from and to Sumatra. So that my voyage to Tonquin at this time, as also another to Malacca afterwards, with my observations in them and the descriptions of those and the neighbouring countries; as well as the description of the island Sumatra itself, and therein the kingdom and city of Achin, Bencoolen, etc., I shall refer to another place where I may give a particular relation of them.

1690. Of Prince Jeoly the painted man, whom the author brought with him to England, and who died at Oxford.

The other passage I shall speak of that occurred during this interval of the tour I made from Achin is with relation to the painted prince whom I brought with me into England and who died at Oxford. For while I was at Fort St. George, about April 1690, there arrived a ship called the Mindanao Merchant, laden with clove-bark from Mindanao. Three of Captain Swan's men that remained there when we went from thence came in her: from whence I had the account of Captain Swan's death, as is before related. There was also one Mr. Moody, who was supercargo of the ship. This gentleman bought at Mindanao the painted prince Jeoly (mentioned in Chapter 13) and his mother; and brought them to Fort St. George where they were much admired by all that saw them. Some time after this Mr. Moody, who spoke the Malayan language very well and was a person very capable to manage the company's affairs, was ordered by the governor of Fort St. George to prepare to go to Indrapore, an English factory on the west coast of Sumatra, in order to succeed Mr. Gibbons, who was the chief of that place.

By this time I was very intimately acquainted with Mr. Moody and was importuned by him to go with him and to be gunner of the fort there. I always told him I had a great desire to go to the Bay of Bengal, and that I had now an offer to go thither with Captain Metcalf, who wanted a mate and had already spoke to me. Mr. Moody, to encourage me to go with him, told me that if I would go with him to Indrapore he would buy a small vessel there and send me to the island Meangis, commander of her; and that I should carry Prince Jeoly and his mother with me (that being their country) by which means I might gain a commerce with his people for cloves.

This was a design that I liked very well, and therefore I consented to go thither. It was some time in July 1690 when we went from Fort St. George in a small ship called the Diamond, Captain Howel commander. We were about fifty or sixty passengers in all; some ordered to be left at Indrapore, and some at Bencoolen: five or six of us were officers, the rest soldiers to the company. We met nothing in our voyage that deserves notice till we came abreast of Indrapore. And then the wind came at north-west, and blew so hard that we could not get in but were forced to bear away to Bencoolen, another English factory on the same coast, lying fifty or sixty leagues to the southward of Indrapore.

Upon our arrival at Bencoolen we saluted the fort and were welcomed by them. The same day we came to an anchor, and Captain Howel and Mr. Moody with the other merchants went ashore and were all kindly received by the governor of the fort. It was two days before I went ashore and then I was importuned by the governor to stay there to be gunner of this fort; because the gunner was lately dead: and this being a place of greater import than Indrapore I should do the company more service here than there. I told the governor if he would augment my salary which, by agreement with the governor of Fort St. George I was to have had at Indrapore, I was willing to serve him provided Mr. Moody would consent to it. As to my salary he told me I should have 24 dollars per month which was as much as he gave to the old gunner.

Mr. Moody gave no answer till a week after and then, being ready to be gone to Indrapore, he told me I might use my own liberty either to stay here or go with him to Indrapore. He added that if I went with him he was not certain as yet to perform his promise in getting a vessel for me to go to Meangis with Jeoly and his mother: but he would be so fair to me that, because I left Madras on his account, he would give me the half share of the two painted people, and leave them in my possession and at my disposal. I accepted of the offer and writings were immediately drawn between us.

Of his country the Isle of Meangis; the cloves there, etc.

Thus it was that I came to have this painted prince, whose name was Jeoly, and his mother. They were born on a small island called Meangis, which is once or twice mentioned in Chapter 13. I saw the island twice, and two more close by it: each of the three seemed to be about four or five leagues round and of a good height. Jeoly himself told me that they all three abounded with gold, cloves and nutmegs: for I showed him some of each sort several times and he told me in the Malayan language which he spoke indifferent well: "Meangis hadda madochala se bullawan": that is, "There is abundance of gold at Meangis." Bullawan I have observed to be the common word for gold at Mindanao; but whether the proper Malayan word I know not, for I found much difference between the Malayan language as it was spoken at Mindanao and the language on the coast of Malacca and Achin. When I showed him spice he would not only tell me that there was madochala, that is, abundance; but to make it appear more plain he would also show me the hair of his head, a thing frequent among all the Indians that I have met with to show their hair when they would express more than they can number. That there were not above thirty men on the island and about one hundred women: that he himself had five wives and eight children, and that one of his wives painted him.

He was painted all down the breast, between his shoulders behind; on his thighs (mostly) before; and in the form of several broad rings or bracelets round his arms and legs. I cannot liken the drawings to any figure of animals or the like; but they were very curious, full of great variety of lines, flourishes, chequered work, etc., keeping a very graceful proportion and appearing very artificial, even to wonder, especially that upon and between his shoulder-blades. By the account he gave me of the manner of doing it I understood that the painting was done in the same manner as the Jerusalem cross is made in men's arms, by pricking the skin and rubbing in a pigment. But whereas powder is used in making the Jerusalem cross, they at Meangis use the gum of a tree beaten to powder called by the English dammer, which is used instead of pitch in many parts of India. He told me that most of the men and women on the island were thus painted: and also that they had all earrings made of gold, and gold shackles about their legs and arms: that their common food of the produce of the land was potatoes and yams: that they had plenty of cocks and hens but no other tame fowl. He said that fish (of which he was a great lover, as wild Indians generally are) was very plentiful about the island; and that they had canoes and went a-fishing frequently in them; and that they often visited the other two small islands whose inhabitants spoke the same language as they did; which was so unlike the Malayan, which he had learnt while he was a slave at Mindanao, that when his mother and he were talking together in their Meangian tongue I could not understand one word they said. And indeed all the Indians who spoke Malayan, who are the trading and politer sort, looked on these Meangians as a kind of barbarians; and upon any occasion of dislike would call them bobby, that is hogs; the greatest expression of contempt that can be, especially from the mouth of Malayans who are generally Mohammedans; and yet the Malayans everywhere call a woman babby, by a name not much different, and mamma signifies a man; though these two last words properly denote male and female: and as ejam signifies a fowl, so ejam mamma is a cock, and ejam babbi is a hen. But this by the way.

He said also that the customs of those other isles and their manner of living was like theirs, and that they were the only people with whom they had any converse: and that one time as he, with his father, mother and brother, with two or three men more, were going to one of these other islands they were driven by a strong wind on the coast of Mindanao, where they were taken by the fishermen of that island and carried ashore and sold as slaves; they being first stripped of their gold ornaments. I did not see any of the gold that they wore, but there were great holes in their ears, by which it was manifest that they had worn some ornaments in them. Jeoly was sold to one Michael, a Mindanayan that spoke good Spanish, and commonly waited on Raja Laut, serving him as our interpreter where the Raja was at a loss in any word, for Michael understood it better. He did often beat and abuse his painted servant to make him work, but all in vain, for neither fair means, threats, nor blows would make him work as he would have him. Yet he was very timorous and could not endure to see any sort of weapons; and he often told me that they had no arms at Meangis, they having no enemies to fight with.

I knew this Michael very well while we were at Mindanao: I suppose that name was given him by the Spaniards who baptised many of them at the time when they had footing at that island: but at the departure of the Spaniards they were Mohammedans again as before. Some of our people lay at this Michael's house, whose wife and daughter were pagallies to some of them. I often saw Jeoly at his master Michael's house, and when I came to have him so long after he remembered me again. I did never see his father nor brother, nor any of the others that were taken with them; but Jeoly came several times aboard our ship when we lay at Mindanao, and gladly accepted of such victuals as we gave him; for his master kept him at very short commons.

Prince Jeoly lived thus a slave at Mindanao four or five years, till at last Mr. Moody bought him and his mother for 60 dollars, and as is before related, carried him to Fort St. George, and from thence along with me to Bencoolen. Mr. Moody stayed at Bencoolen about three weeks and then went back with Captain Howel to Indrapore, leaving Jeoly and his mother with me. They lived in a house by themselves without the fort. I had no employment for them; but they both employed themselves. She used to make and mend their own clothes, at which she was not very expert, for they wear no clothes at Meangis but only a cloth about their waists: and he busied himself in making a chest with four boards and a few nails that he begged of me. It was but an ill-shaped odd thing, yet he was as proud of it as if it had been the rarest piece in the world. After some time they were both taken sick and, though I took as much care of them as if they had been my brother and sister, yet she died. I did what I could to comfort Jeoly; but he took on extremely, insomuch that I feared him also. Therefore I caused a grave to be made presently to hide her out of his sight. I had her shrouded decently in a piece of new calico; but Jeoly was not so satisfied, for he wrapped all her clothes about her and two new pieces of chintz that Mr. Moody gave her, saying that they were his mother's and she must have them. I would not disoblige him for fear of endangering his life; and I used all possible means to recover his health; but I found little amendment while we stayed here.

In the little printed relation that was made of him when he was shown for a sight in England there was a romantic story of a beautiful sister of his, a slave with them at Mindanao; and of the sultan's falling in love with her; but these were stories indeed. They reported also that this paint was of such virtue that serpents and venomous creatures would flee from him, for which reason I suppose, they represented so many serpents scampering about in the printed picture that was made of him. But I never knew any paint of such virtue: and as for Jeoly I have seen him as much afraid of snakes, scorpions, or centipedes as myself.

The author is made gunner of Bencoolen, but is forced to slip away from thence to come for England.

Having given this account of the ship that left me at Nicobar, and of my painted prince whom I brought with me to Bencoolen, I shall now proceed on with the relation of my voyage thence to England, after I have given this short account of the occasion of it and the manner of my getting away.

To say nothing therefore now of that place, and my employment there as gunner of the fort, the year 1690 drew towards an end and, not finding the governor keep to his agreement with me, nor seeing by his carriage towards others any great reason I had to expect he would, I began to wish myself away again. I saw so much ignorance in him with respect to his charge, being much fitter to be a bookkeeper than governor of a fort; and yet so much insolence and cruelty with respect to those under him, and rashness in his management of the Malayan neighbourhood, that I soon grew weary of him, not thinking myself very safe indeed under a man whose humours were so brutish and barbarous. I forbear to mention his name after such a character; nor do I care to fill these papers with particular stories of him: but therefore give this intimation because, as it is the interest of the nation in general, so is it especially of the honourable East India Company to be informed of abuses in their factories. And I think the company might receive great advantage by strictly enquiring into the behaviour of those whom they entrust with any command. For beside the odium which reflects back upon the superiors from the misdoings of their servants, how undeservedly soever, there are great and lasting mischiefs proceed from the tyranny or ignorant rashness of some petty governors. Those under them are discouraged from their service by it and often go away to the Dutch, the Mogul, or the Malayan princes, to the great detriment of our trade; and even the trade and the forts themselves are many times in danger by indiscreet provocations given to the neighbouring nations who are best managed, as all mankind are, by justice and fair dealings; nor any more implacably revengeful than those Malayans who live in the neighbourhood of Bencoolen, which fort has been more than once in danger of being surprised by them. I speak not this out of disgust to this particular governor; much less would I seem to reflect on any others of whom I know nothing amiss: but as it is not to be wondered at if some should not know how to demean themselves in places of power, for which neither their education nor their business possibly have sufficiently qualified them, so it will be the more necessary for the honourable Company to have the closer eye over them, and as much as may be to prevent or reform any abuses they may be guilty of; and it is purely out of my zeal for theirs and the nation's interest that I have given this caution, having seen too much occasion for it.

I had other motives also for my going away. I began to long after my native country after so tedious a ramble from it: and I proposed no small advantage to myself from my painted prince, whom Mr. Moody had left entirely to my disposal, only reserving to himself his right to one half share in him. For beside what might be gained by showing him in England I was in hopes that when I had got some money I might there obtain what I had in vain sought for in the Indies, namely, a ship from the merchants wherewith to carry him back to Meangis and reinstate him there in his own country, and by his favour and negotiation to establish a traffic for the spices and other products of those islands.

Upon these projects I went to the governor and council and desired that I might have my discharge to go for England with the next ship that came. The council thought it reasonable and they consented to it; he also gave me his word that I should go. Upon the 2nd of January 1691 there came to anchor in Bencoolen Road the Defence, Captain Heath commander, bound for England in the service of the Company. They had been at Indrapore where Mr. Moody then was, and he had made over his share in Prince Jeoly to Mr. Goddard, chief mate of the ship. Upon his coming on shore he showed me Mr. Moody's writings and looked upon Jeoly, who had been sick for three months: in all which time I tended him as carefully as if he had been my brother. I agreed matters with Mr. Goddard and sent Jeoly on board, intending to follow him as I could, and desiring Mr. Goddard's assistance to fetch me off and conceal me aboard the ship if there should be occasion; which he promised to do, and the captain promised to entertain me. For it proved, as I had foreseen, that upon Captain Heath's arrival the governor repented him of his promise and would not suffer me to depart. I importuned him all I could; but in vain: so did Captain Heath also but to no purpose. In short, after several essays I slipped away at midnight (understanding the ship was to sail away the next morning and that they had taken leave of the fort) and, creeping through one of the portholes of the fort, I got to the shore where the ship's boat waited for me and carried me on board. I brought with me my journal and most of my written papers; but some papers and books of value I left in haste and all my furniture; being glad I was myself at liberty, and had hopes of seeing England again.

ALSO AVAILABLE FROM AMBERLEY PUBLISHING

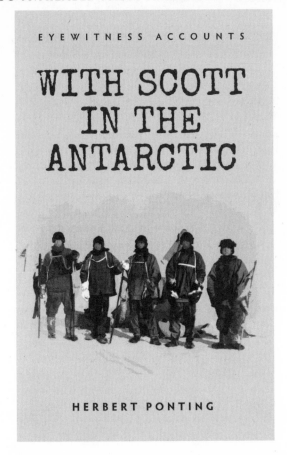

With Scott in the Antarctic

Herbert Ponting

Herbert Ponting was the photographer on Captain Scott's expedition
to the Antarctic in 1910–13. His tale ranks as a classic of travel and
exploration literature.

978 1 4456 3584 2
256 pages, illustrated

Available from all good bookshops or order direct
from our website www.amberleybooks.com

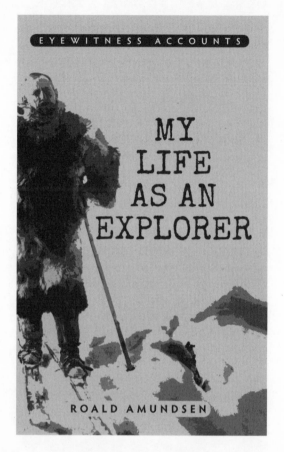

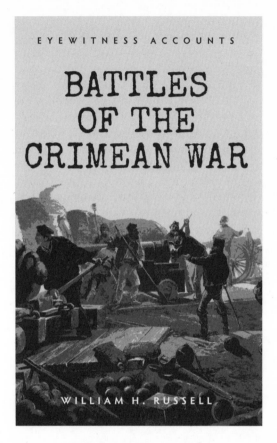

Battles of the Crimean War

William H. Russell

This book reprints Russell's vivid accounts of the battlefields of the
Alma, Sevastapol, Balaclava and Inkerman.

978 1 4456 3789 1

224 pages, illustrated

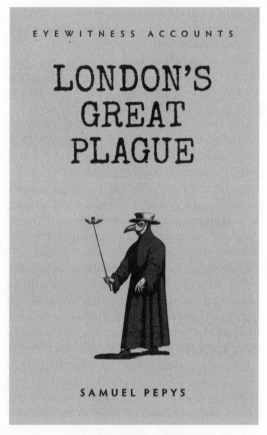

London's Great Plague
Samuel Pepys